**This book is to be returned on or before
the last date stamped below.**

Accommodating the chaos

Accommodating the chaos

Samuel Beckett's nonrelational art

J. E. Dearlove

Duke University Press Durham, N. C. 1982

822 BEC

57306

© 1982 by Duke University Press
Printed in the United States of America
by Heritage Printers, Inc.

Library of Congress Cataloging in Publication Data

Dearlove, J. E., 1949–
   Accommodating the chaos.

   Bibliography: p. 160
   Includes index.
   1. Beckett, Samuel, 1906–   —Criticism and inter-
pretation. I. Title.
PR6003.E282Z6248   848'.91409   81–12465
  ISBN 0–8223–0462–7   AACR2

Contents

Preface

Accommodating the Chaos: Samuel Beckett's Nonrelational Art examines Beckett's unremitting efforts to find a literary shape for the proposition that perhaps no relationships exist between or among the artist, his art, and an external reality. Chapter 1, "The Shape of Ideas," defines Beckett's interest in an art that is nonrelational through his early critical pieces and interviews. The remaining chapters explore both the rationale behind and the variety of strategies and chaos-accommodating forms Beckett adopts in his efforts to create a nonrelational art. Because Beckett's career reflects a progression in narrative strategies, the thematic arrangement of *Accommodating the Chaos* follows, for the most part, a chronological ordering. The main exceptions to a strictly chronological sequence occur in Chapter 4, "The Voice and Its Words," where it was necessary to preview subsequent works in order to clarify the precise contribution of *How It Is*, and in Chapters 5 and 6, "Residual Fiction" and "A Sense of Sufficiency," where the brief fictions written after *How It Is* are arranged not according to dates of composition or publication (debatable issues in themselves), but rather according to the devices, techniques, and moods they display. Although *Company* was not published until after *Accommodating the Chaos* was written, its exploration of the archetypal need for the associations of company places it among the pieces which project a sense of sufficiency. *Company* reconciles the nonrelational with the universal desire for relation. The treatment accorded each of Beckett's works depends not only on the quality of that work, but also on its significance and contribution to Beckett's narrative strategies. Although the trilogy may be discussed specifically in only a certain number of pages, as the culmination of Beckett's processes of fragmentation and tessellation, it is the focus of all of Chapter 3.

For their support and suggestions I wish to thank Daniel Albright, Elgin Mellown, John Pilling, Grover Smith, Leigh DeNeef, Oliver Ferguson, and Dorothy Sapp. Thanks are also due to the *Journal of Beckett Studies* and the *Journal of Modern Literature* for permission to reprint portions of articles previously published by them, and to the American Council of Learned Societies for a summer grant which made possible part of the research for this book.

Accommodating the chaos

1. The shape of ideas

"I am interested in the shape of ideas even if I do not believe in them. There is a wonderful sentence in Augustine. I wish I could remember the Latin. It is even finer in Latin than in English. 'Do not despair; one of the thieves was saved. Do not presume; one of the thieves was damned.' That sentence has a wonderful shape. It is the shape that matters." [1]

Samuel Beckett's interest in the shape as opposed to the validity of ideas pervades and informs his entire canon. Indeed, his narratives are united less by stylistic, metaphoric, and thematic designs than by their unremitting efforts to find a literary shape for the proposition that perhaps no relationships exist between or among the artist, his art, and an external reality. According to Beckett, the artist cannot assume his works exhibit any connection, much less a mimetic one, to an external system. Nor can he be certain that the things he is trying to say are being spoken by his art or heard by an audience. Certainty, meaning, and order disappear as relationships become problematic. Similarly, because the relationships are questioned but not rejected, all sense of assurance, completion, and fixity disappear. Nothing may be affirmed or denied absolutely: all possible permutations must remain available. Ambiguity and fluidity characterize nonrelational arts.

Nonrelational narratives are inevitably paradoxical. Art, especially literature, is inherently ordered: form and structure adhere to even the most avant-garde works. The functions and assumptions of language are intrinsically relational. Language is metaphoric, based on the association of tenor and vehicle, *langue* and *parole*, signified and signifier. It is syntactic, formed from patterns of conventions and structures. It is semantic, designed to communicate meaning and signification. In order to shape a nonrelational narrative Beckett must discover strategies and structures by which his medium may be induced to suggest its antithesis. The task is neither easy nor specious. Beckett challenges not only the restrictions of traditional narrative structures, but also the limitations of human knowledge as he seeks to say the inexplicable, to conceive of the unimaginable. What may initially appear to be a self-gratulatory intellectual game—to examine the shape rather than the soundness of an idea—becomes a profound quest to explore and expand the boundaries of human perception. Although the pieces are stripped of conventional human associations, what remains is nonetheless human.[2] The minima of existence and the imperturbable continuity of life become the center of Beckett's prose. Even the pieces which do not succeed in eliminating correspondences, even his "failures," celebrate our imagination, which irrepressibly fashions orders, meanings, and totalities where perhaps none exist. Beckett's canon, in fact, moves from angry denunciations of relationships to acceptance, if not affirmation, of the impossibility of either disproving their existence or displaying their absence.

Beckett's changing attitudes are intimated in his interviews and early critical pieces. Although these works do not constitute a coherent poetic, they do reveal the evolution of the concept of a nonrelational and self-justifying art.[3] Like Murphy, who divides experience "into jokes that had once been good jokes and jokes that had never been good jokes,"[4] Beckett divides artists into those who assume that authentic relationships exist and those, like himself and Bram van Velde, who do not.

The analysis of the relation between the artist and his occasion, a relation always regarded as indispensable, does not seem to have been very productive either, the reason being perhaps that it lost its way in disquisitions on the nature of occasion. . . . But if the occasion appears as an unstable term of relation, the artist, who is the other term, is hardly less so, thanks to his warren of modes and attitudes. . . . All that should concern us is the acute and increasing anxiety of the relation itself, as though shadowed more and more darkly by a sense of inadequacy, of existence at the expense of all that it excludes, all that it blinds to. The history of painting . . . is the history of its attempts to escape from this sense of failure. . . . My case, since I am in the dock, is that van Velde is the first to desist from this estheticised automatism, the first to submit wholly to the incoercible absence of relation, in the absence of terms or, if you like, in the presence of unavailable terms, the first to admit that to be an artist is to fail, as no other dare fail, that failure is his world and the shrink from it desertion, art and craft, good housekeeping, living. . . . I know that all that is required now, in order to bring even this horrible matter to an acceptable conclusion, is to make of this submission, this admission, this fidelity to failure, a new occasion, a new term of relation, and of the act which, unable to act, obliged to act, he makes, an expressive act, even if only of itself, of its impossibility, of its obligation. I know that my inability to do so places myself . . . in what I think is still called an unenviable situation. . . .[5]

Ironically, the expansion of knowledge is also the discovery of increasingly vast areas of ignorance and uncertainty. Physicists, astronomers, geologists reveal how much we can not know about our universe. Psychiatrists, psychologists, sociologists display how little we can know ourselves. But it is the artist, according to Beckett, who must tell us, not of the uncertainty of universe or individual, but rather of the "incoercible absence of relation" itself. In questioning the validity, adequacy, and existence of a relationship between the artist and his occasion Beckett is questioning the metaphysical traditions which assert not only that there is a rational and harmonious system but also that it is knowable and imitable. Art is denied the justifications and significations provided by external orders. Similarly, in refusing either to turn the absence of relationship into "a new term of relation," or to permit the artistic act to become an expression of its own limitations, Beckett is refusing to accept the replacement of external orders with internal systems that restore meaning and coherence through poetic imagination. It is not enough to assert that there may be no relation between the artist and his occasion. The intelligibility of the words belies their proposition; language cannot be nonrelational; the artist must invariably fail. Nor is it enough to retreat to the individual and speak of the failure and impossibility of the artistic pensum. Art must be self-justifying because all terms of relation, if they exist, are arbitrary, accidental, and self-appointed.

Inherent in the repudiation of a relation between the artist and his occasion is a redefinition of the artist's tasks and capabilities. Langland's allegory and Baudelaire's *symbolisme* are possible if correspondences can be perceived and imitated, or at least intimated, through a careful organization of the linguistic medium. The artist is capable of understanding his context, manipulating his material, and perpetuating through art his conception of an orderly whole. Because most pretwentieth-century conceptions of that whole tend to be of an eternal, absolute, and unchanging structure, the resulting artworks likewise tend to be fixed and final, tend to be what D. H. Lawrence once described as the "poetry of beginning and the poetry of end" which "is the nature of all that is complete and consummate. The completeness, this consummateness, the finality and the perfection are conveyed in exquisite form: the perfect symmetry, the rhythm which returns upon itself like a dance where the hands link and loosen and link for the supreme moment of the end."[6] The creator of an art of completeness, consummateness, finality, and perfection is a person of knowledge and power. If, however, correspondences between the artist and his occasion can no longer be intuited or projected, the knowledge and power, like the consummateness and finality, disappear. The Lawrentian poetry of beginning and end becomes "the poetry of that which is at hand: the immediate present [in which] there is no perfection, no consummation, nothing finished."[7] Repeatedly Beckett describes his own tasks and capability in comparable terms of uncertainty and fluidity.

Beckett's code of uncertainty is articulated in the distinctions he makes between his own art and that of James Joyce:

> With Joyce the difference is that Joyce was a superb manipulator of material—perhaps the greatest. He was making words do the absolute maximum of work. There isn't a syllable that's superfluous. The kind of work I do is one in which I'm not master of my material. The more Joyce knew the more he could. He's tending toward omniscience and omnipotence as an artist. I'm working with impotence, ignorance. I don't think impotence has been exploited in the past. There seems to be a kind of esthetic axiom that expression is an achievement—must be an achievement. My little exploration is that whole zone of being that has always been set aside by artists as something unquestionable—as something by definition incompatible with art.
>
> I think anyone nowadays who pays the slightest attention to his own experience finds it is the experience of a non-knower, a non-can-er. The other type of artist—the Apollonian—is absolutely foreign to me.[8]

While Beckett implicitly defines the Apollonian artist as the "knower" and "can-er," his use of the term evokes Nietzsche's original description in *The Birth of Tragedy* (1872) in which Nietzsche associates the Apollonian mode with sculpture and soothsaying, with restraint, measure, and lucidity; with perfection, the individual, and the glorification of phenomena. The Apollonian artist can do and know because he is concerned with the completed, the spatial, the physical, the individual. The Dionysian, on the other hand, is less interested in the creation of final artifacts than in the celebration of the ongoing, the temporal, the immaterial, and the unified. He is linked with nonimagistic arts, with music, with terror and ecstasy, with intoxicated reality. More important for Nietzsche than either of these "artistic energies" is their interaction and fusion which produced true tragedy. Although Beckett never specifies whether his own artistry should be identified with the Dionysian pole or with the dialectical flux, in either case his dissociation from Apollonian omniscience and omnipotence implies a concomitant dissociation from completed, knowable, and absolute relationships in favor of fluid, unknowable, and uncertain ones. The artist must work with ignorance and impotence.

Beckett's interest in fluidity emerges in his monograph on *Proust* (1931). Instead of discussing the Apollonian and Dionysian dichotomy, in *Proust* Beckett speaks of the classical and romantic antithesis. Posited in opposition to the "classical" artist of omniscience and omnipotence is a romantic artist who is defined less by his knowledge and powers of action than by his multiplicity of responses and by his fluid perceptions of time. Proust is called romantic "in his substitution of affectivity for intelligence."[9] But Beckett's observation, unlike many simplifications, is not merely that romanticism is emotional rather than rational. Indeed, Beckett is less concerned with Proust's "affectivity" than with his replacement, even in purely logical discourse, of singular statements by plural responses, of simple states by multiple corollaries, and of concrete explanations by diverse alternatives.

> He is romantic in his substitution of affectivity for intelligence, in his opposition of the particular affective evidential state to all the subtleties of rational cross-reference, in his rejection of the Concept in favour of the Idea, in his scepticism before causality. Thus his purely logical—as opposed to his intuitive—explanations of a certain effect invariably bristle with alternatives. (*Proust*, p. 61)

Proust's multiplicity of alternatives produces an image not of classic completion and assurance, but rather of expanding possibilities and uncertainty. The same penchant for plurality and alternatives characterizes what Beckett calls Proust's "impressionism," or his apparent presentation of phenomena as they are perceived before any order of intelligibility can be imposed on them. Like the painter Elstir, who paints "what he sees and not what he knows he ought to see," or Dostoevsky, "who states his characters without explaining them" (*Proust*, p. 66), Proust presents experiences without rationalizations or explanations. To the hypothetical objection that Proust does little else except explain his characters, Beckett responds, "But his explanations are experimental and not demonstrative. He explains them in order that they may appear as they are—inexplicable. He explains them away" (*Proust*, p. 67). Multiplicity countermands assurance and finality.

As Watt discovers in Mr. Knott's house, a seemingly endless array of alternatives and plethora of explanations lead not to certain and assured relationships but back to Beckettian ambiguity and doubt.

In a similar fashion Proust's concern with time and its effect on memory and inspiration return him to a world of fluidity distinct from the classical author's realm of timeless, changeless abstraction: "The classical artist assumes omniscience and omnipotence. He raises himself artificially out of Time in order to give relief to his chronology and causality to his development" (*Proust*, p. 62). Instead of "raising himself artificially out of Time" Proust immerses himself and his work in a study of time, "that double-headed monster of damnation and salvation" (*Proust*, p. 1). The individual becomes a function of the passage of time, a succession of discrete and ephemeral moments: "The individual is the seat of a constant process of decantation, decantation from the vessel containing the fluid of future time, sluggish, pale, and monochrome, to the vessel containing the fluid of past time, agitated and multicoloured by the phenomena of its hours" (*Proust*, pp. 4–5). To talk of omnipotence when identity is a process of decantation is patently absurd, for the actions, desires, and aspirations "of yesterday were valid for yesterday's ego, not for to-day's" (*Proust*, p. 3). Omniscience is improbable when the world must be recreated everyday (*Proust*, p. 8), and when continuity is only an illusion of habit protecting the individual from the flux of time, from "the suffering of being" (*Proust*, p. 8). Instead of the classical realms of fixed chronology and causal development, the associations of a Proustian world are plunged into a relativity in which the present moment can be obliterated by an involuntary act of memory, by something as slight as the taste of a teacake. In a world made uncertain by a multiplicity of alternatives and problematic by the relativity of time, the classical and Apollonian artists' powers, tasks, and prerogatives are no longer tenable.

But just as Beckett's disavowal of the Apollonian mode is not coupled necessarily with an endorsement of the Dionysian, so too his repudiation of the classical pattern is not linked inevitably to a participation in the romantic. Indeed, the "Three Dialogues" with George Duthuit (1949) seems to be primarily Beckett's efforts to dissociate himself from even the relative associations of romanticism and from all forms of expressionism. Having denied knowable and absolute correspondences between the artist and his work and world, Beckett, like the romantics, must depend on the internal world of the artist. But, whereas the romantics use their imaginative powers and memory to restore meanings that were formerly external, Beckett tries to prohibit the restoration of meaning and association. Whereas the romantics celebrate the expression of their perceptions and meditations, Beckett seeks to deny the lyrical impulse by questioning both the validity of language and the speaker's powers of perception. He objects, for example, to the paintings of Tal Coat and Masson because they are extensions of traditional art operating on the "plane of the feasible" and participating in the two old maladies "of wanting to know what to do and the malady of wanting to be able to do it" ("Three Dialogues," p. 17). Although they may have denied themselves many of the orders of previous arts, by making that denial itself an expression, the two painters are still "straining to enlarge the statement of a compromise" ("Three Dialogues," p. 16), still seeking to express a relation between the artist and his occasion. Bram van Velde, on the other hand, is the first true revolutionary, according to Beckett, precisely because he is "the first to submit wholly to the incoercible absence of relation . . . the first to admit that to be an artist is to fail, as no other dare fail" ("Three Dialogues," p. 21). Like the Unnamable who summarizes his position saying, "You must go on, I can't go on, I'll go on,"[10] Beckett speaks of an art turning from the plane of the feasible and preferring "The expression that there is nothing to express, nothing with which to express, nothing from which to express, no power to express, no desire to express, together with the obligation to express" ("Three Dialogues," p. 17).

Nonrelational art is obligated to express despite the fact that there is nothing to express, not even the impossibility and necessity of expression itself. The shape of such a statement embodies in its own circularity the perplexing nature of Beckett's endeavor. Because total prohibition of associations is impossible, Beckett's terminology becomes caught on the horns of artificial dilemmas as his dichotomies (Apollonian/Dionysian, classic/romantic) suggest a neatness and order which are alien to a world whose "key word . . . is 'perhaps.' "[11] Even his disavowal of the romantic mode is couched in romantic terms and the failure of his artist echoes the failure in a grand fashion of a Byronic hero. To minimize such inconsistencies Beckett turns increasingly to paradox and metaphor, to oxymoron, negation, and contraction. Language is treated less as a collection of inadequate propositions than as an activity of speaking in vain: "There are many ways in which the thing I am trying in vain to say may be tried in vain to be said" ("Three Dialogues," p. 20). In an effort to achieve structures that will unmake themselves, Beckett fabricates a language that tries to unspeak itself: as if the denial of what has been said could eradicate the fact of its being said. It is not enough to refuse to explain the characters in *Endgame* by insisting that their predication is all the author can manage; even that predication must be undercut as something beyond the playwright's powers:

"Hamm as stated, and Clov as stated, together as stated, nec tecum nec sine te, in such a place, and in such a world, that's all I can manage, more than I could." [12] Nor is it enough to counteract every statement by asserting its opposite; Beckett must undercut even that opposition by focusing attention not on his words, but on the silence they interrupt. "Every word is like an unnecessary stain of silence and nothingness." [13]

The difficulties of his paradoxical quest are compounded in the critical pieces by Beckett's confusion of terminology. In the early pieces especially Beckett treats *form* as a synonym for *structure, style, meaning, order, stasis*. The conflation of formal concepts, structural devices, and stylistic techniques is complicated further by Beckett's tendency to identify these elements with their functions in conventional narratives. Art is condensed into the characteristics, restrictions, and capabilities of the traditional novel: every aspect of every art is reduced to precisely the generic relationships Beckett attempts to avoid.

Given such a system, the bellicosity and obscurity of Beckett's early prose are understandable. The fusion of definitions has deprived Beckett of a language—even a paradoxical one—for articulating his objections to relational art. He resorts to the polemics of the champion of a new art form, but neither his theories nor his structures and techniques are unique. For example, in opposition to the rhetorical traditions which would relegate form to ornamentation, Beckett postulates, in the essay on Proust, the equally conventional theory that form is a spatial configuration of meaning.

> For Proust, as for the painter, style is more a question of vision than of technique. Proust does not share the superstition that form is nothing and content everything, nor that the ideal literary masterpiece could only be communicated in a series of absolute and monosyllabic propositions. For Proust the quality of language is more important than any system of ethics or aesthetics. Indeed he makes no attempt to dissociate form from content. The one is a concretion of the other, the revelation of a world. The Proustian world is expressed metaphorically by the artisan because it is apprehended metaphorically by the artists: the indirect and comparative expression of indirect and comparative perception. The rhetorical equivalent of the Proustian real is the chain-figure of the metaphor. It is a tiring style, but it does not tire the mind. The clarity of the phrase is cumulative and explosive. One's fatigue is a fatigue of the heart, a blood fatigue. (*Proust*, pp. 67–68)

An idea resides in its shape, and style reflects more accurately than any content a speaker's vision of the universe. The linguistic equivalent of the

Proustian real is the "chain-figure of the metaphor" and not the flux of a Heraclitian river. By its very nature, however, the metaphor assumes a world of correspondences Beckett will seek to avoid. Albertine's laugh can be described as possessing the color and smell of a geranium only if some relationship can be perceived between Albertine and her world—or indeed, between Albertine and her laugh. In his encomiums of Joyce's work Beckett similarly lambastes the ignorant reader who might accuse Joyce of obscurity in his language by retorting that precisely the fashion in which Joyce speaks comprises the beauty of his work. Indeed, it is as if Beckett could not argue strongly enough for the identity of form and content for he insists on underscoring his points: "Here form *is* content, content *is* form. You complain that this stuff is not written in English. It is not written at all. It is not to be read—or rather it is not only to be read. It is to be looked at and listened to. His writing is not *about* something; *it is that something itself*. . . . When the sense is sleep, the words go to sleep. . . . When the sense is dancing, the words dance."[14]

More important here than the underscored passages and the misleading sense of novelty is Beckett's effort to circumvent the relationships of conventional narratives through references to other genres. A work is not merely to be read; like a ballet it is to be looked at and listened to. The stasis of printed material is subverted by the mobility of dancing words. At another point in the same essay Beckett defines structure not in terms of an inflexible outline or bare skeleton, but rather as the sinuous, intertwining of motifs: "By structure I do not only mean a bold outward division, a bare skeleton for the housing of material. I mean the endless substantial variations of these three beats, and interior intertwining of these three themes into a decoration or arabesques—decoration and more than decoration" ("Dante . . . Bruno . Vico . . Joyce," p. 7). Like the dancer's movements, the fugue's arabesques invite the audience to follow the graceful and complicated turns of the design.

The Proust essay likewise turns to other genres to avoid the restrictions placed on art by a conflation of terminology. As impossible or improbable as Schopenhauer's theory of music might be, Beckett finds its influence on Proust "unquestionable."

Schopenhauer rejects the Leibnitzian view of music as 'occult arithmetic,' and in his aesthetics separates it from the other arts, which can only produce the Idea with its concomitant phenomena, whereas music is the Idea itself, unaware of the world of phenomena, existing ideally outside the universe, apprehended not in Space but in Time only, and consequently untouched by the teleological hypothesis. This essential quality of music is distorted by the listener who, being an impure subject, insists on giving a figure to that which is ideal and invisible, on incarnating the Idea in what he conceives to be an appropriate paradigm. (*Proust*, pp. 70–71)

Music is seen (rather inaccurately because of its dependence on physical properties such as wave length and vibration) as an Ideal art, freed from the associations and constraints of the physical world. It is the perfect abstraction, unveiled only in time, unrelated to space and concomitant phenomena. But Beckett acknowledges that even this perfect art is distorted by relationships—if not between the artist, his art, and an external reality, then between the art and its audience. The listener insists on giving shape to the ideal and invisible.

The relationship between an artwork and its audience becomes especially important in the last half of Beckett's career as his cryptic pieces increasingly demand that the reader be involved with and responsible for whatever "meaning" the works entail. The reader's responsibility intensifies when Beckett alters the artist's role by reversing his earlier pronouncements and by acknowledging that form does not have to *be* content.

What I am saying does not mean that there will henceforth be no form in art. It only means that there will be new form, and that this form will be of such a type that it admits the chaos and does not try to say that the chaos is really something else. *The form and the chaos remain separate. The latter is not reduced to the former.* That is why the form itself becomes a preoccupation, because it exists as a problem separate from the material it accommodates. To find a form that accommodates the mess, that is the task of the artist now.[15] (My emphasis.)

The shape of an artwork can be separate from the idea it accommodates. No longer can a reader presume to know what is being said by noticing only how it is said: structure may, in fact, work in opposition to chaos.

The shift in his aesthetic theories from identity ("form *is* content") to adaptation, adjustment, and reconciliation ("find a form that accommodates the mess") enables Beckett to impart a greater flexibility and ambiguity to his works. Instead of absolutes, Beckett presents possible shapes of ideas. Instead of embodying a formal context and making an abstraction concrete, Beckett accommodates fluidity and uncertainty: "I think perhaps I have freed myself from certain formal concepts. Perhaps, like the composer Schönberg or the painter Kandinsky, I have turned toward an abstract language. Unlike them, however, I have tried not to concretize the abstraction —not to give it yet another formal context."[16] Instead of a print-oriented literature, Beckett posits the verbal art of the "narrator/narrated."[17] The visual is replaced by the audible. The difficulty of Joycean language dissolves before a simpler vocabulary. Although the early Beckett signed the initial Verticalist manifesto advocating use of language as "a mantic instrument . . . which does not hesitate to adopt a revolutionary attitude toward word and syntax, going even so far as to invent a hermetic language, if necessary,"[18] the later Beckett writes a nonmantic prose whose complexity lies neither in the words nor the syntax, but in the propositions themselves. As Beckett observes in contrasting his works to those of Kafka, the consternation lies not in the form, but behind it.

> I've only read Kafka in German—serious reading—except for a few things in French and English—only "The Castle" in German. I must say it was difficult to get to the end. The Kafka hero has a coherence of purpose. He's lost but he's not spiritually precarious, he's not falling to bits. My people seem to be falling to bits. Another difference, you notice how Kafka's form is classic, it goes on like a steamroller—almost serene. It seems to be threatened the whole time—but the consternation is in the form. In my work there is consternation behind the form, not in the form.[19]

According to Beckett, Kafka's classic work threatens to disperse, but the structure is ultimately serene. The reader recognizes the completed spatial patterns characteristic of the novel and realizes, even at the moment of greatest anxiety, that the threatened breakdown will be contained within the literary patterns. The form provides a security in its very nature. Beckett, on the other hand, seeks to indicate the consternation behind the form. Instead of assurances inherent in shape itself, Beckett tries to get to the shapelessness beyond. His quest is to find a form for the possibility of nonrelationship.

The shifts and contradictions of Beckett's critical works concerning the concept of nonrelation are made manifest in the narratives (as the following chapters will attempt to show). His earliest prose parodies the traditions and conventions of relational art without proposing an alternative vision. The resulting pieces are brilliantly witty but disingenuous as they mock the structures upon which they depend. Like the belligerent critical works, the early pieces fall prey to the errors of relationship and generic characteristics against which they protest. It is not until *Murphy* that Beckett finds the first of his shapes for dealing with uncertainty and fluidity. There he expands and distorts the assumptions beneath relational art until they explode into intentional ambiguity. Once *Murphy* has destroyed conventional structures, however, Beckett must find other shapes for his art. The pieces written during Beckett's most prolific period (1944–50) seek the shape of nonrelational art in the dual processes of fragmentation and tessellation. Like the narrator of the trilogy progressively stripping away layers of material reality in order to say himself, the pieces written during this period persistently shatter traditional associations of time, space, identity, and even language in an effort to attain the "nothingness" Watt discovers at Mr. Knott's house. The more former patterns are broken apart, the more the works give rise to alternative interpretations. The difficulty of the pieces is not that they are fragmented, but rather that they provoke an agonizing surplus of possible reintegrations. The dual processes not only provide Beckett with new forms to express the possibility of a formlessness beneath art, but they also enable him to infuse his narratives with the abstraction and dynamism of other art forms. Conventional characters, settings, and plots yield to a verbal score in which negation and contraction force vestigial patterns and meanings to collapse. By the time he writes *How It Is*, Beckett no longer insists on equating form and content. Instead of belaboring the lack of associations between a speaker and his world, Beckett explores the possibilities of a voice unrelated to any world and hence unrestricted. Instead of focusing attention upon the divorce of the mind from the external world, he explores the internal, arbitrary, and self-appointed worlds the mind creates. This interior focus in turn makes possible the highly self-conscious and arbitrary constructions of the "residua" in which artifice and intricacy themselves suggest a more fundamental absence of order. Structure works in opposition to content. In the most recent fictions, rather than attempting to deny, explode, implode, ignore, or controvert the metaphysics of a relational art, Beckett permits the elements of traditional narrative to commingle with those of a nonrelational narrative. It is no longer necessary to isolate or exacerbate either realm. The pieces reconcile, but do not reunite, an impotent speaker with an unknowable world. Beckett accepts both the impossibility of a nonrelational art and the improbability of a relational one, and in doing so he finds yet another shape for the ambiguity, fluidity, and uncertainty of the human condition.

2. The unwilling Apollonian

Although Beckett resists comparisons of his own art to that of Joyce, his early pieces are based on the same conceptions of language and form, which he attributes to Joyce. Such conceptions accept the Apollonian assumptions that an artist can do and know, that viable relationships exist among the artist, his art, and the surrounding world, and that complete and absolute structures can be fashioned and communicated. Artworks in the "Joycean" tradition affirm an order antithetical to Beckett's fluid postulations. In Beckett's early works the resulting conflict between structure and hypothesis leads to ambivalent pieces in which language contradicts its own subject, to parodic works in which satire denigrates its own foundation, to parasitic arts in which conventions debunk their own allusions. In *Murphy*, on the other hand, instead of trying to controvert the assumptions beneath his structures, Beckett pursues them to their logical ends. Relationships are multiplied until their excess destroys meaningful orders, until Apollonian associations crumble beneath their implications.

1

Beckett's relationship to James Joyce was complicated and complex. In his interviews Beckett carefully separates himself from Joyce, denying not simply the supposition that he was Joyce's secretary, but more significantly, the suggestion that he was influenced by Joyce's work. Joyce's effect was moral, not stylistic: "He made me [Beckett] realize artistic integrity."[1] In fact, the Shenker interview establishes Joyce and Beckett as opposing types of artists. Beckett is the artist of ignorance and impotence; Joyce is the omnipotent, omniscient, Apollonian artist—the "superb manipulator of material."[2] The descriptions accurately distinguish Beckett's trilogy from Joyce's *Finnegans Wake*, but the very same descriptions also distinguish

Beckett's trilogy from his earlier pieces. Although they appear highly original, the early pieces assume a traditional relationship between world and art. Like Joyce before him, Beckett creates a densely textured and coterie language full of obscure allusions, foreign quotations, arcane references, and learned word games; but it is a language whose conventions can be traced (as Beckett does in his essay on Joyce) to the traditions of Vico, Bruno, and Dante. What may be perceived as obscurity is a return to "direct expression": the abstractions which treat words as "mere polite symbols" are replaced by a language in which word, gesture, and object are united, in which "form and content are inseparable."[3] Beckett's effort to fuse words and the objects they represent reflects the underlying assumption that relationships exist between word and world. The confusion of the physical manifestation of words with the objects they represent also contributes to the essentially print-oriented nature of an Apollonian literature. We are asked to savor not merely the *mot juste* but more importantly what Joyce described as "the perfect order of words in the sentence."[4] An interlocking plethora of meanings requires the media of print to be understood or appreciated fully. Joycean language demands a visual and spatial perception of its intricacies and unities: "the Beauty of '*Work in Progress*' . . . depends as much on its visibility as on its audibility."[5] Whether or not Beckett's early works are influenced directly by Joyce, they do participate in a Joycean attitude toward language and art. Although Beckett claims the Apollonian mode is absolutely foreign to him, it is precisely this mode, in which external order and meaning can be found and conveyed through interlocked images and printed words, that best explains the verbal pyrotechnics and biting satire of his earliest prose.

2

Beckett's "Apollonian" use of language is perhaps most clearly displayed in "Text,"[6] a published extract of the unpublished *Dream of Fair to Middling Women*. Like the later works, "Text" derives its energy more from its own verbal structures than from any external orders. Unlike the later pieces, however, "Text" reasserts through language its adherence to and belief in external reality. Basically, the piece portrays an exchange between a "lust-be-lepered" lover and the woman he unsuccessfully importunes to be his "bonny bony doublebed cony." The real interest, however, lies not in the situation, but in the language which compounds aural devices into one long (approximately 180-word) sentence. Within the first two dozen words alone there is a remarkable accumulation of alliteration, assonance, consonance, and internal rhyme: "Come come and cull me bonny bony doublebed cony swiftly my springal and my thin Kerry twingle-twangler comfort my days of roses days of beauty. . . ." The words create a pulsing rhythm that thrusts us through the piece to the conclusive beats of the final phrase, "of whom clapdish and foreshop." Like the lover, our mounting expectations are abruptly deflated by the woman's emphatic refusal and the end of the piece. As Beckett says of *Work in Progress*, here sound has united with meaning. Indeed, sound replaces meaning as the interpersonal relationship is subsumed under a verbal one. We are more interested in the way words tumble about each other's meanings than we are in the lover's frustrated efforts to tumble about with his cony. We are more affected by the musical rhythms of the words than by their specific denotations. Although "Text" deals with one of the most basic of human situations, its audience must necessarily be a coterie one capable of enjoying neologisms and allusions. Its very density of texture makes "Text" difficult and obscure. The piece celebrates not humanistic concerns but rather the power of the artist.

The artist's ability to create verbal structures, metaphors, and allusions is a power which itself returns us to external orders. Instead of focusing, as the later works do, on the hollow, the imaginative, and the analytic, "Text" concentrates on the full-to-bursting, the earthy concrete, and the emotionally evocative. Its images are insistently individual, yet they stem from familiar realms of order and reason. They are the kinds of images Robbe-Grillet objected to in "Nature, Humanism, Tragedy" (1958) because they imply a solidarity between perceiver and perceived through the mediation of art, because they assume a universe of significations, because they make man the justification of the world. These images glorify the skill of the author who forces his words to operate on all levels of meaning simultaneously, who makes each word refer both forward and backward in a flowing prose. For example, both standard denotations of "cony"—a Kerry-hunted rabbit and a man-duped woman—are present throughout the piece in references to defoliation ("gone the hartshorn and the cowslip vine gone and the lettuce nibbled up nibbled up and gone") and to the refusal to have "toadspit about this house." In a dazzling display of metaphysical transitions, Beckett transforms the woman into a hunted rabbit, to the nibbled-up lettuce, to a plant covered by an insect's secretion, and back to a woman. The very density of images in which human, animal, and vegetable allusions interconnect and overlap to create a piece bursting with movement and life, testifies to an underlying belief in the possibility of order, in the reality of the external, and in the capacity of language to project and display that order and that reality.

While its brevity prevents "Text" from being sundered by the tensions between a belief in hermeticism and a language of associations, Beckett's other early short stories do not fare as well. "Assumption," "Sedendo et Quiesciendo" (sic), and "A Case in a Thousand,"⁷ show the strains of pieces that mock the forms upon which they depend. They are the works of a learned and satiric author who seems finally indifferent to whether his obscure allusions, his acrid wit, and his recondite and foreign vocabulary leave his reader dazed and dumbfounded or not. Unlike the later pieces in which the narrator appears as powerless as the reader, in which the energy of the work is directed to making us imagine that imagination is dead, these early pieces imply a narrator who revels in his intellectual and artistic superiority, who is not interested in making certain that we are "in" on the joke. The resulting distance tempts us to reject certain passages as cheap satire or intellectual sniping. Unlike *Murphy* and subsequent works in which the dissolution of images is consistent with and exemplary of thematic, metaphysical, and epistemological concerns, the destruction in these stories is unrelated to content. Structure is denied, but that denial is without purpose or meaning; destruction becomes self-destruction and parody, self-parody.

If the portrayal of an eccentric individual's struggle to create his own divinity is as petty an issue as "Assumption" implies, then there is little reason to write "Assumption" itself. The story tells of a man whose existence depends upon keeping silent a "wild rebellious surge that aspired violently towards realization in sound" (p. 269). The man eventually meets a woman who nightly saps "a part of his essential animality" (p. 270) until he dies in "a great storm of sound" (p. 271). Although the story discusses themes that will intrigue Beckett throughout his career—the tensions between speaker and spoken, between inhibition and creation—the real focus of the piece is on a conventional treatment of character and story. Instead of seeing a narrator create himself through the act of narration, we are told about a man who defines his individuality in terms of an "involuntary inhibition" (p. 269) and a struggle to keep silent. It is this artist of silence and his endeavors, not his underlying theories, which confronts us. Indeed, those theories remain ill-defined. We are uncertain why "our whispering prestidigitator" (p. 269) should locate humanity in silence, divinity in sound. Nor do we know if his last "great storm of sound" (p. 271) is a cry of victory or of defeat; if that "flesh locked sea of silence" achieves its glorious consummation in spite of the artist's will or because of his hunger to be "engulfed in the light of eternity" (p. 271). We are concerned with the emotions, not the logistics of the struggle. Moreover, although a "cosmic discord" (p. 269) is postulated, the aesthetic impetus is toward a world that still contains other people, concrete settings, and reduced but nonetheless heroic actions. The romantic ideal of art, though relegated to a rather insignificant artist of silence, still persists:

> To avoid the expansion of the commonplace is not enough; the highest art reduces significance in order to obtain that inexplicable bomb shell perfection. Before no supreme manifestation of Beauty do we proceed comfortably up a staircase of sensation, and sit down mildly on the topmost stair to digest our gratification: such is the pleasure of Prettiness. We are taken up bodily and pitched breathless on the peak of a sheer crag: which is the pain of Beauty. (p. 269)

Caught between Beckett's concerns with silence and the heroic ideals of perfection, "Assumption" fails to take us up bodily and pitch us breathless on the peak of a sheer crag. The pain of Beauty and even the pleasure of Prettiness are lost in the confusion of theory and practice, in the desire for a new ideal and the grudging adherence to an old one.

Similarly, if a psychological story is as preposterous as "A Case in a Thousand" suggests, then a deliberately overwritten example of such a story is even more meaningless. Without its psychological suggestions, the plot of "A Case in a Thousand" is uninteresting: Dr. Nye operates on a boy who, by coincidence, is the son of Mrs. Bray, his former nanny; the boy dies; and Dr. Nye asks his nanny an unspecified question before they part. Throughout the story Beckett baits the reader, leading him to expect that some traumatic, sexual childhood experience will clarify events and explain that "sad" young man, Dr. Nye, whose very name suggests negation (cf. the French *nier*, to deny). Beginning with Dr. Nye's melodramatic recognition of Mrs. Bray, the story consistently creates innuendoes about their earlier relationship without ever disclosing "the trauma at the root of this attachment" (p. 242). What are otherwise natural responses—a boy's desire to marry his nurse, a kiss upon being reacquainted, a desire to ask an unasked question, a hand gesture—all become suspicious as the narrator of this exceedingly brief story chooses to dwell upon them—and to describe them in suggestive terms. Mrs. Bray feels Dr. Nye's hand upon her hat as an "imposition too pregnant for words" (p. 242). She is moved by his aghast and rapt expression during a therapeutic trance in a number of ways: ". . . to trouble, at such dissolution of feature; to gratification that at last she saw him as she could remember him; to shame, as the memory grew defined; to embarrassment, as though she were intruding on a privacy or a face asleep. She forced herself to look at her son instead. Then, very sensibly, she closed

her eyes altogether" (p. 242). The whole story vibrates with sexual under-
tones from Dr. Nye's preference for buttocks (p. 241) to his departures
from Mrs. Bray, once to "visit an old school fellow professionally" (p. 241)
and again to "carry out Wasserman's test on an old schoolfellow" (p. 241).
After the reader's curiosity has been carefully and almost perversely aroused
about the thing Dr. Nye had been wanting to ask and Mrs. Bray has been
wanting to tell, all is ironically and paradoxically dismissed as something
"so trivial and intimate that it need not be enlarged on here" (p. 242). Beginning in a quasi-psychological mode that invites identification, the story
rapidly and self-consciously distances us through parody. Ultimately, however, this movement is self-defeating as the reader learns to care for neither
the characters, nor the story, nor even the parody itself. Beckett has broken
a contract with his reader: the only way into his story is through acceptance
of the very conventions Beckett denies.

Like "Text," "Sedendo et Quiesciendo" was written in 1932 as part of
the unpublished *Dream of Fair to Middling Women*. Like "Text," the
piece uses a language that is self-consciously obfuscating, learned, and self-
gratulatory. Our attention is directed not to the characters and their interre-
lationships, but to sorting out the incredibly long sentences, foreign terms,
and recondite allusions. Unlike "Text," however, this section of *Dream* begins to suggest an interest in the persona of the narrator. The stream of
words is seen as issuing from a pompous, exuberant, satirical narrator who
refuses to fade into the background. Repeatedly he draws attention to his
own cleverness and control over the story as he addresses the reader directly
(pp. 15–16), edits his story (p. 16), or plays with his characters' name (p.
14). Increasingly he reveals his own personality through the language he
uses to describe the protagonist, Belacqua, and the women he meets, the
Smeraldina-Rima. The narrator's indelicacy of description matches Belacqua's coarseness of behavior in everything from Belacqua's nose-picking
to his role as a peeping tom (pp. 16, 18). His narrative omniscience does not
quite conceal the narrator's own voyeurism (pp. 18–19). The piece is a
prototype of the Beckettian "novel" in which characters, actions, and style
are a backdrop for the narrator himself. Although the language of "Sedendo
et Quiesciendo" is still the dazzling, print-oriented language of Beckett's
earliest period, the piece begins to replace the concerns in "Assumption"
for character, in "A Case in a Thousand" for parody, and in "Text" for
scintillating sound with an interest in the speaker of those sounds. The
narrator is beginning to emerge as interesting in his own right.

The liberation of the Beckettian narrator from the assumptions of the
Apollonian mode is continued in the stories collected in *More Pricks Than*

Kicks (1934).[8] Although many of these stories are successful by themselves, all of them benefit from their presentation as a collection dealing with Belacqua and his relationships with various women. Instead of having to recreate character, setting, or attitude with each new story, Beckett is freed by the accumulative nature of the work to concentrate on the expansion of his themes. While it is still very much an early work exhibiting Joycean influence, coterie language, interlocked images, and master craftsmanship, *More Pricks Than Kicks* is enabled by its larger context to emphasize an increasingly important narrative element. Suddenly, not only the *telling*, but also the *possibility* of telling a story become issues. Images of impotence begin to qualify those of control. The narrator becomes a figure whose comments are part of rather than intrusions on the story being told. Texture, though still a long way from the relaxed simplicity of spoken texts, inclines toward the less dense, the more manageable.

Belacqua, the main character of the stories, provides the central images of impotence. While he is not plagued by the degenerative processes that dissolve both names and bodies of the trilogy's figures, Belacqua is a modern antihero: not merely unendowed with superhuman powers, he is inferior to even the average man. Although a young man, Balacqua is already curiously aged and decayed, suffering from spavined feet (p. 14), impetigo (p. 24), and weak eyes (p. 83). He always looks "ill and dejected" (p. 15). He is a "grotesque person" (p. 15), a self-made hermit, a "creepy-crawly" voyeur (p. 108). Having denied Belacqua the power for external action, Beckett also deprives him of internal fortitude. Belacqua does not believe in the faiths he preaches: his self-sufficiency is belied by his anxiety to explain himself (p. 38), by his desire to return to the caul (p. 29), by his botched suicide (p. 99), by his indifference to this world, and by his fear of death (p. 161).

The satire which makes Belacqua a "non-knower, a non-can-er" also prevents him from being a Beckettian "hero." He only begins to replace the Apollonian with the Murphian outlook. Like Murphy, he seeks to dissociate mind and body through the refuge of a chair (p. 10), and he "scoffs at the idea of a sequitur from his body to his mind" (p. 29). He feels intimacy with the inmates rather than the doctors of the Portrane asylum ("Fingal"). He is troubled by problems of order and permutation (p. 79). But Belacqua is "an impossible person in the end" because he is not "serious" (p. 38): he is only a dilettante of the Murphian consciousness. While Murphy acknowledges the reality and attractions of the body (making music, Music, MUSIC with Celia is an earthly version of the pleasures offered at the M.M.M.), Belacqua pretends to be above such desires. He seeks to confine his musical relationship with Lucy to the gramophone but finds titillation in slipping off to the woods to watch "Fraulein and friends" ("Walking Out"). While Murphy's "vicarious autology" and responses to Mr. Endon are spontaneous, Belacqua's are constrained by rationality. He is incapable either of communicating with the Portrane inmates (p. 27), or of acting upon his own desires. Although he "could on no account resist a bicycle" (p. 27), Belacqua takes his joy ride only when no one else is in sight (p. 31). His solipsism yields to a "relish" for the world (p. 36). Belacqua's impotence is artificial and self-imposed. Ultimately he is neither Apollonian nor Beckettian, only satiric.

Although he is closer to a traditional hero than Beckett's later figures are, Belacqua is far less appealing. Whereas the wanderings of subsequent characters are ennobled by participation in quest motifs (if for nothing else, the figures are still impelled to search unendingly for an end to searching), Belacqua's motions are aimless and easily "come to anchor" at some "low public-house" (p. 42). Whereas other figures will continue their quests even when reduced to crawling by inexplicable and uncontrollable processes of decay, Belacqua, forced to crawl because of his own vices (drunkenness, p. 83, and voyeurism, p. 113), moves only to get away from his scenes of ignominy. Instead of struggling to define himself against the threatening chaos, Belacqua petulantly criticizes a society he is himself unwilling to leave. Less impotent than Beckett's later characters, Belacqua is nevertheless a weaker figure than they.

Belacqua's shortcomings are indicative of the shortcomings of *More Pricks Than Kicks*. Just as satire prevents Belacqua from being the hero of either "Assumption" or of the trilogy, so too the self-destructive nature of its satire prevents *More Pricks Than Kicks* from being viable as either a conventional or an innovative structure. As Beckettian criticism suggests, the work satirizes society, literature, and language without proposing any alternatives. It is a comedy of manners without an acceptable social norm.[9] Like "A Case in a Thousand," *More Pricks Than Kicks* has an almost decadent dependence upon the forms it debunks. One critic generously attributes this self-defeating satire to Beckett's early effort to break from literary conventions by destroying them.[10] But even granting Beckett the parodic impulse and the desire to demolish conventions by making them fail, it is hard not to accuse him of tilting at self-constructed windmills. His position is analogous to the one another critic attributes to Belacqua of suffering from a torment he has chosen himself and from which he could escape.[11] Beckett's anguish remains intellectual, for he can end his discontent—either by accepting conventional structures, or by creating new ones. Moreover, his satire is itself often incidental to the work, serving no other function than that of exhibiting the author's own cleverness. Rather than being the inevitable outgrowth of character and situation, the Alba's observation that we go through this world "like sunbeams through the cracks in cucumbers" ("A Wet Night," p. 69) is an academic allusion to one of the absurd labors undertaken at Swift's Royal Academy of Lagado. Similarly, self-conscious references to the book as a whole[12] serve only to highlight the differences between this centrifugal type of work which seems to be coming apart at the seams, and Joyce's centripetal kind of art which organically bonds every word into a seemingly indivisible totality.

Although Beckett's satire diverts him from creating a new and viable form, his parodies themselves are often brilliant. No longer merely imitating Joyce's style, Beckett consciously mimics it:

> A divine creature, native of Leipzig, to whom Belacqua, round about the following Epiphany, had occasion to quote the rainfall for December as cooked in the Dublin University Fellow's Garden, ejaculated:
> "Himmisacrakrüzidirkenjesumariaundjoseundblütigeskreuz!"
> Like that, all in one word. The thing people come out with sometimes! ("A Wet Night," p. 82)

Gerty McDowell's uneducated, romantic thoughts become the even more illiterate Smeraldina's billet doux, Stephen's Martello tower is located next to the Portrane Lunatic Asylum (p. 26), Mrs. Purefoy's labor pains are resolved into triplets (p. 126). Nor is Beckett content to confine his parodies to Joyce. It is humorous and disconcerting to find Belacqua implicitly transformed into Yorick by a drunken cemetary groundsman (p. 183) or to find the Smeraldina day-dreaming in the language of Valéry's mediation, "far far away with the corpse and her own spiritual equivalent in the boneyard by the sea" (p. 190). Beckett attacks his predecessors' big scenes and theories, transforming unity, meaning, and nobility into chaos, absurdity, and pathos. Wordsworth's epiphanical "spots of time" are turned by Belacqua into an excuse for indolence. Union and insight are replaced with a pure blank moment which can be passively endured: "Not the least charm of this pure blank movement, this 'gress' or 'gression,' was its aptness to receive, with or without the approval of the subject, in all their integrity the faint inscriptions of the outerworld. . . . This sensitiveness was not the least charm of this roaming. . . . But very nearly the least" ("Ding-Dong," p. 38). Not content with making the solipsistic Belacqua the antithesis of

D. H. Lawrence's sensual new man, Beckett offers in "Walking Out" his own version of the "real man" complete with rugged beauty, natural superiority, simple pride, and unpretentious dialect (pp. 103–04). All this nobility is somewhat dampened, however, as the Kerry blue makes herself at home upon the "real" man's trouser leg, " 'Wettin me throusers,' said the vagabond mildly, 'wuss'n meself'" (p. 104). Similarly, Birkin's pole-star equilibrium theory is undercut by the pathetic and disappointed life of Ruby Tough:

> Her sentimental experience had indeed been unfortunate. Requiring of love, as a younger and more appetising woman, that it should unite or fix her as firmly and as finally as the sun of a binary in respect of its partner, she had come to avoid it more and more as she found, with increasing disappointment and disgust, its effect at each successive manifestation . . . to be of quite a different order. The result of this erotic frustration was, firstly, to make her eschew the experience entirely; secondly, to recommend her itch for syzygy to more ideal measures. . . . ("Love and Lethe," pp. 87–88)

Like Beckett's other early pieces, *More Pricks Than Kicks* depends on associations with a traditional, knowable, material, external world. Instead of undifferentiated mud or geometrical shapes, we are presented with the bridges, hills, towers, and advertisements of a recognizably Irish setting (cf. especially "Fingal" and "A Wet Night"). The characters we meet are eccentric but stable and identifiable. Beckett even insinuates himself into the stories. He foists his own unpublished *Dream of Fair to Middling Women* upon poor Walter Draffin ("What a Misfortune," p. 143), and credits a "Mr. Beckett" with a pretentious German word (p. 176). But unlike some of Beckett's other early works, the stories in *More Pricks Than Kicks* are comprehensible without any knowledge of the biographical background. The stories are beginning to be understandable in spite of their coterie wit. The narrative elements are beginning to be important in themselves.

The narrative voice dictates the arrangement of the diverse stories moving the collection from an identification with, to an alienation from, Belacqua. The work begins in "Dante and the Lobster" with a third person, omniscient voice that lets us into Belacqua's thoughts and emotions. Although we may find him bizarre, we, like the narrator, are willing to suspend our own judgments in order to learn of Belacqua's. Indeed, the effect of the story depends on our being jolted by the last line, which contradicts Belacqua's opinion by asserting a superior point of view.

She lifted the lobster clear of the table. It had about thirty seconds
to live.

Well, thought Belacqua, it's a quick death, God help us all.

It is not. (p. 22)

The distancing begun by the line "It is not" is continued in "Fingal" as we
are excluded from more of Belacqua's mind. Like Winnie, we are never told
what Fingal means to Belacqua: "He would drop the subject, he would not
try to communicate Fingal, he would lock it up in his mind. So much the
better" (p. 26). By the third story, "Ding-Dong," the narrative strategy
has shifted from demanding a willing suspension of judgment, to requiring
a critical appraisal. Our narrator, the "sometime friend" (p. 36) of Belacqua,
emerges as a character in his own right, and it is his overthrow of Belacqua
and their former relationship as "Pylades and Orestes" (p. 37) that most
insistently forces us to recognize Belacqua's hypocrisies:

> He was at pains to make it clear to me. . . . In his anxiety to explain him-
> self he was liable to come to grief. Nay, this anxiety in itself, or so at least
> it seemed to me, constituted a breakdown in the self-sufficiency which he
> never wearied of arrogating to himself. . . . But he wriggled out of every-
> thing by pleading that he had been drunk at the time. . . . He was an
> impossible person in the end. I gave him up in the end because he was
> not *serious*. (pp. 37–38)

Belacqua's increasing drunkenness in "A Wet Night" proportionately distances us until we are ready, in "Love and Lethe," to switch our allegiance
from Belacqua to Ruby. In fact, the force of the story requires our at least
subconscious desire that Ruby gain "what she has missed and . . . what
she was missing" (p. 88). We too tolerate Belacqua and even his suicide pact
"in the hope that sooner or later, in a fit of ebriety or of common or garden
incontinence, he would so far forget himself as to take her in his arms"
(p. 88). Not only have the readers become removed from Belacqua, but
even the narrator no longer claims access to his mind: "Who shall judge
of his conduct at this crux? Is it to be condemned as wholly despicable? Is it
not possible that he was gallantly trying to spare the young woman embarrassment? Was it tact or concupiscence or the white feather or an accident
or what? We state the facts. We do not presume to determine their significance" (p. 99). The slow evaporation of concern for Belacqua continues
through the next two stories until, at the end of "What a Misfortune,"
Belacqua even loses interest in himself: "It was from this moment that he
used to date in after years his crucial loss of interest in himself, as in a grape

beyond his grasp" (p. 150). In the following story he is present only as the subject and recipient of "The Smeraldina's Billet Doux." "Yellow" momentarily allows us back into Belacqua's thoughts and feelings. This modicum of identification is necessary in order to make us feel the irony of Belacqua's life and death, and in order to set up the final story. Although Belacqua himself becomes increasingly unimportant, in "Draff" his satiric and indolent attitude prevails. Just as he had sought to dismiss the lobster's death as a quick one, so too we attempt to dismiss the absurd world Belacqua leaves behind with the anaesthetizing comment, "So it goes in the world" (p. 191). But the shifting focus has also taught us to expect an answering, "It is not."

By altering the narrator's relationship with Belacqua, Beckett is able to distance us from him without damaging, as in "A Case in a Thousand," either character or story. By altering the narrator's attitude, Beckett is able both to increase the narrator's importance and to affect our responses. How the story is told is becoming important. Although it is still told in very much an early period style, *More Pricks Than Kicks* initiates the quest for an adequate mode of saying the inexplicable.

3

Murphy (1938) [13] is Beckett's first successful accommodation of shape and the hypothesis that there may be no relationships among an artist, his art, and an external world. Although superficially the most conventional of Beckett's novels, *Murphy* ultimately expands and distorts Apollonian assumptions until they dissolve into intentional ambiguity. Language is made to deal with uncertainty; structure, to intimate fluidity. As traditional as *Murphy*'s form might appear initially, its language, characters, settings, and viewpoints are in fact products of and consistent with the Beckettian themes presented.

The best vehicle for conveying the Beckettian themes in *Murphy* is Murphy's mind itself. Instead of being drawn into the mind and developing the kind of rapprochement we have with a Stephen Dedalus, we are taken on a scientific tour of what Murphy felt his mind to be. It is a "large hollow sphere, hermetically closed to the universe without" (p. 107). It is a closed system, self-sufficient, subject to no principle of change but its own, impermeable to the vicissitudes of the body, and exclusive of "nothing that it did not itself contain" (p. 107) in either "actual" or "virtual" form. The "actual" are forms deriving from both mental and physical experience, while the "virtual" are forms involving solely mental experience. Murphy is unaware how these mental and physical experiences may overlap. Like Geulincx he reverts to "supernatural determination" (p. 109) to resolve (or more precisely to circumvent) Cartesian dualism and the disparity between the mind and "the big world" (p. 178). Ambiguity and ambivalence are preserved because no necessary and irrefutable connection exists between subject and object. Each individual arbitrarily imposes his own pattern of figures upon a universe that is entirely ground. As knowledge of this external and physical ground becomes impossible, movement within it becomes comparable to molecular motion in a gaseous system. Analogically, the familiar Beckettian paralysis becomes the exhaustion of random physical movement. *Murphy* is about Murphy's entropic quest to reach the point "where he could love himself" (p. 7) by annihilating that physical part of himself "which he hated" (p. 8). Although Murphy feels that his body can "think and know after a fashion . . . sufficient for his parody of rational behavior" (p. 110), physical motion must be done "carefully" (p. 84) and with an awareness that the necessary energy might dissipate "before he had half ended" (p. 138). True freedom exists only when the body is still and the mind is free to move through its various zones (p. 110).

The first zone of Murphy's mind, that of light, contains forms which imitate the external world. But since Murphy is free and sovereign in this zone, he can correct and adjust the torments of the physical world. "Here the kick that the physical Murphy received, the mental Murphy gave. . . . Here the whole physical fiasco became a howling success" (p. 111). The second zone, that of the half-light, contains forms which do not exist in any other mode. Hence, no effort of readjustment, no initiative, no choice is necessary. The pleasure is that of pure contemplation and peace—the Belacqua bliss. In the dark zone, the zone that Murphy prefers, there exists a perpetual flux of forms becoming, disintegrating, and becoming again without any intelligible principle of change. Here opposites are simultaneous and identical rather than mutually exclusive. All permutations are still possible; no physical contingencies exert arbitrary limit and order upon free-flowing potential. In this zone, "so pleasant that pleasant was not the word" (p. 113), Murphy approaches inertia as he becomes freed from his physical part. He is a "mote in the dark of absolute freedom . . . a point in the ceaseless unconditioned generation and passing away of line" (p. 112). Here he attains the intellectual irresponsibility of a mind made independent of body. He becomes "a missile without provenance or target, caught in a tumult of non-Newtonian motion" (p. 113). He achieves a state conventional society would term insanity based upon "the complacent scientific conceptualism that made contact with outer reality the index of mental well-being" (pp. 176–77).

The paradox of Murphy's quest is that it, like all Beckettian quests, is impossible and doomed to failure. Murphy seeks in this spatial, temporal world an existence beyond space and time; he seeks himself in a realm where the self does not exist; he seeks an ultimate expansion of self that inevitably leads to the ultimate contraction. The universe Murphy seeks is a curious combination of Einstein's relativity and Heraclitus's unity and sameness. Newtonian physics with its ordered but limited universe is rejected for a relative universe. The simple, mathematical, and precise are replaced by the ambiguous, paradoxical, and unknowable. The laws of gravity become the enigmatic "the way up and down is one and the same," [14] while the laws of motion yield to the concept that ". . . these things having changed round are those, and those things having changed round 'again' are these ones." [15] Where all is flux, the only principle of consistency is that all possibilities are possible. In fact, Murphy's quest necessitates learning a lesson: where one is nothing, one can prefer nothing. As long as Murphy prefers to eat the anonymous biscuit first and the ginger last, his permutations are limited from a full 120 to a paltry six: "Overcome by these perspectives Murphy fell forward on his face on the grass, beside those biscuits of which it could be said as truly as of the stars, that one differed from another, but of which he could not partake in their fulness until he had learnt not to prefer any one to any other" (p. 97). The ending of *Murphy* is appropriately ambiguous as Beckett refuses to tell us if Murphy has learned his lesson. We do not know if Murphy's epiphanical moment (pp. 245–53) leads to the realization that he would become an Endon only when he ceased to have preferences, even preferences for the Mr. Endons, or if his insight is of limitation—that he cannot help preferring the Endons and thus never will be more than "a speck in Mr. Endon's unseen" (p. 250). We do not know if Murphy's last rock with its surrealistic visions indicates Murphy's successful immersion of self into the dark zone, or if it is, on the contrary, a gesture of despair. Through his ambivalence Beckett skillfully keeps open all the permutations of meaning in *Murphy*. Our final image becomes an embodiment of the paradoxical flux and negation of the book rather than a key to its ultimate answers. Mr. Kelly's kite attains ultimate freedom and expansion as it pierces the dome of the visible universe to escape into the "unseen" (p. 280), to become a "mote in the dark of absolute freedom" (p. 112). Yet, at the same moment, the kite also reaches the ultimate contraction as it ceases to exist in the world of Celia and Mr. Kelly, as it becomes the nothingness sounding in the off-stage cries of the rangers, "All out. All out" (pp. 281–82). By careful manipulation of the themes of flux, permutation, ambivalence, and negation, Beckett creates a quest that presents simultaneously both sides of a paradox. The same careful manipulation of these paradoxical processes is present in the structure of *Murphy* itself.

Although *Murphy* might appear Apollonian in its ability to do and know, in its density of texture, and in its sheer exuberance, even these elements are consistent with the Murphian consciousness as Beckett's vitality and excess lead to the explosion of his language into artificiality. In his later works Beckett deals with "the sounds the mind makes in actually grappling with words."[16] The result is a sense of the distance between the words and the panting voices that mutter them in the mud. The narrators can find no words weak enough to describe their positions. In *Murphy* the same effect is achieved by opposite means. Words contain a plethora of meanings as secondary and tertiary meanings, etymological implications, and even synonyms, antonyms, and homonyms are all made present to us. This superabundance of meanings collapses into a sense of the real vacuity and meaninglessness of words, just as the gesture that points in several directions ultimately distinguishes none. Beckett's insistence upon maintaining all possible permutations of meanings leads to ambivalence and flux, to a language of paradox and negation.

One of the simplest ways of introducing the concepts of permutation and paradox into a language is through the use of word games. Beckett, like Joyce, is a master of the janus-faced word. He delights in the overt word game that self-consciously announces itself, in the more subtle game that almost escapes detection, and in the complex game that joyfully compounds itself. Murphy reads in his "blackmail" (p. 32) Nativity that a fruitful life is to be obtained by cultivating his lucky color, lemon, with a "dash in apparel, also a squeeze in home decorations" (p. 33). Cooper professes that Celia's features have escaped his detection because of the dusk, the distance, "the posterior aspect (surely a very thin excuse), and so on" (p. 203). Cooper himself never sat, "his acathisia was deep-seated and of long-standing" (p. 119).

The shifting sense of Beckett's words begun by his games is continued in more sophisticated associations. Some knowledge of Latin, Greek, and behaviorist psychology is necessary to savor the full fragrance of Celia's "happy inspiration" in talking with the incurably smelly Miss Carridge (pp. 68–69), to order Murphy's random comments on chaos (p. 175), and to appreciate the "Skinner House" as providing the perfectly controlled atmosphere for learning the pecking order of "lit, indicated, extinguished" (p.

247). In *Murphy's Bed,* Sighle Kennedy gives an entertaining study of these "mantic meanings" in *Murphy,* tracing Murphy's name from the Greek word for form (*morphe*) through Morpheus, Endymion, *Ulysses,* a murphy bed, biscuits, and Greenwich Mean Time. Whether or not we are willing to go to Kennedy's extremes, we discover that the "crystalline" structure Oliver Wendell Holmes attributed to words begins to liquify and flow into new areas under Beckett's influence. We begin to think of hands as "pocketed" (p. 15), of chairs as the "massive upright upholstered armchairs, similar to those killed under him by Balzac" (p. 63), and of social decorum as maintaining "a little conduction" (p. 221). We become attuned to the juxtaposing of literal and figurative meanings: "Celia . . . dragged her tattered bust back into the room, the old boy's. 'Bosom friends of Mr. Murphy,' said Miss Carridge" (p. 229). Words are permutable and ambivalent essences that begin to flow into their opposites whenever the mind tries to capture the physical world through them.

Beckett's art is not content to play only with words. One of the triumphs of *Murphy* is the way it subverts our own assumptions and perceptions. Suddenly, innocuous phrases no longer say what we expected them to say. Although the characters are able to move with ease through the coruscating prose, we are often pulled up short or made to do a double-take. We may suddenly find ourselves floundering in a world of grotesque propositions: Celia storms "away from the callbox, accompanied delightedly by her hips, etc." (pp. 10–11); Murphy enjoys the sensation of a sit (p. 80); Cooper enters a room with "his glass eye bloodshot" (p. 119). We alone seem to be aware of the absurdity of Dr. Killiecrankie asking if "Mrs. Murrrphy" is the Dutch uncle (p. 268) or of the narrator saying, "In the presence of such grief Wylie felt purer than at any time since his second communion" (p. 51). Joycean irony flavors Pandit Suk's claim, "Famous Throughout Civilized World and Irish Free State" (p. 32) and Murphy's "maiden night" run of "virgins and Irish virgins" (pp. 242–43).

Perhaps the most striking devaluation of our efforts to connect word and world, arises from Beckett's use of negation and identified contrarieties. He presents a statement with one hand, while the other hand subtly takes it away. He controverts the expectations he raises by negating the cliché and twisting the aphorism. The result is that we read two sentences simultaneously—the one we "virtually" anticipated and the one we are "actually" given. Notice, for example, how the phrase "*in*adequate to *conceal*" reverses our expectations and understandings: "He stood with his back to the door, one hand behind him holding the handle, the other describing the gesture that he always used when words were inadequate to conceal what he felt" (p. 130). Similarly, perhaps only Milton could surpass the bewildering complexity of negatives used in describing Murphy's mind: "This was not an impoverishment, for it excluded nothing that it did not itself contain" (p. 107). By slightly modifying and negating familiar phrases Beckett creates an eccentric and extraordinary universe containing curios like a "little bull of incommunication" (p. 31), "one chest, not of drawers" (p. 162), and the "encounter, on which so much unhinges . . ." (p. 112). The doubletake effected by negation and ambivalence reaches its apex in Wylie's irrefutable conundrum: " 'Tut! Tut!' said Wylie, 'I may not be a trueborn jackeen, but I am better than nothing. My superiority to nothing has often been commented on' " (p. 220).

In its very expansion the language of *Murphy* falls into contraction in much the same way that Bosch's unlimited fertility turns paradise into a "surreal" nightmare. Words with multiple meanings collapse into meaninglessness and man is left exiled from the physical sphere. Gestures, phrases, and sentences challenge us as their ambivalence and permutability make us take a second look at them and what they stand for. The Apollonian qualities of the language plunge the prose of *Murphy* into the dark zone where all is flux and where "neither darkness nor light, neither bad nor good are different, but one and the same thing. . . . And good and evil are one." [17]

Similarly, seemingly traditional characters are slowly perverted by the pervasive Murphian consciousness into figures more appropriate to the *noveau roman*. In an essay "On Several Obsolete Notions" Robbe-Grillet summarizes the attributes of a conventional literary figure. He has a name, background, profession, possessions, recognizable features, distinct personality. He reacts in a predictable fashion, is able to be judged by the reader, and is both universal and unique. Above all he "is not a banal *he*, anonymous and transparent, the simple subject of the action expressed by the verb." [18] At least some of these terms could be applied to almost all of *Murphy*'s figures. Unlike the self-negating characters in the French trilogy, *Murphy*'s characters are identifiable, relatively stable, and recognizably human. They possess, at least partially, the unique personalities, backgrounds, and features of traditional characters. They are not merely the "banal *he*" implied by a predicate. But just as negation and flux erode the supports of language, so too they silently alter the fixed quantities of our characters.

Although their names are more human than the nonsense syllables given Pim and Bom and more dependable than the stream of names given the protagonist(s) in the trilogy, they still tend toward caricature. While

Murphy ("the man was unbaptised," p. 268) and Celia Kelly have relatively conventional names, others, like Neary, Needle Wylie, Rosie Dew, Miss Carridge, Bom and Bim Clinch, Austin Ticklepenny, and Dr. Killiecrankie have progressively more comic and self-conscious names, which call attention to the characters as characters of a fiction. Their pseudo-realism is annulled. Their "traditionalism" is undermined as they are turned into cartoon figures who waddle through life plagued by "Panpygoptosis" (p. 97), sedately endure "acathisia" (p. 119), or are sensitized by "insmell" to a peculiar infirmity (p. 32). Beckett even vivisects his characters in embodying the Cartesian schism. Murphy has trouble deciding where to put the receiver of the phone when Celia calls (p. 8). Mr. Kelly is incapable of answering Celia's questions until he has gathered together the pieces of his mind which are scattered about his body: "Part was with its caecum, which was wagging its tail again; part with his extremities, which were dragging anchor; part with his boyhood; and so on" (p. 19, cf. also p. 115).

The removal of an individual character's underpinning is accompanied by an excavation of realistic characterization in general. Beckett blatantly refuses to allow even the most willing suspenders-of-disbelief to retain faith in the "realism" of his figures. Not only do we see them placed in various scenes by the narrator's stage directions (pp. 208, 231, 232), but we even have point-blank references to their artificiality: "All the puppets in the book whinge sooner or later, except Murphy, who is not a puppet" (p. 122). Moreover, we begin to realize the essential sameness of all the characters. They are interchangeable elements in an equation. In spite of their scintillating badinage Wylie, Miss Counihan, and Neary begin to sound alike. Neary, without any alteration in his own character, can facilely substitute Celia for Murphy for Miss Counihan for Miss Dwyer just as Miss Counihan seems finally indifferent to whether the provider of the finer things to which she has become accustomed is Murphy, Neary, or Wylie. Our Heraclitian sense of the unity of all things is underlined as we see characters repeating each others' actions and gestures. Neary's aborted hand gestures that so annoy Murphy (p. 5) are more successfully repeated by Mr. Kelly (p. 24) and Celia (p. 35) and faintly reappear even in the "wild gesture of metaphysical liquidation" of Miss Counihan's Hindu (p. 255). Our initial vision of Celia sitting upon Mr. Kelly's bed (pp. 23–24) and his pinioning her wrists as she rises to go (p. 25) is repeated in Celia's position on Murphy's bed (p. 29) and his pinioning of her wrists (p. 40). Both scenes are visually alluded to when Miss Counihan sits on Neary's bed (p. 208). Likewise, Murphy's distinction of experience based upon good and bad jokes (p. 65) is parodied in Ticklepenny's distinction of reprimands (p. 170) and is negatively duplicated in Wylie's lack of distinctions (p. 277). Thematic issues are underlined as Cooper's negative capability and Mr. Kelly's fondness for his own chair (p. 277) emphasize Murphy's obsession with his chair. Celia's attempts to be seen by Murphy (pp. 13, 14) are important foreshadowings of Murphy's futile efforts to be seen by Mr. Endon (p. 248). In the most important repetition of the novel Celia imitates Murphy's mental motion. Not only does she give up street walking for the pleasures of sitting nude in the rocking chair, not only does she "understand as soon as he gave up trying to explain . . . [that] where livings were being made . . . they were being made away" (p. 67), but most significantly she moves through the mental zones Murphy envisions, ending in the dark flux where she no longer exists, no longer has any history:

> She got out of her clothes and into the rocking-chair. Now the silence above was a different silence, no longer strangled. The silence not of vacuum but of plenum, not of breath taken but of quiet air. The sky. She closed her eyes and was in her mind with Murphy, Mr. Kelly, clients, her parents, others, herself a girl, a child, an infant. In the cell of her mind, teasing the oakum of her history. Then it was finished, the days and places and things and people were untwisted and scattered, she was lying down, she had no history. (pp. 148–49)

She, like Geulincx (p. 178) and Murphy (p. 179), learns to want nothing in order to be nothing, "So Neary and Celia cease slowly to need Murphy. He, that he may need her; she, that she may rest from need" (p. 256). Although she returns to prostitution (p. 277), Celia has become detached from the external world. She no longer notices "the ludicrous fever of toys struggling skyward, the sky itself . . . the wind tearing the awning of clouds to tatters . . . the light failing . . ." (p. 281).

Although *Murphy* begins as if it will follow Robbe-Grillett's definition of traditional characters, it ends in character descriptions and movements closer to his concept of the new novel: "A few paragraphs more and, when the description comes to an end, we realize that it has left nothing behind it: it has instituted a double movement of creation and destruction. . . . The entire interest of the descriptive page—that is, man's place in these pages—is therefore no longer in the thing described, but in the very movement of the description." [19] We have left only Murphy, and possibly Celia. They remain distinct for us because of all the characters they alone are presented in both their mental and physical spheres. We see them acting as perceiver and perceived. In a dualistic world we cannot know characters presented in their physical realm only. A character who opts for the "big world" (p. 178) can "comfort himself with the society of others in the same predicament" (p. 177), but our perception of him is limited to the sameness of his predicament.

Our first impression of the "big world" in *Murphy*—its time, space, and place—is one of traditional, Newtonian limits and realities. We are securely located in positive space. We know that we are in London in 1935 on Brewery Road in Miss Carridge's house, or in the Skinner House of the M.M.M. "ideally situated in its own grounds on the boundary of two counties" (p. 156). The architecture of buildings (pp. 165–66) and the decor of rooms (pp. 63, 64, 162) are given to us. It is possible to determine the precise day and sometimes even the very hour or minute in which an event occurs.[20] Unlike *Molloy*, *Malone Dies*, and *The Unnamable* where time is discontinuous, where we are unsure *when, where, why* or even *if* an event happened, in *Murphy* we have a distinct past, present, and future which our own reading experience supports. Memory is thus validated, linear patterns substantiated, causal relations intimated.

But, even as he establishes this "realistic" setting of time, space, and place, Beckett discards it by ascribing true existence and freedom to the atemporal, nonspatial dark zone. The elaborate overlay of time is seen precisely as an overlay, incidental to the real center of the book. Its function is as a structuring principle on which to hang the story. It is present not because it is necessary, but because it has no choice. "The sun shone, having no alternative, on the nothing new" (p. 1). Any intercourse between the "realistic" setting and the characters is limited to the accidental mingling embodied in Murphy's final spatial arrangement: "By closing time the body, mind and soul of Murphy were freely distributed over the floor of the saloon; and before another dayspring greyed the earth had been swept away with the sand, the beer, the butts, the glass, the matches, the spits, the vomit" (p. 275). Time and space are tempered by the same negating irony to which the language and characters are subjected. Murphy hears a cuckoo-clock strike "between twenty and thirty" (p. 2); Celia dispenses with even the mention of time and place as she tells Murphy, "Meet me at the usual at the usual" (p. 8). Even Beckett's astrology is debunked when one discovers that Murphy's Nativity—drawn up without reference to the time "of the unhappy event" of Murphy's birth (p. 23)—describes an all but impossible positioning of the heavens.[21] Space becomes the external factor Murphy "can't talk against" (p. 39) and time, though it does not stop—"that would be asking too much" (p. 246)—becomes relegated to the cessation of "the wheel of rounds and pauses" (p. 246).

The antagonism the characters feel toward space and time is further revealed in their actions. In relatively violent protests Murphy and Celia retreat to the chair, Neary ensconces himself in bed, Mr. Endon immures himself in his mind (p. 180). But subtle protests against the outer world are also evident. One of the major motifs is the closing of one's eyes to block out the external world. In fact, the book is an exploration of "how various are the ways of looking away!" (p. 264). Murphy can "see" only in the dark, his own dark which excludes the "big world." In order to see Miss Counihan "he had to close his eyes" (p. 90). Likewise, he does not see Celia until she is physically absent and his mind is free to meet her in the dark flux (pp. 90–91). His mind can produce better images than the external order can: he can improve on time and space:

. . . by closing his eyes he could be in an archaic world very much less corrupt than anything on view in the B.M. (p. 95)

. . . he might lie down, cease to take notice and enter the landscapes where there were no chandlers and no exclusive residential cancers, but only himself improved out of all knowledge. (p. 79)

The prejudice for the inner world is intimated in the directional change of Murphy's prepositions. Opening one's eyes is a coming "from," not a coming "to" (p. 105). Mr. Endon's perspicacity here surpasses Murphy's as he manages to eliminate even the desire to see. The sad truth is that Murphy for Mr. Endon is neither felt as the friend's eye (p. 241), nor as Murphy's eye (p. 242), nor as the chessy eye (p. 242). Rather he is only "a speck in Mr. Endon's unseen" (p. 250). According to the opacity of their mind's eyes, other characters are able to imitate to varying degrees Murphy's partial and Mr. Endon's total exclusion of time and space. Even the coroner shuts out the mortuary in order to sink a long putt (pp. 260–61).

A motif closely related to this visual attempt to block out the realities of setting concerns the problems of "meeting." In a world of closed systems it is perhaps inevitable that most of the characters enter vain quests to break out of themselves. Celia tries to "meet" Murphy and Mr. Kelly; Neary seeks Miss Dwyer, Miss Counihan, Murphy, Celia; Miss Carridge longs for anyone who seems immune to her peculiar problem. The futility of their searches lies in the confusion of mutually exclusive realms. Neary tries to make virtues of his intellectual walls making "meeting" the "repudiation of the known . . . a purely intellectual operation of unspeakable difficulty" (p. 222). But it is Miss Counihan who comes closest to articulating the Murphian resolution of the problem: "It is only in the dark that one can meet" (p. 234). Just as Murphy must close his eyes to block out time and space in order to "see" Celia or Miss Counihan, so too must physical "realities" be overcome by submersion in the dark flux where "one can meet." Time and space are the obstacles about which the real motion of *Murphy* revolves.

Murphy's orbit around a traditional novel structure attains its perigee in the realm of narrative consciousness. The narrator self-consciously orders characters and actions. He knows the end of the story and is able to anticipate events (e.g., pp. 7 and 9 anticipate Section Six) and pass judgments (e.g., "So all things hobble together for the only possible," pp. 227, 235). As might be expected, however, Beckett expands the narrator's self-conscious omniscience until it negates itself and contracts into impotence. Beckett deliberately draws attention to the artifice of fiction and specifically questions the nature of his own art. We are forced to reevaluate our assumptions about narrative form when we hear Mr. Kelly denounce setting and motive as the "beastly circumstantial" and "demented particulars" (p. 13). Like Mr. Kelly we begin to feel that the contingencies of the physical world with which Celia fills her narration are obfuscating, "Hell roast this story . . . I shall never remember it" (p. 15). The introduction of Ticklepenny's "poetry" (pp. 84, 85) presents another challenge to art. His poems, like his radiator, can neither bridge the gap between, nor reside within the realms of either imagination or reality: "He related how the crazy installation had developed, step by step, typically, from the furthest-fetched of visions to a reality that would not function" (p. 17). Our questions about the role and function of art are increased as the narrator reveals that, in spite of his professed control, he is obligated to express elements he would prefer to leave unmentioned (pp. 86 and 107). Furthermore, the narrator's caustic comments force us to reexamine our own relation to *Murphy*. Blatant references to the narrator's control (e.g., his stage directions and his "expurgated, accelerated, improved and reduced" accounts given to Celia, p. 12; Neary, p. 48; Ticklepenny, p. 87, Cooper, p. 119) draw our attention to our voluntary submission to the fiction. This submission is in turn made painful and questionable as the narrator's asides become more pointed. He introduces passages to satisfy "the filthy censors" (p. 76), catch the "gentle skimmer" (p. 84), "deprave the cultivated reader" (p. 224). The narrator even seems to transpose us into the fictive world as he gives warnings in the imperative mood, "Do not come down the ladder, they have taken it away" (p. 188). We are no longer the "gentle skimmer" but characters capable of falling down the empty ladderway. Beckett's extraordinary ability to create and simultaneously destroy his fiction and its narrative voice enables him to capture our interest in his characters at the very moment he is exposing them. "He [Murphy] tried with men, women, children, and animals that belong to even worse stories than this" (p. 251).

Just as Murphy's attempts to penetrate Mr. Endon's chess game fail (pp. 243–44) and just as his association with the patients of the M.M.M. can only be one of "vicarious autology" (p. 189), so too are the narrator's attempts to penetrate the closed systems of the characters doomed to failure. Beckett allows the narrator to describe what Murphy felt his mind to be, but he never lets the narrator actually enter that "little world." The narrator, like astrology, is one of the external systems of "subordination" and meaning that Murphy refutes. Although the narrative voice is skillful, glib, and ironic, its stream of words can describe the flux only metaphorically; the words can never actually *be* the flux. In contrast to Beckett's assertions in "Dante . . . Bruno. Vico . . Joyce," writing here can only be *about* something, "it is [not] *the something itself.*" The real center of Murphy remains ambivalent and elusive. Our "omniscient" narrator is ultimately unable to close the fissure begun by Descartes, unable to penetrate another's closed system, unable to resolve ambivalences. His self-conscious control flows into impotence before final questions. He holds two visions at one time, the traditional vision "that depends on light, object, viewpoint, etc., and the vision that all those things embarrass" (p. 90).

Although *Murphy* might seem at first to emulate a traditional structure, to be a work of omniscience and omnipotence, its structure is consistent with Beckettian impotence and ignorance. The principles behind "Murphy's mind"—Cartesian dualism, ambivalence, permutation, flux, negation, and paradoxical expansion into contraction—are the same principles operating on the structural elements of *Murphy*. The symbiotic relationships between the Murphian mind and the novel's language, characters, setting, and viewpoint, turn an expanding traditional structure into a contracting inconoclastic one. The self-defeating dependence of earlier works upon the conventions they debunked is overcome as Beckett places the conventions themselves into a fluid world. Traditional, fixed, and certain relationships dissolve as Beckett discovers a way to make structure intimate fluidity and language confront uncertainty. *Murphy* is the first of Beckett's works to find a shape to accommodate the chaos.

3. Fragmentation and tessellation

"These fragments I have shored against my ruins."[1] —T. S. Eliot

"I think if I could be given a month of Antiquity and leave to spend it where I chose, I would spend it in Byzantium a little before Justinian opened St. Sophia and closed the Academy of Plato. I think I could find in some little wine-shop some philosophical worker in mosaic who could answer all my questions, the supernatural descending nearer to him than to Plotinus even. . . . I think that in early Byzantium, maybe never before or since in recorded history, religious, aesthetic and practical life were one, that architect and artificers . . . spoke to the multitude and the few alike. The painter, the mosaic worker, the worker in gold and silver, the illuminator of sacred books, were almost impersonal, almost perhaps without the consciousness of individual design, absorbed in their subject-matter and that the vision of a whole people. They could copy out of old Gospel books those pictures that seemed as sacred as the text, and yet weave all into a vast design, the work of many that seemed the work of one, that made building, picture, pattern, metal-work of rail and lamp, seem but a single image: and this vision, this proclamation of their invisible master had the Greek nobility, Satan always the still half-divine Serpent, never the horned scarecrow of the didactic Middle Ages."[2] —W. B. Yeats

"The forms are many in which the unchanging seeks relief from its formlessness."[3] —Samuel Beckett

When *The Waste Land* first appeared T. S. Eliot was seen to be giving voice to the modern age and to its sense of alienation and confusion caused by the collapse of traditional beliefs. The poem seemed to range through

Western culture gleaning images, quotations, and symbols by which modern man might sustain himself in the midst of the universal breakdown. As the last lines suggested, the poem offered us the fragments of civilization which it had shored against our ruin. In doing so, *The Waste Land* provided both an image of the age and a pattern for the artist in the early decades of the century: out of the scraps and pieces of a broken culture the artist fashioned a design and thus transcended the surrounding fragmentation by synthesizing his own order. For many artists, however, this heroic act of synthesis was destroyed by the advent of World War II. The gap between the orders of art and the shards of society became simply too large to bridge. Postwar artists could not put civilization back together; indeed critics often doubted that they could put the novel together again. The contemporary artist, it seems, must choose between accepting and even celebrating the artificiality of his orders (cf. Vladimir Nabokov in *Pale Fire*) or seeking a disintegrative art form that reflects the chaos itself.

Beckett is often considered the latter type of artist, the artist of fragmentation. Whereas T. S. Eliot created from the broken segments about him a bulwark against uncertainty and fluidity, Beckett rigorously and unflinchingly explodes even those segments. His works progressively break down and strip away the tatters of conventional associations. The fragmentation is the result of Beckett's unremitting efforts to find a shape for the possibility that no relationships exist between or among the artist, his art, and an external world. Once his earliest fictions had mocked traditional relationships and once *Murphy* had exploded them by following them to their logical ends, Beckett sought to create a nonrelational art by breaking apart whatever pieces of identity, time, space, and language remained. Like the emergence of the first person narrator and the switch to composition in French, fragmentation is one of the identifying characteristics of Beckett's most prolific period (1944–50). *Watt* splits once and for all the logic of language from the world of events. The chapter summaries of *Mercier and Camier* sever the illusions of plot and narrative time. The trilogy is a masterpiece of negation, contradiction, and disruption. As a glance at the list of works written and translated between 1944 and 1950 reveals, the period is astounding in its quantity, quality, diversity, and disintegration.

1944 *Watt*
1945 "Saint-Lô" (poem)
1946 "Mort d'A.D." (poem)
     "La Fin" ("The End"—1954)

"L'Epulsé" ("The Expelled"—1962)
"Premier Amour" ("First Love"—1972)
"Le Calmant" ("The Calamative"—1967)
Le Voyage de Mercier et Camier autour du Pot dans les Bosquets de Bondy (*Mercier and Camier*—1974)
1947 *Molloy* (translated into English 1951)
Eleuthéria (unpublished)
1948 *Six Poèmes* (translated into English 1961)
Malone meurt (*Malone Dies*—1956)
En attendant Godot (*Waiting for Godot*—1954)
1949 *L'Innommable* (*The Unnamable*—1958)
1950 *Textes pour rien* (*Texts for Nothing*—1967)

As disintegrated as these pieces apparently are, they are nonetheless still works of literature. It is inadequate to describe them in terms of fragmentation only. Beckett does take conventional literary shapes and structures and break them apart, but his works are intelligible only if the reader assumes partial responsibility for them and accepts the task of reconstructing the disruptive and broken forms. Although Beckett may not provide T. S. Eliot's cultural synthesis, he does demand that his reader be involved in the reconstruction of a discourse. Although his works may never proffer completed conventional structures, his pieces depend on the reader's perceptions of the disparity between the recognizable fragments he is given and the traditions they deliberately do not fulfill. The "failures" of Mercier and Camier's trip or of Moran's report are evident only in contrast to our unsatisfied expectations about the nature of the quest or detective report. Like the reader, the narrator of Beckett's fictions devotes much of his energy to shaping and reshaping the fragments available to him. Watt obsessively explores all possible explanations of the appearance of two piano tuners. Malone keeps rearranging his possessions and stories. The Unnamable orders and reorders the images and words that might constitute his pensum. They are all, as the narrator of *Enough* suggests of himself, cursed by the "art of combining."

Beneath the reduction and negation of Beckett's fragmentation is always the implicit coherence of tessellation. The works may never be recombined into an absolute truth, but at least they may be shaped into a story freed from the constraints of former associations. Yeats once located his vision of perfection in sixth-century Byzantium where he felt even the mosaic worker was a philosopher in tune with the supernatural, where life was so unified that the artisans instinctively and impersonally spoke to a whole people, where every act contributed to the vast design and single image of Greek nobility. Yeats's harmony and unity of vision are never the reward of Beckett's mosaic workers who recombine fragments that never produce the anticipated pattern. It is as if important pieces and colors of the mosaic had been lost so that the resulting image is rife with gaps comparable to the gaps in our knowledge. Just as there is no rational number for the square root of two, so too there is no mosaic, image, or word for the unnamable of Beckett's fiction. In fact *Watt* and *Mercier and Camier* emphasize the inabilities of the pieces to produce a single image and of language to say the unspeakable. In Beckett's other works, the effects of his tessellation may be compared to the effects of an irreparably jumbled collection of jigsaw puzzles in which the individual tesserae are interchangeable but the pictures are not. The pieces will all fit together, just as Beckett's fictions all cohere and adhere to amazingly rigid rules of composition, but the images produced are not familiar and recognizable ones—the abstractions are not concretized.[4] The advantage of this analogy is that it parallels a movement in Beckett's works that becomes increasingly pronounced in the years from 1944 to 1950: the fragmented and tessellated pieces begin to suggest an archetypal story. Having broken apart false distinctions and fragmented artificial structures in *Watt* and *Mercier and Camier*, Beckett has his narrators in the four short stories and in the trilogy confront the human condition stripped to its most essential ingredients. Amid the fragments man's only story, indeed his identity itself, becomes the act of narration. Beneath the disparate surfaces lies the vast, continuous buzzing heard in *Malone Dies, The Unnamable, How It Is, Not I*: "What I mean is possibly this, that the noises of the world, so various in themselves and which I used to be so clever at distinguishing from one another, had been dinning at me for so long, always the same old noises, as gradually to have merged into a single noise, so that all I heard was one vast continuous buzzing" (*Malone Dies*, p. 207). The buzzing is continuous, but the shapes in which it is manifested are multifold. In *Texts for Nothing* Beckett combines the universal buzzing and archetypal story-teller with the earlier impetus toward nothingness. The result is a work in which the thirteen different versions of the narrator's identity combine to suggest an image of the underlying void. The void and the uncertainty and fluidity of the chaos remain because Beckett's reintegrations refuse to restore us to the associations of relational art. Although he does not follow Eliot's example and synthesize fragments of our civilization into a new and saving version of reality, and although he does not provide Yeats's vast and noble design, Beckett does transcend mere disintegration. His dual processes of fragmentation and tessellation provide new shapes for the possibility of a nonrelational art. As Malone observes: "The forms are many in which the unchanging seeks relief from its formlessness" (*Malone Dies*, p. 197).

1

The picture in Erskine's room and Watt's reaction to it offer an emblem not only of Watt's experience in Mr. Knott's house, but also of the reader's primal experience in confronting Beckett's works. The picture is of the black circumference of a circle, "obviously described by a compass, and broken at its lowest point," and a blue dot in the eastern background, "the rest was white."5 The picture is abstract and precisely defined. But Watt is unable to view this simple picture without attempting to explain it, to attribute to it an effect of perspective and an illusion of movement (pp. 128–29). He imposes motivation upon the picture and speculates about the artist's intentions: "Watt wondered how long it would be before the point and circle entered together upon the same plane. . . . Watt wondered if they had sighted each other, or were blindly flying thus. . . . He wondered if they would eventually pause and converse. . . . And he wondered what the artist had intended to represent . . ." (*Watt*, p. 129). Although there is no definite top to the picture, Watt prefers, in remotely sexual terms, to have the breach below (p. 130). Moreover, Watt seems to derive a curious consolation from the picture. He is driven to tears which refresh him greatly by the proposition (characteristically devoid of hope) that the picture represents a circle in search of its center, and a center in search of its circle, but the center and circle respectively required are not present in the picture (p. 129). Like the picture, Beckett's pieces offer stark and reduced images which the reader seeks to explain. Precisely because they are more stark than conventional works, Beckett's pieces provide us with less evidence from which to formulate our interpretations. Like Watt, we invoke aesthetic terms, effects, and illusions to justify our preference for certain stories, interpretations, and combinations of shapes. But, just as the circle and dot cannot be transformed into a triangle and square, so too we cannot impose an infinite number of readings upon the works. We are restricted in our tessellations by the bits of narration actually presented to us. Just as Watt can never provide an absolute explanation of the picture in Erskine's room, so too we can never assert with certainty what Beckett's works ultimately "mean."

Similarly, the consolation provided by Beckett's broken mosaics is the same bittersweet relief implicit in Watt's tears before the impossible, incomplete quest he sees represented by the picture.

Watt's experience with the picture is characteristic of his experience in Mr. Knott's house generally. The underlying uniformity of Watt's experiences leads the narrator to speculate whether the incidents related by Watt "as separate and distinct . . . are not in reality the same incident variously repeated" (p. 78). Watt is confronted by events "of great formal brilliance and indeterminable purport" (p. 74), which he attempts to explain in much the same way as he attempts to fashion from the circle and dot an interpretation that encompasses motivation, signification, and consolation. But his efforts at explication fail, not, as many critics have suggested, because his system of logic is internally inconsistent, but rather because that system is irretrievably split from the world of phenomena it is supposed to describe. Logic depends upon systematic application of the process of elimination in a field of limited possibilities. In *Watt*, Beckett preserves the system, but places it in a field of unlimited possibilities in which all alternatives are equally available. The limitations of common sense and probability are themselves eliminated so that, for example, in exploring the instructions "to give what Mr Knott left of this dish, on the days that he did not eat it all, to the dog" (p. 91), Watt is free not only to hypothesize entire generations of needy local men and famished dogs (pp. 91–115), but also to treat his hypotheses as reality and refuse "to assist at the eating, by the dog, of Mr Knott's remains" (p. 115). The structures of logic become useless in an absurd world, but, nonetheless, the structures are jealously maintained despite mathematical error (p. 104) and the nonsequiturs of idiomatic language:

> For if Erskine's room had been *always* locked, and the key *always* in Erskine's pocket, then Erskine himself, for all his agility, would have been hard set to glide in and out of his room, in the way he did, unless he had glided in and out by the window, or the chimney. But in and out by the window he could not have glided, without breaking his neck, nor in and out by the chimney, without being crushed to death. (*Watt*, p. 124)

Empirical evidence to the contrary, Watt persists, because "logic was on his side" (p. 219), in striving to correct the poor fit of his mismatched boots by wearing two socks on one foot and none on the other. The same careful attention to preserving patterns and permutations is evident in Beckett's manuscript copies of *Watt*. In the materials for the French translation,[6] for example, we find Beckett underlining difficult words, laboring to give French equivalents to English word games and nonsense utterances, dividing and numbering sentences so that he misses none of the seventy-nine phrases describing Mr. Knott's changing appearance, nor any of the thirty-six prepositional phrases describing Mr. Knott's movements about his room. In fact, Beckett minimizes the possibility of repeating or mistranslating any of the thirty-six movements by meticulously drawing each of them in his notebooks. The marked British copy of Watt (pp. 203, 204) from which the French translation was made divides the sentence as follows:

Here he moved, to and fro, from the door to the window,
from the window to the door; / from the window to the door,/
from the door to the window; / from the fire to the bed, from 2
the bed to the fire; / from the bed to the fire, from the fire 3
4 to the bed; / from the door to the fire, from the fire to
5 the door; / . . .

On the left hand side of the corresponding pages of the notebooks we find drawings similar to the following:

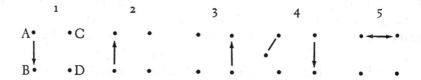

Like Beckett, who explores more the shape than the validity of ideas, Watt employs the patterns of logic and the laws of combinational mathematics more to attain "semantic succor" (p. 83) than to reach an absolute truth. His concern is not with what events and figures are in reality, but only with what they appear to be (p. 227). He seeks to make "a pillow of old words" (p. 117) to label external phenomena and thus exorcise them: "For to explain had always been to exorcize, for Watt" (p. 78). Watt's need to name objects is akin to the Unnamable's desire for an end to speaking: both urges are toward the ultimate elimination of language and its subject matter.

The problem for Watt in Mr. Knott's house is that, placed in a field of unlimited possibilities, language no longer obliterates itself. Yet Watt feels compelled to restate and relive events until he successfully has eliminated them, until he was evolved "a hypothesis proper to disperse them" (p. 78).

The failure of logic and language to provide Watt the succor he seeks can be traced to the "slight" change Arsene describes.

> For my—how shall I say?—my personal system was so distended at the period of which I speak that the distinction between what was inside it and what was outside it was not at all easy to draw. Everything that happened happened inside it, and at the same time everything that happened happened outside it. I trust I make myself plain. I did not, need I add, see the thing happen nor hear it, but I perceived it with a perception so sensuous that in comparison the impressions of a man buried alive in Lisbon on Lisbon's great day seem a frigid and artificial construction of the understanding. (*Watt*, p. 43)

The borders between inner and outer, between word and world begin to blur and disappear. The breakdown of these borders and the destruction of what were formerly discrete identities deprive Watt both of separate objects to label and of empirical data about those objects. There can be no objective viewpoint in an indiscrete and contiguous world. Information in such a world is like being told it is precisely 5:17 and hearing Big Ben strike 6:00 immediately after (p. 46). Watt can neither draw conclusions from what he sees (p. 69) nor accept any reasons "offered to the understanding" (p. 68). Yet there are no other alternatives available to him as long as he insists that the incidents he perceives actually do occur and are significant in themselves, as long as he is unable to accept "that nothing had happened, with all the clarity and solidity of something, and that it revisited him in such a way that he was forced to submit to it all over again" (p. 76). Watt cannot accept the fluidity and uncertainty of the phenomenal world as being simply processes of light and sound. Instead he seeks signification for the events he cannot obliterate:

> And Watt could not accept them for what they perhaps were, the simple games that time plays with space, now with these toys, and now with those, but was obliged, because of his peculiar character, to enquire into what they meant, oh not into what they really meant, his character was not so peculiar as all that, but into what they might be induced to mean, with the help of a little patience, a little ingenuity. (*Watt*, p. 75)

When he discovers that events are not significant in themselves and that externality is itself dissipating, Watt turns to images and symbols for guidance: "This fragility of outer meaning had a bad effect on Watt, for it caused him to seek for another, for some meaning of what had passed, in the image of how it passed" (p. 73). But the imposition of meaning upon images is like the attribution of motivation to inanimate representations of a circle and a dot. The fragments simply exist, and any effort to explain them reflects not the fragments, but the need to find meaning where perhaps none exists, the need to make a pillow of words and symbols to comfort one in a nonrelational world.

The fragmentation of word and world which destroys Watt's purpose (p. 58) is repeated in the structural fragmentation of *Watt*. From Mr. Hackett's prelude to the final Addenda, the book is a conglomeration of broken and self-consciously disruptive literary techniques. Although Mr. Hackett's poem (pp. 11–12), Mr. de Baker's song (p. 193), Arsene's farewell speech (pp. 39–63), and Arthur's tale of Louit (pp. 169–97), might be justified as conventional literary digressions, the inclusion of musical scores (pp. 34–35 and 254), charts of solutions and objections (pp. 97–98), and choruses of Krak, Krek, Krik (pp. 137–38) diverts attention from the story being told to the artificiality of the telling. The narrator seems intent on severing the readers from his words, if not through qualifications of his ability to hear and report the tale (e.g., pp. 75 and 156), then through dismemberment of the text itself by self-defeating footnotes (pp. 8, 33, 102, 104, 153) and gaps in the manuscript marked either with a question mark (e.g., pp. 228, 236) or with the notation, "(Hiatus in MS)" (p. 238). These disruptions repeatedly jolt us out of any semantic succor we have fabricated and insist that we, like Watt, become aware of the fragility of outer meaning. The structure of *Watt* refuses to let us enter imaginatively any secondary world of the story. We cannot complacently observe in the inversions Watt undergoes in his methods of locomotion (p. 30 and p. 159) and in his patterns of speech (pp. 164–69), without being made aware of having similar reversals thrust upon us by much of the book from its word games and puns to its ordering of the tale (p. 215). Our experience of *Watt* is disconcertingly similar to Watt's experience, as we too try to piece together fragmented incidents into some meaningful whole.

The similarity of the reader's experience with that of Watt is supported by the narrative apparatus of the book. Our narrator, Sam, is clearly unreliable despite his painstaking notations. In addition to providing an account dependent upon his admittedly questionable ability to hear and report Watt's disjointed, almost inaudible murmurs, Sam may be himself an inmate of a mental asylum, sharing with Watt at first a pavilion (p. 151) and then an adjoining pavilion (pp. 158ff). But more important than either of these limitations of Sam's credibility are the implications that Sam has been one of the long line of servants at Mr. Knott's house. According to

Arsene, the servants in Mr. Knott's house alternate between two contrasting physical types (p. 58). Although Sam seems to share an emotional, perhaps even mental bond with Watt, his features are distinct. Watt resembles, as Sam does not, the "Christ believed by Bosch" (p. 159). Again according to Arsene, the experiences at Knott's house are passed down orally from one fleeting generation to the next, or, as is more usual to the next but one (p. 60). Although Watt does not give a farewell speech to his replacements (p. 222), the book we read testifies that the tradition has not been broken as Watt gives his speech, neither to Arthur nor Micks, but to Sam. Moreover, Sam hears Watt's tale with the same imperfect hearing and through the same fits and starts that characterize Watt's hearing of Arsene's speech (p. 80). In explaining that all he knows comes from Watt, Sam links himself with earlier servants at Mr. Knott's house: "For all that I know on the subject of Mr. Knott, and of all that touched Mr. Knott, and on the subject of Watt, and of all that touched Watt, came from Watt, and from Watt alone. . . . For Erskine, Arsene, Walter, Vincent and others had all vanished, long before my time" (pp. 125–26). Finally, even if one rejects the circumstantial evidence linking Sam and Watt, the thematic suggestion of the book is that the experience of Mr. Knott's house is both unchanging and universal. What happens to Arsene and Watt will happen to Sam, will "happen to us all" (p. 45). As Arsene admits, even "if I could begin it all over again, knowing what I know now, the result would be the same" (p. 47).Watt similarly senses "that nothing could be added to Mr. Knott's establishment, and from it nothing taken away, but that as it was now, so it had been in the beginning, and so it would remain to the end . . ." (p. 131). The results are the same and nothing is ultimately changed if we are presented with Watt trying to make sense of the picture in Erskine's room, or with Sam attempting to understand Watt's "impetuous murmur" (p. 156), or with ourselves sorting out the structures and themes of Watt. Just as in musical composition in which bar one hundred is ordained by bar ten (p. 136), so too here the reader's experiences (like Sam's and like Watt's) are determined once Arsene begins to unravel the continuous cycle of non-events that constitute life at Mr. Knott's house: "For in truth the same things happen to us all, especially to men in our situation, whatever that is, if only we chose to know it" (p. 45). Like Watt attributing motivation to the picture in Erskine's room, we seek to explain the fragments we are given. But the disappearance of subjective and objective borders and the inefficacy of logic before unlimited possibilities prevent us from attaining "semantic succor." We cannot know the "unutterable or ineffable" (p. 62).

Instead we become caught in a nonrelational world where we unendingly recombine fragments in search of an elusive significance, where there are "no symbols where none intended" (p. 254).

2

The breakdown begun in *Watt* between word and world is continued and expanded in *Mercier and Camier*.[7] Indeed, Watt himself appears in the book as a spiritual father of Mercier and Camier. They refer to him as "daddy" and obliquely to themselves as his unique, bigeminal child (p. 115). Whether or not one takes Watt's paternity seriously, Mercier and Camier clearly belong to a subsequent generation. They accept, as Watt cannot, that external incidents are irrevocably separated from language and from human understanding. They move through their trip untouched by the events that befall them or by the people they encounter. For them nothing does happen with all the clarity and solidity of something. Whereas Watt labors to comprehend events by working through all possible explanations of them, Mercier and Camier are indifferent to questions and answers alike (p. 87). They are willing to pursue their quest without recalling either its cause or their concerns (p. 60). Moreover, they are relatively unperturbed by their inability to do anything but circle about their starting point— indeed they are unruffled by their inability to do anything at all: "One does what one can, but one can nothing" (p. 84). In contrast Watt makes a definite, physical pilgrimage to and from Mr. Knott's house where he undergoes the blurring of borders between inner and outer, a blurring which destroys purposeful action for him. As Watt observes to Mercier and Camier, "I too have sought . . . all on my own, only I thought I knew what" (pp. 113–14). After his experience at Mr. Knott's house, Watt no longer knows what he sought to achieve through his "pillow of words," but Mercier and Camier go one step further into uncertainty. They do not know even the words to describe their nonjourney:

So they raised their glasses and drank, both saying, at the same instant or almost, Here's to you. Camier added, And to the success of our ——. But this was a toast he could not complete. Help me, he said.

I can think of no word, said Mercier, nor of any set of words, to express what we imagine we are trying to do. (p. 83)

Mercier said, Let us resume our ——. At a loss he gestured, with his free hand, towards his legs and those of his companion. There was a silence. Then they resumed that indescribable process not unconnected with their legs. (p. 83)

Whereas Watt seeks for words that will eliminate external events by labeling them, and whereas the Unnamable seeks for words that will delve into the unutterable mysteries of the self, Mercier and Camier are content to remain in the gap between external and internal, content to explore the "great formal brilliance" with which nothing happens.

Mercier and Camier succeeds in exploring the formal brilliance with which nothing happens, and succeeds in the restitution of conventional signification, by generating tensions between theatrical and novelistic devices. Beginning with his earliest pieces, essays, and interviews, Beckett manifests a fascination for the possibilities of mixing genres. In *Mercier and Camier* instead of blending generic structures, Beckett sets them in opposition to each other so that the conventions which provide meaning in a novel are offset by those that yield signification on the stage. Ultimately the dual conventions cancel each other out and turn the book into a verbal portrayal of an empty set. *Mercier and Camier* is unique among Beckett's works not only because it is content to present the formal brilliance of the null set, but also because it achieves that nullity through a forced and incompatible yoking of genres.

The tension in *Mercier and Camier* between novelistic and theatrical devices is reflected in the difficulty one has in finding descriptive terms appropriate to the work. If it is discussed in strictly novelistic terms, *Mercier and Camier* seems at best perplexing, artificial, and contradictory. The absurd characters are incompatible with their realistic setting,[8] the chapter summaries obscure the central design of the double hero,[9] the piece is "an experiment in coherence" employing "a number of disintegrative, antinovelistic devices."[10] In order to speak about the work in positive terms, critics have turned to stage terminology and theatrical comparisons. The most frequent comparison is to Beckett's first stage success.[11] If *Waiting for Godot* is, as Vivian Mercier once observed, "a play in which nothing happens twice,"[12] then *Mercier and Camier* is a book in which that nothing is repeatedly discussed. Written within two years of each other, the play and the novel share many themes, techniques, and images. Mercier and Camier even sound like Vladimir and Estragon speaking in order to fill time's void.[13] Despite its similarities to *Godot*, however, *Mercier and Camier* is written to be read, not performed. Although it depends far more than any of Beckett's preceding pieces upon the spoken word, the work is not simply or purely theatrical. Indeed, *Mercier and Camier* is the forerunner of both *Waiting for Godot* and the French narrations of Beckett's subsequent works.

Mercier and Camier's dual legacy is the result of the narrative strategies Beckett adopts. On the one hand, he casts his narrator as an actor in the unfolding drama rather than as an omniscient, impartial observer. On the other hand, he allows the narrator to assert intermittently his novelistic prerogatives and intrude on the story. The tension between the narrator's roles as actor and intruder leads to a deprivation rather than expansion of knowledge and enables Mercier and Camier to stay in the rift between word and world, between pattern and signification.

Claiming to report a journey he has witnessed ("The journey of Mercier and Camier is one I can tell if I will, for I was with them all the time," p. 7), the narrator recounts only what he himself hears. Any "off-stage" business must be reported by a "messenger" as, for example, George reports on the condition of the sleeping couple to Mr. Conaire, who is looking for Camier (p. 55). Descriptions are similarly given by figures talking either to themselves or to others. In anticipating a trip Mercier and Camier provide the only picture we have of the canal.

> The very water, said Mercier, will linger livid, which is not to be despised either. And then the whim, who knows, may take us to throw ourselves in.
>
> The little bridges slip by, said Camier, ever fewer and farther between. We pore over the locks, trying to understand. From the barges made fast to the bank waft the waterman's voices, bidding us good-night. Their day is done, they smoke a last pipe before turning in.
>
> Every man for himself, said Mercier, and God for one and all.
>
> The town lies far behind, said Camier. Little by little night overtakes us, blueblack. We splash through puddles left by the rain. It is no longer possible to advance. Retreat is equally out of the question. (p. 22)

In the above passage Mercier and Camier must set the scene, provide exposition, and articulate customarily unspoken observations. It is Camier who must impart the sense of motion and of passing time that in a more conventional novel would be provided by a transitional passage such as, "They travelled down the river as evening approached." The narrator seldom violates his restricted point of view to provide such transitional passages or to penetrate beneath the surfaces of his characters' words and thus explore their emotions and thoughts. As a participant in a drama, rather than creator of a tale, the narrator can assert no real control over or certitude about the story (pp. 10 and 104).

Yet despite his limitations, the narrator insists on calling attention to himself. He haunts his characters, giving them "the strange impression sometimes that we are not alone" (p. 100). He is not the quite off-stage observer, the "vague shadowy shape" (p. 19) whose presence modifies our perceptions of the characters. He intrudes on the unfolding drama, playing games with the characters' names ("... George [as the barman now is called] ... ," p. 37), obtruding self-conscious comments ("They advanced into the sunset [you can't deny yourself everything] ... ," p. 112), and inserting unnecessary observations ("I'm cold, said Camier. It was indeed cold. It is indeed cold, said Mercier," p. 21). Instead of enriching our knowledge, the narrator's intrusions undermine his authority and dismantle the novelistic patterns he evokes. In spite of his ability to cite the *Iliad* (p. 39) and allude to Wordsworth (p. 24) and Poe (p. 77), in spite of his knowledge of the particulars—of, for instance, the name of Mercier's wife (p. 84) or the wording of Camier's business card (p. 54)—the narrator knows little of importance about the characters or their trip. He never tells us why they are setting out (p. 8), nor where they are going (p. 90), nor even how closely the narration corresponds to the actual course of events (p. 107). Moreover, the narrator places Mercier and Camier in the quest tradition, and then denies them a goal which might make such a quest meaningful and the hardships which might make it heroic: "They had to struggle, but less than many must, perhaps less than most ... " (p. 7). He provides realistic details but in the form of pseudo-scientific textbook descriptions (p. 14). He reduces time to the artifice of tables (p. 9), direction to the fall of a tossed umbrella (p. 24), and life to the contents of pockets (p. 66). Descriptive passages are included, but by pointing them out the narrator fictionalizes the worlds they describe (pp. 97–98). He turns causality into a joke Camier appreciates (p. 60). In fact, he subverts the idea of order itself, and translates God into "Omniomni, the all-unfuckable" (p. 26). The narrator's interruptions negate the narrative structures he invokes.

Having deprived himself of the novelistic conventions which intimate order and meaning, the narrator cannot supplement his prose with the non-verbal expressions, intentions, and gestures which suggest motivation in a play. Having rejected traditional interpretive and transitional passages, the narrator cannot rely on lighting, costuming, scenery, and stage business to clarify moods and meditations. The narrator's divided role as actor and intruder successfully prevents him from providing the associations and certainties of relational art.

The opposition between the novelistic and the theatrical which fore-stalls signification in *Mercier and Camier* effects not only the book's narra-tive strategies but also its central structuring devices: its dialogues and chap-ter summaries. As in a play, the book depends on words spoken in dialogue. Mercier and Camier are less important as individuals with distinct per-sonalities, motivations, and desires than as respondents in a dialogue dis-cussing the events that befall them and the characters they meet.

They need each other to sustain the work's verbal games and repartee. Strength may be necessary to remain as a couple, but less strength than is needed for the agonized memories and self-examination of soliloquy and dramatic monologue: "Admittedly strength was needed for to stay with Mercier, but less than for the horrors of soliloquy" (p. 78). Although some distinctions are made between them—Mercier is the more intellectual, Camier the more physical; Mercier is tall and bony, Camier is small and fat; Mercier has a wife, Camier a profession—Mercier and Camier's sig-nificance resides in their interdependence rather than independence. To-gether, like a vaudeville team with Camier usually playing the straight man for Mercier's lines, the couple can pass its time in banter reminiscent of the music-hall:

> What have we done to God, he [Mercier] said.
> Denied him, said Camier.
> Don't tell me he is all that rancorous, said Mercier. (p. 75)

> Yes, said Mercier.
> What do you mean, Yes? said Camier.
> I beg your pardon, said Mercier.
> You said yes, said Camier.
> I said yes? said Mercier. I? Impossible. (p. 84)

Just as Mercier and Camier rely on each other to sustain the dialogues, so too they rely on the figures they encounter to provide occasions for that dialogue. It is the rangers, barmen, and policemen who set Mercier and Camier literally and figuratively in motion by driving them out of shelters (p. 15), saloons (p. 115), and alleys (p. 94), and by providing them with subjects for conversation. It is the Mr. Maddens and Mr. Conaires who fill the interludes with stories and questions. It is the Watts who momentarily reunite the couple. Mercier and Camier are acted upon by others, but those other figures assume importance only as they are filtered through the con-versations. Figures from the primary world of the reader, figures like policeman and rangers, are engulfed by the same language that is applied to a whole world of imaginary beings from the past (Murphy and Watt, pp. 111 ff.), the nonexistent (Quin, p. 119),[14] and the yet to come ("One shall be born, said Watt, one is born of us, who having nothing will wish for nothing, except to be left the nothing he hath," p. 114). The impalpability of characters and events is irrelevant. What matters is their accessibility as subject matter for the couple's improvisations.

Although the improvisations provide the energy of the book, they are interrupted after every two chapters by summaries that tend to read like scene titles, stage directions, and players' notes. Any illusion of reality or conventional signification the "actors" may have achieved in their dialogues is broken by the interruption. Moreover, the artificiality of the summaries draws attention away from the characters and focuses it on the narrator, who is self-consciously and arbitrarily reducing the dialogue to lists emphasizing the recurrence of an ultimately useless object (e.g., the umbrella) or the repetition of ineffectual actions (e.g., the looks at the sky):

Evening of the eighth (?) day.
At Helen's.
The umbrella.
Next day at Helen's.
Pastimes.
Next afternoon in the street.
The bar.
Mercier and Camier confer.
Result of this conference.
At Helen's.
Next day noon in front of Helen's.
The umbrella.
Looks at the sky.
The umbrella.
More looks at the sky.
Ladysmith.
The umbrella.
More looks at the sky.
The umbrella.
Mercier departs.
Mercier's encounters.
Mercier's mind.
The chains. (p. 95).

By stripping away the conversations, the summaries emphasize the absurdity of material reality and physical motion in the world of Mercier and Camier. In a book dependent upon the spoken word, the possession of a bicycle and the condition of an umbrella are important only as occasions for discourse. Objects and places are the things "too tedious to enumerate, in the long run too tedious" (p. 108) which keep us from grasping "more or less what [has] happened" (p. 108). They are the nothings with which we fill our vain quests. But the summaries offer us only these "nothings." We are told that "Mercier and Camier confer" and that a chapter contains the "results of this conference" (p. 35), but neither the conference nor the results are suggested. Instead of conveying the ideas, prejudices, and conclusions which Mercier and Camier draw, the summaries reduce their conversations to the mere fact of having spoken. We are given entries such as "Mercier and the children" and "Distress of Mercier" (p. 36), but the outlines pass over Mercier's objections to children, birth, and propagation (pp. 32 and 83). "Mercier's contribution to the controversy of the universals" (p. 96) is duly recorded, but the specifics of that contribution (p. 84) are not mentioned. In a similar fashion the narrator refrains from incorporating his own opinions and observations into the summaries, but his presence nonetheless pervades them. The narrator compiles and edits the lists, purposely misleading the reader and playing games as he does so. The hose and the blowpipe (p. 96) are not objects Mercier and Camier encounter, but rather metaphors in one of Mercier's speeches (p. 87). The notion "Mercier and Camier mount" (p. 68) suggests not only the couple's retirement upstairs, but also their sexual proclivities. "The gulf" (p. 96) is a hyperbolic reference to a large square Mercier and Camier choose not to enter (pp. 89–90). "The goat" (p. 69), an entry which initially looks like a minor detail randomly selected from a pastoral description (p. 56), sets up one of the book's more subtle ironies. As the story draws to a close and Mercier and Camier reminisce, Camier admits that what he remembers from their whole affair is precisely that inconsequential and irrelevant goat (pp. 117, 121). Because the lists follow the chronology of the chapters, "the endocranian blows" mentioned for Chapter VI cannot refer to the grotesque and shocking beating in that chapter (p. 93), but must refer to the relatively placid final sentences: "They went then mostly in silence the short way they had still to go . . . for they were weary, in need of sleep, buffeted by the wind, while in their skulls, to crown their discomfiture, a pelting of insatiable blows" (p. 94). In fact the summary never explicitly acknowledges the beating and probable murder of the constable. Repetition of the phrase "the fatal ally" calls attention instead to the meaninglessness of place in the world of Mercier and Camier, in a world where quests are undertaken without goals, and where all roads lead to Helen's. By extracting from the chapters minor details and objects, the narrator destroys the rhythms of the dialogue revealing in the gap between word and world Mercier's "blessed sense of nothing, nothing to be done, nothing to be said" (p. 87).

The nothingness of which Mercier speaks so highly is carefully fabricated out of the tensions between the work's novelistic and theatrical impulses. Beneath the central image of the couple lies the fractured surface of the chapter summaries: beneath the burnished surface of the dialogue lies the narrator's disruptive voice. The result of these tensions is a book that denies relationships by insistently staying on the surface of events. The forced and deliberately incompatible yoking of genres enables *Mercier and Camier* to explore the great formal brilliance with which nothing happens.

3

The four nouvelles[15] are not content to present the burnished surface of an empty set. Instead of exploring the great formal brilliance with which nothing happens, the words together discover an archetypal situation beneath broken external structures. Having fragmented "the big world," language, and meaning in *Murphy*, *Watt*, and *Mercier and Camier* respectively, Beckett discovers in the aggregate of the four short stories a basic pattern which enables his art to exist without resorting to the orders and associations of conventional literature. The particularities of existence prove to be irrelevant. Beneath their artificial diversity is the elemental condition of man alone, isolated from the surrounding world and from others, telling himself stories to pass the time. The stories are themselves unimportant and can be substituted easily one for another. Their individual truths and meanings are accidental and insignificant. What is significant is the image of man unendingly combining words he may not even understand, much less control. Language is unreliable and uncertain—it is man's weapon, victim, solace, and pensum. But language is all that is left in a nonrelational world.

Although a Heraclitean unity of opposites is postulated in *Murphy*, *Watt*, and *Mercier and Camier*, the four nouvelles are the first works to equate the continuity beneath diversity and flux with the primal role of a narrator telling himself stories. Like the currents of a flowing river, the stories are ever changing, but like the unity of the entire stream, the stories are part of a universal condition of man speaking in the midst of the chaos. Although the four nouvelles only intimate the persistence of an archetypal image beneath the fragmentation, it is this underlying image which will provide the energy and coherence of the trilogy. Much as *Mercier and Camier* has been considered an ur-*Godot*, the four short stories can be seen as an embryonic trilogy. Both multipart narrations are written in French, from a first person point of view, about similar figures, problems, and issues. Even more specific parallels can be traced between the three short stories published in *Stories and Texts for Nothing* and the trilogy:

> Beckett's French novels, *Molly, Malone meurt*, and *L'Innommable*, could suitably have been called "L'Expulse," "Le Calmant," and "La Fin." Moran of *Molloy* is "expelled" from middle-class cliches, Molloy from all repose, and they are both condemned to frenetic quests. Malone on his deathbed tries, even as the protagonist of "Le Calmant," to attain some tranquillity through his fictions. And finally, an unnamable protagonist comes to a conclusion as inconclusive as that of "La Fin"; "you must go on, I can't go on, I'll go on." [16]

Whether or not the stories are perceived as a miniature trilogy, they, like the novels, blend into a single image into diverse versions of the same basic story.

The basic story of the four nouvelles is easily recounted: a figure, forced from an asylum, wanders about in search of some undefined thing; he meets someone who offers him an affectional relationship, but he rejects that offer and continues his search, ending alone. The figures have similar interests, habits, and attitudes. All are attracted to some type of flower. All talk to themselves. All raise their eyes to the sky, "whence cometh our help" ("The Expelled," p. 13), whence cometh no help "notwithstanding its reputation" ("the Calmative," p. 32) whence cometh nothing worth focusing on, "For why focus it?" it is "always the same sky and never the same sky" ("The End," p. 64, and "First Love," p. 26). They dress in nondescript hats and great coats of the now familiar Beckettian "bums," walking with the peculiar Beckettian gait, suffering from typically degenerating bodies. They come to us with bits and fragments of an external world still clinging to them. As though trying to dismiss the problems of subsistence once and forever, Beckett provides his figures with a small inheritance ("The Expelled"), with donated money and clothes ("The End"), with a hard-working girl friend ("First Love"). But in spite of lingering tatters of material reality, the narrators remain indistinct, presented without names or identifying backgrounds, professions, or motivations. They are simply postulated. We never learn who it is that ejects the narrator of "The Expelled," nor why he is thrown out. We are never told how the figure in "The End" came to be in his initial refuge, nor if it is a hospital, rest home, or asylum. We are never certain of the situation, nor of the location of the narrator in "The Calmative"—be he dead (p. 27), alive (p. 27), dreaming (p. 43), reminiscing (p. 46), or experiencing (p. 28). Having been reduced to the elemental, the figures became interchangeable. In fact, through his allusions to the other stories (p. 23), the narrator of "First Love" identifies himself with the other narrators. He implies that his is the continuing voice behind Beckett's works as he dissociates his present way of loving from the earlier manner described in *Murphy*: "That must have been my way of loving. Are we to infer from this I loved her with that intellectual love which drew from me such drivel, in another place?" ("First Love," p. 23). Stripped of customary associations, and given meagre characteristics revealing more what is not than what is, our figures force us to consider not individuals but the human condition.

The lack of distinctions and blurring of borders between the narrators are repeated in the blurring and merging of the settings of the stories. Specific details decline as the external world fades. While the world still contains towers, woods, plains, and towns, the scenes are not recognizably Dublin or London. Instead the narrator moves through an elemental wasteland containing a sea, a forest surrounded by a ditch, a lush pasture, and a walled town. Passages describing a lovely and ordered, external reality do infrequently occur, but always they are undercut and deflated: "Now I was making my way through the garden. There was that strange light which follows a day of persistent rain, when the sun comes out and the sky clears too late to be of any use. The earth makes a sound as of sighs and the last drops fall from the emptied, cloudless sky. A small boy, stretching out his hands and looking up at the blue sky, asked his mother how such a thing was possible. Fuck off, she said" ("The End," p. 50). The narrator is left in an archetypal world where trees come as a surprise—"trees, oh look trees" ("The Calmative," p. 28)—where landscapes may be only hallucinatory— "we are needless to say in a skull" ("The Calmative," p. 38). The simplified settings, like the narrators, become interchangeable.

The merging of the figures and of their setting is possible because former patterns are broken and distinctions rejected. Like Murphy, the narrators seek "supineness of the mind," which is achieved through indifference to "the self and [to] that residue of execrable frippery known as the nonself and even the world" ("First Love," p. 18). The details and diversity of external orders fade and dissolve. Objects are shunned as "a nightmare of thingness" ("The Calmative," p. 36). The varieties of experience, like the uncertainties of a "lover," are dismissed as "perplexities . . . closer to Giu-

decca in the hell of unknowing than the existence of God, or the origins
of protoplasm, or the existence of self, and even less worthy than these to
occupy the wise" ("First Love," pp. 32–33). Common experiences such as
"the colour of an eye half seen, or the source of some distant sound" ("First
Love," p. 32) are perhaps less worthy of consideration than the inexplicable
origin of life or the unfathomable existence of God, but they are equally
unknowable. Even the mundane is beyond understanding and unworthy
of consideration. Understanding is itself rejected. The explanations and
hypotheses that sustained Watt are reduced to "Poor juvenile solutions,
explaining nothing" ("The Expelled," p. 15). Self-knowledge disappears.
It is no longer possible to know why one laughs ("The Expelled," p. 17) or
even when one dies ("The Calmative," p. 27). Connections may exist, but
the narrator is unaware of them ("First Love," p. 21). Although he associates his marriage with the death of his father, the narrator of "First Love"
does not pretend that his association is either accurate or complete (p. 11).
Connection with another being is similarly rejected. Whereas *Mercier and
Camier* evolved out of the tensions between the dramatic need for a couple
and the narrative emphasis upon isolation, the four nouvelles consistently
and persistently deny affectional relationships. As soon as he is preferred
to a funeral, the narrator of "The Expelled" grows sick and tired of his
companion the cabman (p. 21). The impecunious, hungry, crippled speaker
of "The End" prefers isolation to acceptance of the money, food, and shelter offered him by the modern good samaritan and his ass (pp. 57–60).
Generosity and friendship are refused: "He was kind. Unfortunately I did
not need kindness" ("The End," p. 60). Even the unintentional ministra-
tions of a cow end with the animal being driven away ("The End," p. 62).
The words and gestures of the figures the narrator meets are as irrelevant to
them as the speech of the street-corner orator is to the beggar in "The End":
"Union . . . brothers . . . Marx . . . capital . . . bread and butter . . . love.
It was all Greek to me" (p. 66). In the most definitive rejection, the narrator of "First Love" walks out on Lulu/Anna when he hears the birth cry
of the child she claims is his (p. 35). In these stories of alienated, isolated,
and exiled figures, even love is a "banishment" ("First Love," p. 18). Emotions, ideas, explanations—the deceptively particular details of life—are
all broken apart and rejected. In their place we find the basic uniformity of
the human condition.

The merging of stories, narrators, and settings in the four nouvelles is a
process more dependent upon reductions and simplifications than upon
additions and accretions. For example, in blurring the borders of time,

Beckett eradicates not only memories of the past and the hope for a future, but more importantly a sense of time itself. The archetypal figures always have been and always will be telling themselves stories. There is no other possibility. Proust's timelessness, on the other hand, comes less from negating time, than from folding it back upon itself by making the past vividly available to the present. The past and the present coexist in involuntary memories. The taste of a tea-cake or the strain of a sonata can recreate entire worlds, sensations, and emotions for Proust's characters. For Beckett's figures, even the remembrances of such experiences are undermined. Unlike the memories of Proust's Marcel, the narrator's memories "come faint and cold" ("The End," p. 72). Instead of causing him to relive previous scenes, they help him forget those earlier moments ("First Love," p. 18–19). Just as the narrator stays with Lulu in order to forget her ("First Love," pp. 27–28), so too he consciously uses "voluntary memory" to destroy the past: "Memories are killing. So you must not think of certain things, of those that are dear to you, or rather you must think of them, for if you don't there is the danger of finding them, in your mind, little by little. That is to say, you must think of them for a while, a good while, every day several times a day, until they sink forever in the mud. That's an order" ("The Expelled," p. 9). Proust's vases of world-creating perfume are reduced to the strange and unopened phials of "The Calmative" (pp. 41–42) and "The End" (p. 60), and Marcel's epiphanical moments amid the pink hawthorns are likewise diluted in our indolent narrator's passing daydreams:

> Under these circumstances nothing compelled me to get up immediately. I rested my elbow on the sidewalk, funny the things you remember, settled my ear in the cup of my hand and began to reflect on my situation, notwithstanding its familiarity. But the sound, fainter but unmistakable, of the door slammed again, roused me from my reverie, in which already a whole landscape was taking form, charming with hawthorn and wild roses, most dreamlike. . . . ("The Expelled," p. 10)

Any connection between the narrator's desires and his experiences is similarly accidental and unsatisfying. While Proust speaks with melancholy and disappointment about the inability of today's ego to enjoy attainment of yesterday's desires, Beckett, characteristically, reverses the responses. Instead of pleasure turning into disappointment, he speaks of disappointment as a relief: "I came home disappointed, and at the same time relieved. Yes, I don't know why, but I have never been disappointed, and I often was in the early days, without feeling at the same time, or a moment later, an undeniable relief" ("The Expelled," p. 13). The rejection even of expectations is a relief to the figure being stripped of artificial diversity and reduced to an archetypal existence.

Having been denied distinguishing personalities and settings, and having rejected the external world, others, self-knowledge, memory and desire, the narrators are left with only themselves telling stories. Unlike Belacqua and earlier figures, the narrators take their roles as storytellers seriously. Instead of attacking the society that rejects them, they credit their tormentors' actions ("The Expelled," pp. 10–11 and 12) and can acknowledge their own flaws ("The End," pp. 61–62). Some satire remains, but it is muted. We are not forced to see traces of other scenes in a retreat to a horse-drawn cab ("The Expelled") or an encounter with a youth and a goat ("The Calmative"). But if the similarities between these scenes and those of Laurence Sterne in A Sentimental Journey and The Life and Opinions of Tristram Shandy are noticed, they add to our understanding of character and story. Instead of mocking and destroying both his own work and Sterne's, Beckett uses the parallels to reveal how very limited the world of his narrators actually is. Not even the fragile bonds of feeling are left to save man from his solipsism. Sympathy and sentiment cannot make a disintegrating world cohere.

The four nouvelles not only encourage the narrators to take seriously their roles as storytellers, but they also make those roles the focal points of each story. The tensions in Mercier and Camier between narrative and dramatic impulses are resolved by making the narrator the main actor in each piece. Indeed, the narrator's identity is precisely that of a figure telling himself stories to calm himself, "So I'll tell myself a story, I'll tell myself a story, I'll try and tell myself another story, to try and calm myself, and it's there I feel I'll be old . . ." ("The Calmative," p. 27). The actual stories are irrelevant: "I don't know why I told this story. I could just as well have told another. Perhaps some other time I'll be able to tell another. Living souls, you will see how alike they are" ("The Expelled," p. 25). Like living souls, the tales are alike and tend to blur. Meaning is similarly less important than is the act of speaking. Because the narrator relies on language, his stories may be "grammatically unexceptionable" and "on close inspection" perhaps not devoid of meaning entirely. The speeches, however, are entirely devoid of foundation ("First Love," p. 31). The narrator views purpose and foundation with indifference.

Although he would like perhaps to find the words to put an end at last to both deeds and words—to tell "this story that aspires to be the last" ("The Calmative," p. 35)—the narrator lacks the urgency and determination which drive the Unnamable to seek an end. The four nouvelles discover the mythic urge to combine phrases, but they do not explore its implications. They are content to intimate universality. Instead of agonizing over the unending, they provide metaphors of merging. In the unity of timelessness, all evenings are the same: "I say this evening as if it were always the same evening, but are there two evenings?" ("The Calmative," p. 35). Everything merges: "graves and nuptials and the different varieties of motion" are all muddled in the narrator's head ("First Love," p. 15). Whereas the trilogy probes the depths of the archetypal figure, the four nouvelles find a release in the blurring of the borders. As the narrator observes in response to the faulty last line of his epitaph, "The second and last or rather latter line limps a little perhaps, but that is no great matter, I'll be forgiven more than that when I'm forgotten" ("First Love," p. 12). The individual is forgotten as former distinctions are broken and rejected. Beneath the fragmentation is a figure whose story, in the simplest sense, is the story of us all. Man is expelled into life where he makes a quest for a hypothetical grail which he never finds and may not believe in. During that journey he meets others who offer him order and relationships he ultimately rejects, ending alone—an isolated figure moving uncomprehendingly through his own version of the wasteland.

4

The trilogy—*Molloy, Malone Dies,* and *The Unnamable*[17]—marks the culmination of Beckett's efforts to avoid relational art through the dual processes of fragmentation and tessellation. The trilogy not only carries fragmentation and its corollary patterns of tessellation further than any preceding work, but more importantly, it also derives its meaning from the dual processes themselves. Whereas the four nouvelles were content simply to discover the archetypal substratum beneath a disintegrating external reality, the trilogy examines the implications of that substratum. Beneath the apparent and artificial diversity of traditional associations is the universal figure of a self coming into being via its self-perceptions, of a narrator creating himself through his own narration. Like the dual processes, the narrator/narrated is irretrievably split between antithetical impulses. On the one hand, he is the formless, fluid speaker who rejects all that is alien to the nonverbal core of himself. On the other hand, he resides in the fixed shapes and external orders of his spoken words. He exists, as the Unnamable observes, in the interstice between internal and external (pp. 382–83), in the balance between fluidity and fixity, in the tension between fragmentation and tessellation. Unlike the narrator of *How It Is,* who seeks to understand his identity by examining the very act of narration and the imaginary worlds his words create, the narrator of the trilogy still seeks to define himself in terms of the nonself of the external world. But because his existence is kinetic and noncorporeal, residing in the dynamic tensions between contradictory impulses, the narrator cannot identify with the knowable, quantifiable certainties of conventional associations. He can relate to time, space, philosophy, and literature only by breaking apart their conventional depictions to reach the universal substratum underlying superficial distinctions. Although the universal emerges out of simplification and reduction, it is itself neither simple nor reduced. As in the dual processes generally, so too here: the more the narrator fragments and eliminates traditional associations, the more he expands the implications and potential interpretations of his works. Despite his consistent efforts to refine his descriptions of himself and reject all irrelevant categories, the narrator never will be able to describe himself completely: some larger dimension always will be necessary to contain both the speaker (no matter how minute) and his self-definition. Zero never will be attained because, in addition to producing an infinite series of diminishing fractions, the narrator inevitably evokes a converse progression of accreting explanations. Although he seeks the words that "can put an end to it" (*The Unnamable,* p. 324), the narrator discovers that speech is incapable of saying nothing, that words proliferate, and that some small term always starts the process over: "If I could speak and yet say nothing, really nothing? Then I might escape being gnawed to death. . . . But it seems impossible to speak and yet say nothing, you think you have succeeded, but you always overlook something, a little yes, a little no, enough to exterminate a regiment of dragoons" (*The Unnamable,* p. 303). The "little yes," the "little no" always emerge: the urge for tessellation, like the act of fragmentation, is inexhaustible. The difficulty of the trilogy is not that it is devoid of meaning, but rather that, having been shaped by the dual processes, it presents an "agonizing surplus of possible meanings."[18]

The surplus of meanings adhering to the narrator/narrated arises in part from the gradual merging of the various narrators in the trilogy into one voice which consistently shatters all external associations in an effort to reach the unspeakable essence of the speaking self. Instead of distinct figures, the narrators present stages or levels in the continuous search for self-definition. Beginning with Moran, who feels himself superior to things (p. 165) and capable of moving, if not at a brisk walk at least with the assistance of a broken bicycle, the narrators steadily decompose, losing their ability to move about in an external world. While Molloy resorts to crutches and a crawl, Malone propels himself and his bed with a pole and Mahood becomes an appendageless figure stuck in a jar. The progression from Moran's full-bodied involvement with an outside world to The Unnamable's disembodied voice is a refinement of identity from the diffuse and "immediate vexations" that keep Moran from confronting the "kernel of the affair" (*Molloy*, p. 98) to the essential act of narration. In this progression the further the narrator moves from an identification with the outer world, the more inseparable he becomes from the only material left him, his words. The Unnamable may be wrong in assuming that he must speak some particular pensum in order to be done with speaking (p. 311), but he is correct in assuming that his presence, for the reader anyway, is over once his words have ended.

Although the narrators are compressed into a single voice, their identity as the archetypal storyteller is inherently dual. Although the speaker and his words are not quantitatively or qualitatively the same, it is impossible to separate them. Without words the narrator does not exist for us. Without a speaker the words never come into being. Indeed the act of speaking is the central leitmotif of the trilogy. The significances and paradoxes of language are established early as Molloy is shown trying to communicate with his mother (p. 18), the police (p. 20), and Lousse, "assuming the words were the same when [he] heard them as when first spoken" (p. 33). The Unnamable defines himself in terms of the paradoxes of language: "Yes, in my life, since we must call it so, there were three things, the inability to speak, the inability to be silent, and solitude, that's what I've had to make the best of" (*The Unnamable*, p. 396). He is made of words, but words belong to others (p. 386); they are outside of him and hence an "excess" (*Molloy*, p. 116). Even the stories the narrator tries to tell of himself and the memories he tries to invent belong to others (p. 396). The powers of creation are denied the narrator; all he can do is stammer out a lesson he got once by heart: "Saying is inventing. Wrong, very rightly wrong. You invent nothing, you think you are inventing, you think you are escaping, and all you do is stammer out your lesson, the remnants of a pensum one day got by heart and long forgotten, life without tears, as it is wept" (*Molloy*, p. 32). The narrator invents nothing. His words are both essential and irrelevant to the "senseless, speechless, issueless misery" that is his identity (*Molloy*, p. 13). Even his pronouns prove to be unmanageable "red herrings" which must be seen through the "adjusted later" (*The Unnamable*, p. 343). Their distinctions of gender, number, and possession are meaningless devices the narrator adopts for convenience: "In the meantime no sense in bickering about pronouns and other parts of blather. The subject doesn't matter, there is none. Worm being in the singular, as it turned out, they [the beleaguerers] are in the plural, to avoid confusion, confusion is better avoided, pending the great confounding" (*The Unnamable*, p. 360). There is no pronoun for the unspeakable self. In the Unnamable's words, ". . . it's the fault of the pronouns, there is no name for me, no pronoun for me . . ." (p. 404). In trying to reach himself, the narrator would do better to eliminate words than to compound them, "to obliterate texts than to blacken margins" (*Molloy*, p. 13). At best, the narrator tries to make language gesture to a silence beyond both words and desires: "Not to want to say, not to know what to say, not to be able to say what you think you want to say, and never to stop saying, or hardly ever, that is the thing to keep in mind, even in the heat of composition" (*Molloy*, p. 28). But of course language cannot be its absence and the narrator cannot stop narrating and continue to exist. He must go on "as long as there are any words, until they find him, until they say him" (*The Unnamable*, p. 414).

The narrator's condition of dependence upon the act of speaking, but not upon the words spoken, affects his relationship to his characters. Like the narrative voices, the characters blur. Sapo is arbitrarily renamed Macmann (*Malone Dies*, p. 229). Basil is likewise rechristened Mahood (*The Unnamable*, p. 309), who in turn is called Worm (p. 337). The narrator himself becomes confused by the merging characters and attributes Macmann's hat to Malone (*The Unnamable*, p. 293). More important than his confusion of the characters, however, is the narrator's fusion of his own identity with those of his figures. Just as Moran at least figuratively becomes Molloy, so too Molloy merges with his mother: "I am in my mother's room. It's I who live there now. I don't know how I got there. . . . I have taken her place, I must resemble her more and more. All I need now is a son. Perhaps I have one somewhere. But I think not" (*Molloy*, p. 7). Malone's narration ends at the moment Macmann is killed (p. 308). The Unnamable suggests that he is Worm until he realizes Worm is by definition beyond language and sensation: ". . . I'm like Worm, without voice or reason. I'm Worm, no, if I were Worm I wouldn't know it, I wouldn't say it, I wouldn't say anything, I'd be Worm" (*The Unnamable*, p. 347). Having failed to be Worm, to be beyond language, "wrapped in a namelessness often hard to penetrate" (*Molloy*, p. 31), the narrator suggests that perhaps by trying to be Worm he'll finally succeed in being Mahood (p. 399). Because the narrator's characters are both the products of his narration and his "vice-existers" (p. 315), his sporadic identification with them is not surprising.

If the self is, as the trilogy suggests, separable from, and unrelated to, the accidents of physical arrangement (poised in the tension between disintegration and reintegration), then all of the stories and all of the words that compose them are extraneous to the self. As the Unnamable admits, "the fable must be of another" (p. 398). It is the characters, not the narrators, who move about in an external world, encounter others, endure hardships. The characters are the narrator's "delegates" (p. 297) who teach him what he knows "about men, the light of day" (p. 297), who live in his stead and provide him with words and stories: "It was he [Basil-Mahood] told me stories about me, lived in my stead, issued forth from me, came back to me, entered back into me, heaped stories on my head. I don't know how it was done" (*The Unnamable*, p. 309).

As the last sentence in the preceding quotation implies, the attribution of words and actions to his delegates does not explain, however, how the narrator can learn anything from them, from external figures with whom he never can have been in contact (p. 291). Unlike Descartes, the narrator does not postulate a pineal gland, does not attempt to explain how his irreconcilable realms are reconciled. At the same moment that he identifies with the characters and their stories, he also repudiates them and their versions of who he is. He hates Basil, who, "without opening his mouth, fastening on me his eyes like cinders with all their seeing, he changed me a little more each time into what he wanted me to be" (p. 298). He rejects Mahood, whose voice was woven into his, preventing him from saying who he was (p. 309). He overthrows all of Beckett's previous characters and speakers who taught him how to proceed:

First I'll say what I'm not, that's how they taught me to proceed, then what I am, it's already under way, I have only to resume at the point where I let myself be cowed. I am neither. I needn't say, Murphy, nor Watt, nor Mercier, nor—no, I can't even bring myself to name them, nor any of the other whose very names I forget, who told me I was they, who I must have tried to be, under duress, or through fear, or to avoid acknowledging me, no the slightest connexion. (*The Unnamable*, p. 326)

Just as the trilogy resides in the dynamic balance of fragmentation and tessellation, so too the narrator exists at once in the union with the characters who provide him with his fictions, and at the same time, in opposition to the incomplete pictures they portray. He speaks of them because he cannot speak of himself. He attributes to them the wordless pain he has suffered, but in their mouths the pain is unrecognizable and in himself it is unalleviated:

All these Murphys, Molloys and Malones do not fool me. They have made me waste my time, suffer for nothing, speak of them when, in order to stop speaking, I should have spoken of me and of me alone. But I just said I have spoken of me, am speaking of me. I don't care a curse what I just said. It is now I shall speak of me, for the first time. I thought I was right in enlisting these sufferers of my pains. I was wrong. They never suffered my pains, their pains are nothing, compared to mine, a mere tittle of mine, the tittle I thought I could put from me, in order to witness it. Let them be gone now, them and all the others, those I have used and those I have not used, give me back the pains I lent them and vanish, from my life, my memory, my terrors and shames. (*The Unnamable*, pp. 303–04)

The life from which the narrator would banish preceding characters is a nontemporal, nonspatial one. Objects such as hats come as a surprise (*The Unnamable*, p. 293) and offer no comfort. Even Malone ultimately is indifferent about the possessions he tallies. Landscapes dissolve from Molloy's forest and walled town to the vast space extending before the Unnamable's fixed viewpoint (pp. 293–95). Molloy seeks to navigate a linear course by crawling in spirals (p. 90). He purports to relate consecutive days, but the moon at his window indicates a two-week gap. The reader, having no reason to find Molloy's perceptions of the moon more viable than Molloy's sensations of passing time, is deprived of any reliable chronology. Time becomes "the mythological present" of a narrated story (*Molloy*, p. 26). Whereas earlier works were content simply to break apart conventional postulations of space and time, the narrator of the trilogy goes on to immerse himself in the resulting nonspatial, nontemporal substratum. He imagines himself waiting alone for a show that never will start (p. 382); he is on both sides of the threshold that is his story (p. 414); he hears without an ear, speaks without a mouth (p. 382). The narrator is the dimensionless tympanum between inner and outer:

. . . I'll have said it inside me, then in the same breath outside me, perhaps that's what I feel, an outside and an inside and me in the middle, perhaps that's what I am, the thing that divides the world in two, on the one side the outside, on the other the inside, that can be as thin as foil, I'm neither one side nor the other, I'm in the middle, I'm the partition, I've two surfaces and no thickness, perhaps that's what I feel, myself vibrating, I'm the tympanum, on the one hand the mind, on the other the world, I don't belong to either. . . . (*The Unnamable*, p. 383)

He resides in the evanescent act of speaking: he is created and destroyed in the same exhalation: ". . . I'm in words, made of words, others' words. . . . I'm something quite different, a quite different thing, a wordless thing in an empty place, where nothing speaks" (*The Unnamable*, p. 386).

As a nonspatial, nontemporal speaker, the narrator is denied conventional boundaries. Beginnings and endings, like places and times, are illusions the narrator fabricates to give himself the momentary configuration of a form fading among fading forms. The tasks, the pensums, the journeys, the endings are all inventions adopted by a narrator who, having nothing to say, must nonetheless continue to speak:

> All this business of a labour to accomplish, before I can end, of words to say, a truth to recover, in order to say it, before I can end, of an imposed task, once known, long neglected, finally forgotten, to perform before I can be done with speaking, done with listening, I invented it all, in the hope it would console me, help me to go on, allow me to think of myself as somewhere on a road, moving, between a beginning and an end, gaining ground, losing ground, getting lost, but somehow in the long run making headway. All lies. I have nothing to do, that is to say nothing in particular. I have to speak, whatever that means. Having nothing to say, no words but the words of others, I have to speak. No one compels me to, there is no one, it's an accident, a fact. Nothing can ever exempt me from it, there is nothing, nothing to discover, nothing to recover, nothing that can lessen what remains to say. . . . (*The Unnamable*, p. 314)

Because he is the immediacy of a voice speaking, nothing, no passage of time nor change of locale, can free the narrator from his narration. There is no escape and no end in the words. The narrator must and will go on: ". . . you must go on, I can't go on, I'll go on" (*The Unnamable*, p. 414).

The endless process of narration is reflected in the structure of the trilogy. Although books inevitably are bound by openings and closings, the trilogy negates the authority of its boundaries. *Molloy* seems to tell the first half of its tale last, and even that half seems to be erased as Moran ends his report by contradicting its opening words: "Then I went back into the house and wrote, It is midnight. The rain is beating on the windows. It was not midnight. It was not raining" (p. 176). Similarly, the Unnamable undermines his opening queries in the process of asking them: "Where now? Who now? When now? Unquestioning. I, say I. Unbelieving. Questions, hypotheses, call them that. Keep going, going on, call that going, call that on" (p. 291).

The narrator is not so much beginning as going on (p. 292), and his gestures toward the conventions of a well-made novel come primarily "for the sake of clarity" (p. 295). Not only are the beginnings and endings of the individual works undermined, but the whole trilogy is similarly denied resolution. As the Unnamable informs us, he is seeking for the words that will put an end to words and speaking. But he is uncertain what those words might be, whether he has already spoken them, and if they will produce the desired silence or merely carry him to the threshold of a door which will open on the story of himself:

> . . . you must go on, I can't go on, you must go on, I'll go on, you must say words, as long as there are any, until they find me, until they say me, strange pain, strange sin, you must go on, perhaps it's done already, perhaps they have said me already, perhaps they have carried me to the threshold of my story, before the door that opens on my story, that would surprise me, if it opens, it will be I. . . . (*The Unnamable*, p. 414)

Intimating a circularity reminiscent of *Finnegans Wake*, the opening paragraphs of *Molloy* can be seen not as a beginning but rather as the continuation of the stream of words that issue from the other side of the Unnamable's opening door, "The threshold scarcely crossed that's how it is" (*Molloy*, p. 8). Molloy specifically tells us that what we are reading is a flashback: the words are the beginning of his story, but the narrator himself is at his end, all has grown dim, sounds fade, the speaker is going dumb—in short, Molloy's condition from the outset is that of the Unnamable at the end of his quest:

> Here's my beginning. . . . I took a lot of trouble with it. . . . It was the beginning, do you understand? Whereas now it's nearly the end. Is what I do now any better? I don't know. That's beside the point. Here's my beginning. It must mean something or they wouldn't keep it. Here it is.
>
> This time, then once more I think, then perhaps a last time, then I think it'll be over, with that world too. Premonition of the last but one but one. All grows dim. A little more and you'll go blind. It's in the head. It doesn't work any more, it says, I don't work any more. You go dumb as well and sounds fade. The threshold scarcely crossed that's how it is. It's the head. It must have had enough. So that you say, I'll manage this time, then perhaps once more, then perhaps a last time, then nothing more. (*Molloy*, p. 8)

The trilogy can never conclude because of the impossible nature of the narrator's endeavor. He attempts to use words to speak of the inexplicable;

he tries to shatter relationships, but the process of speaking is inherently relational. He is caught, like his figures, on an infinitely spiralling course.

It has been observed that "The trilogy is, among other things, a compen-
dious abstract of all the novels that have ever been written reduced to their
most general terms."[19] The same point might be made of the trilogy's
treatment of metaphysics. Having been denied conventional conceptions of
identity and character, time and space, beginning and end, the narrator is
cut off not only from the external world, but also from the philosophical systems used to explain it. The philosophies that comforted earlier characters
are parodied and dismissed. Murphy's admiration for Geulincx is reduced
to Malone's futile efforts to teach Geulincx's ethics to a parrot (p. 218) and
to phrases that must be guarded against: "But I am easily frightened now.
I know those little phrases that seem so innocuous and, once you let them
in, pollute the whole of speech. *Nothing is more real than nothing.* They
rise up out of the pit and know no rest until they drag you down into its
dark. But I am on my guard now" (*Malone Dies*, p. 192). The words that
justified the third zone of Murphy's mind pollute a discourse by taking it
over with their assumptions and implications. To avoid such subservience
to the ideas of others, the narrator shatters previous philosophical systems.
Ethics becomes meaningless as Molloy is taught only the details of behavior and not the "essence of the system" (p. 25). Logic becomes en-
tangled in word games as Molloy wonders how he can repay the compliment
of being ignored (p. 23). Epistemology is subverted as both knowledge and
the desire for knowledge are passed over in favor of being beyond knowledge
and desire: "For to know nothing is nothing, not to want to know anything
likewise, but to be beyond knowing anything, to know you are beyond knowing anything, that is when peace enters in, to the soul of the incurious seeker"
(p. 64). Meditation is self-negating: the less one thinks of something, the
more certain one can be of it (*Molloy*, p. 12). Instead of adhering to the
comforts of previous orders, the narrator creates from the shards of those
orders his own fluid systems, inventing "loves, music, the smell of flowering
currant, to escape from me" (*The Unnamable*, p. 305). *Ex nihilo* he re-
creates philosophical theorems, making himself the Ptolemaic center of a
universe of orbiting bodies (*The Unnamable*, p. 295) and making Worm's
dark den the successor of Plato's firelit cave (p. 358). The philosopher's
search for truth, however, is irrelevant to the narrator's postulations. Sup-
positions are offered only "to get on a little" (*The Unnamable*, p. 311). Hypotheses are built up until they "collapse on top of one another" (*The Unnamable*, p. 372). Metaphysical issues are reduced to a single problem with
diverse manifestations: "Mahood I couldn't die. Worm will I ever get

born? It's the same problem" (*The Unnamable*, p. 352). The narrator's problem is to speak the words that define himself. As the Unnamable's summary of his questions (pp. 388–89) indicates, all of his stories and theories, personage and problems, have tried to explain his dual role as speaker and spoken, as self and noise: "... I sum up, now that I'm there it's I will do the summing up, it's I will say what is to be said and then say what it was, that will be jolly, I sum up, I and this noise, I see nothing else for the moment, but I have only just taken over my functions, I and this noise . . ." (*The Unnamable*, p. 388). The role remains inexplicable, but the questions evoked encompass the entire trilogy and most of Western philosophy. In respect to the noise, the narrator cannot determine what it is, how it comes, how it is perceived, or by what intelligence it is apprehended. In respect to himself, he does not know what he is, where he is, whether he is in words or silence, what he is doing, how he manages to hear (if it is he who hears), how he understands, how he speaks without ceasing (if it is he who speaks), if it is he who seeks, what he seeks, finds, loses, finds, throws away, seeks, etc., if it is not he who seeks, who it is, what it is, why he tells himself things to pass the time, and why the time doesn't pass (pp. 388–89). Similarly, when he wearies of his unanswerable question, the narrator can entertain himself (and incidentally create himself) by making resolutions which, if followed, would produce a very different and more conventional narration without altering the basic situation of a narrator/narrating. He resolves to make abundant use of the principle of parsimony, to assume the thing said and the thing heard have a common source, to situate that source in himself without specifying where, to abandon all other postulates except that of a deaf half-wit, hearing nothing of what he says and understanding even less, to evoke an image of a mouth spewing words whenever discouragement arises, to set aside forever the ideas of beginning and end, to overcome the fatal leaning to expressiveness, to equate himself with him who exists, to ascribe to himself a body and mind, to speak of an inner world without choking, to doubt no more, to seek no more, to speak of time and space without flinching (p. 390). But these resolutions are quickly forgotten in the fragmenting prose. They, like the questions, theories, and hypotheses of philosophy merge into the obligation felt by the narrator "to begin again, to start again from nowhere; from no one and from nothing, and to win to me again, to me here again, by fresh ways to be sure or by ancient ways, unrecognizable at each faring" (*The Unnamable*, p. 302).

Not too surprisingly, like the philosophical systems upon which they are based, literary conventions linking an unidentifiable narrator to a knowable world are consciously disrupted. Wordsworth's affirmative theory of the creative imagination is changed into Molloy's gloomier perception that "It is in the tranquillity of decomposition that I remember the long confused emotion which was my life, and that I judge it, as it is said that God will judge me, and with no less impertinence" (*Molloy*, p. 25). The Romantic education of the emotions through imagination, through long and deep meditation, and through association with the sublime yields, in Molloy's world, to a confused emotion recalled only in the processes of decay. The transcendent vision is not attained: the epiphany never coheres. Although the moment when Moran meets a shepherd seems propitious in respect to both the setting ("The silence was absolute. Profound in any case. All things considered it was a solemn moment. The weather was divine," p. 158) and to Moran's condition (his journey almost over and his son restored, Moran longs to serve someone "faithfully," p. 159), nothing comes of the encounter:

> I came finally to halt about ten paces from the shepherd. . . . How I would love to dwell upon him. . . . I longed to say, Take me with you, I will serve you faithfully. . . . But now I felt the man turning towards me again, and the dog, and the man drawing on his pipe again, in the hope it had not gone out. And I knew I was all alone gazing at that distant glow that would get brighter and brighter, I knew that too, then suddenly go out. And I did not like the feeling of being alone. . . . And I was wondering how to depart without self-loathing or sadness, or with as little as possible, when a kind of immense sigh all round me announced it was not I who was departing, but the flock. (*Molloy*, pp. 158–59)

Moran is left more desolate than before. His shepherd fails to act either as a Joycean catalyst for synthesis or as a counterpart to the Christian parable and gather Moran into his herd of black sheep. The moment of salvation doesn't come, and Moran turns instead to a violent fight with his son (p. 159).

Other literary patterns are likewise alluded to, but never completed. For example, the names of the characters evoke expectations they never fulfill by referring to truncated psychological patterns. Obidil may well be an anagram for libido, Youdi for you id, and Lousse for soul plus *se* (the French reflexive),[20] but such references are fleeting and disconnected. The motivations, anxieties, desires, and passions that give significance to the psychological terms are omitted. Similarly, instead of enforcing the connections between his tales and those of other times and places, the narrator's allusions enlarge the gaps. Joyce belonged to a tradition of artists that believed art could turn the surrounding chaos back into its proper order. His references to Greek mythology help connect Stephen's and Bloom's stories to each other, to the past, and to Western civilization. In contrast, Beckett's borrowings disrupt the past and diminish the present. Consider the parallels Dieter Wellershoff has pointed out between Molloy and the Greek god Hermes.[21] The fleet-footed god of travelers and thieves, the eloquent deceiver, the guide to the underworld, capable of predicting the future from the position of pebbles, is reduced to a crippled tramp and petty thief incapable, with his hesitant speech, of persuading the police to accept the truth and preoccupied with thoughts of extinction and with the arrangement of sucking stones. Molloy does not belong to the traditions of gods. The divine attributes and heroic powers shrink and crumble whenever they are associated with him. Both the Olympians and Molloy are diminished by the comparison. Moreover, Beckett's comparisons tend to refer to the superficial rather than the significant. Although scraps of Joyce's *Ulysses* appear frequently in the trilogy, Molly's affirmation, Bloom's compassion, and Stephen's talent never do. Instead of the diaphane of existence, Molloy echoes the accidents of time (his trip occurs the second or third week of June, i.e., the weeks in which Bloom's 16 July trip would take place) and space (he shares Bloom's physical peculiarity of testicles which hang lower on the right side). Joyce becomes the compounded pun in Molloy's reminiscences: "I who had loved the image of old Geulincx, dead young, who left me free, on the black boat of *Ulysses,* to crawl towards the East, along the deck. . . . And from the poop, pouring upon the wave, a sadly *rejoicing* slave, I follow with my eyes the proud and futile *wake* (*Molloy,* p. 51, my emphasis). The literary traditions by which characters in the past made sense of themselves and their world become in the trilogy the proud and futile wake from which the narrator is steadily borne.

The trilogy's fragmentation of literary traditions, Western philosophy, and the external world compels the reader to confront the primal act of a narrator narrating. Beneath the apparent complexity, is the archetypal storyteller. Beneath irrelevant associations is the human condition at its most elemental level. Even the narrator's words are less important than his process of speaking: "There is no great difference here between one expression and the next, when you've grasped one you've grasped them all" (*The Unnamable,* p. 388). All things—identity, time, space, philosophy, literature, and language—merge into the universal substratum. Although uncovered by reductions and simplifications, the substratum itself is neither simple nor reduced. Its lack of irrelevant associations makes the substratum powerfully evocative. For example, the absence of details from Molloy's description of A and C enables their meeting to assume parabolic dimensions.

Their story is a paradigm of all human encounters: they meet, pause, and depart. We know neither the names, pasts, or purposes of the figures; nor are we aware if the figures know each other, whether they speak, whither they go. But in their very anonymity and lack of specificity, the figures become emblems of the encounters of all mankind beginning with Cain and Abel and including the stories of Sapo, Macmann, Basil, Mahood, and even the two figures that collide before the Unnamable (p. 292).

Paradoxically, the breakdown of traditional relationships yields, not a dearth of meanings, but a plethora of possible interpretations. Like the Saposcats who draw "strength to live from the prospect of their impotence" (*Malone Dies*, p. 188), the narrator evokes the materials to continue his discourse from the rejection of speech: "The search for the means to put an end to things, an end to speech, is what enables the discourse to continue" (*The Unnamable*, p. 299). Despite its fragmentation, the discourse does continue. The reader responds by recombining the pieces he is given into a larger whole. Because Beckett's words offer no ultimate and absolute order, however, the effort to explain through tessellation produces not single answers but rather multiple patterns and interpretations. Consider, for example, the diverse critical response to the two-part structure of *Molloy*. Upon first reading, the novel seems to be sundered by a radical break in character, plot, and style. Molloy's meandering and confused perceptions are in sharp contrast to Moran's precise report. But on closer inspection the two parts reveal several similarities. For example, the characters in both see a herd of black sheep, enter gardens, hear gongs, are cared for temporarily by a woman, possess a knife rest, write reports, and claim to kill a man they meet in the woods.[22] From the suggestive but not conclusive similarities critics have fashioned compelling but not identical interpretations. David Helsa suggests the novel presents two versions of the same event—the meeting of Molloy and Moran. Ironically, neither Molloy nor Moran is aware he is meeting the other.[23] In a Jungian reading John Fletcher[24] sees the story as a study in sado-masochism in which the reconciliation of the masochistic antiself (Molloy) to the sadistic self (Moran) is represented by the metamorphosis of Moran into Molloy. In his quest for Molloy, Moran increasingly loses control of his body and mind until he kills a figure resembling himself and assumes instead the postures, attitudes, and confusions of Molloy on his journey to his mother's bed (womb). G. C. Barnard offers a more Freudian account, seeing all the figures as schizophrenic phases of the anal character Moran.[25] David Hayman merges not only characters but also times, suggesting that the two narrators are simultaneous descriptions of one event with Molloy presenting the viewpoint of the libido and

Moran that of the superego.[26] To Ludovic Janvier ". . . Moran and Molloy are two consecutive moments in a single process of becoming."[27] The list of interpretations continues as each reader reenacts the narrator's experience of attempting to discover the most convincing and satisfying explanation of uncertain and fluid events by recombining the given pieces and by merging characters and events into some more explicable whole. Like the narrator, indeed like the trilogy itself, the reader is caught by the dual processes of fragmentation and tessellation, unable to go on, yet compelled to continue: " . . . I don't know, I'll never know, in the silence you don't know, you must go on, I can't go on, I'll go on" (*The Unnamable*, p. 414).

5

Once he has written the trilogy, once he has created a work of art which embodies the dual processes of fragmentation and tessellation, Beckett must discover new ways to continue his quest for nonrelational art. According to Israel Shenker, Beckett observed of his next work, *Texts for Nothing*, that it failed to release him from the attitude of disintegration in which he had been placed by *The Unnamable*.[28] Although reflecting accurately the fragmentation of *Texts*, the observation obscures the new mood which *Texts* achieves by combining the archetypal narrator/narrated with the concern for the "nothingness" postulated by *Watt* and explored by *Mercier and Camier*. By shifting the primary focus of the narrator away from his identity and back to the uncertainty and fluidity in which he exists, *Texts* not only provokes a more emphatic consideration of the void itself, but also reduces the dependence upon disintegration. Instead of simply fragmenting external orders or progressively rejecting definitions of the self, *Texts* posits uncontested images of the way it is. These images are prevented from reasserting the orders and meanings of relational art by their juxtapositionings. Counterpoint replaces contradiction as propositions and moods are more frequently intertwined with their antitheses than undermined by negations. Depictions of despair are balanced with images of hope; existence in the dark, with memories of life above in the light; the dwindling of language, with the emergence of stories. The urgency with which the Unnamable seeks a relief from life dissipates before the reconciliation with which the voice in *Texts* can sometimes accede that "life alone is enough."[29] While *Texts* does not proffer the affirmation and acceptance of Beckett's minimalist literature, it does avoid the direct negation and immediate contradiction of preceding pieces. Although less certain than the fragments T. S. Eliot shores against our ruin, and more fluid than the unified picture Yeats projects for his mosaic worker, *Texts for Nothing* does counterbalance the impetus to disintegration with ephemeral images of reintegration: "Soon there will be nothing where there was never anything, last images" ("Text 13," p. 139).

Lacking the sustained plot and shared characters that bind together chapters in a conventional novel, the texts are self-contained and can be, and have been, published individually.[30] Their self-sufficiency liberates them from the constraints, such as temporality and causality, inherent in a continuous narration. Each text may present its own impression of the way it is without taking into consideration any earlier or later impressions. The completeness of the various impressions is emphasized by the ordering principles within each section. Often, for example, the final sentence rounds out a vignette by returning to the themes introduced in its initial words. "Text 4" begins with questions reminiscent of the Unnamable's aporia: "Where would I go, if I could go, who would I be, if I could be, what would I say, if I had a voice, who says this, saying it's me?" ("Text 4," p. 91). The piece ends with evasive answers to these questions:

> Yes, there are moments, like this moment, when I seem almost restored to the feasible. Then it goes, all goes, and I'm far again, with a far story again, I wait for me afar for my story to begin, to end, and again this voice cannot be mine. That's where I'd go, if I could go, that's who I'd be, if I could be. ("Text 4," p. 94)

The circle has been completed and although we cannot succinctly state who it is the narrator would be, if he could be, we are satisfied by the vignette's illusion of an answer. Similarly, "Text 3" opens with a call for a departure (p. 85) and closes with a dismissal of the possibility of departing (p. 90); "Text 5" starts with the narrator's assertion that he is a scribe (p. 95) and finishes when he drops his quill (p. 99); "Text 11" begins with the narrator's thoughts of those who knew him (p. 127) and ends with him left alone by the others (p. 131). Even the texts which do not in some way resolve their opening issues may return to their initial propositions to suggest an unchanging endlessness. "Texts 9 and 10," for instance, end where they began, on the one hand speculating that if the narrator could say there was a way out, the rest would come (pp. 117 and 121), and on the other acknowledging that giving up is nothing new and the narrator will go on giving up (pp. 123 and 125).

Although the texts are self-contained, they also reflect a subtle pressure for tessellation. The thirteen distinct versions of the narrator gradually blend into "the same voice, the same ideas" ("Text 1," p. 76). From the first text on, the seemingly disparate voices are treated as a collective, "all of one mind, fond of one another, sorry for one another, unable to do anything for one another" ("Text 1," p. 77). All the voices confront the same threefold problems of saying themselves with a language that must inevitably fail, of creating art in a fluid and uncertain universe, of presenting meaningful images in the midst of disruption. The uniformity of their problems makes the apparent diversity of their narrations irrelevant. Although we are presented with thirteen different segments of narration, for the voices all acts of narration produce "for ever the same murmur, flowing unbroken, like a single endless word and therefore meaningless, for it's the end gives meaning to words" ("Text 8," p. 111). The merging of their words into a single, unending stream denies conventional meaning by destroying conventional limitations and borders. The denial of meaningful boundaries is supported and compounded by the merging in the texts of time and space. Past, present, and future blend into one moment: "All mingles, times and tenses, at first I only had been here, now I'm here still, soon I won't be here yet . . ." ("Text 1," p. 78). Similarly, locations blur until it makes little difference if the voice gives himself up for dead at the sea, or at the mountains, or at the forest, city, or plain ("Text 1," p. 78).

More interesting than the simple fusion of tenses or of settings, however, is the voice's perception that time is itself becoming spatial: ". . . time has turned into space and there will be no more time, till I get out of here" ("Text 8," p. 112). As long as the narrator is in his present location, time will not pass and there will be no change, only an eternal stasis. But just as time is becoming spatial, so too space becomes temporal, and the narrator is caught, not so much in a location, as in the unending and unchanging present condition: he exists "deep in this place which is not one, which is merely a moment for the time being eternal, which is called here . . ." ("Text 11," p. 131). *Here* is merely the word the narrator uses to name "this unnamable thing that I name and name and never wear out" ("Text 6," p. 104). *Here* is a label for the narrator's archetypal role of a voice speaking. As long as the narrator exists, he cannot alter or escape the unchanging present of his condition. Just as Murphy cannot be Murphy and enter the dark flux, so too the narrator cannot dissociate himself from the immediacy of a voice speaking here and now. Moreover, since the here and now is always the known and experienced, since change requires other times and places, nothing can ever happen to the narrator. "Here, nothing will happen here, no one will be here, for many a long day. Departures, stories, they are not for tomorrow. And the voices, wherever they come from, have no life in them" ("Text 3," p. 90). The act of narration is associated with the nothingness the *Texts* strive to attain. The words of a narration produce only fantasies of change ("Ever since nothing but fantasies and hope of a story for me somehow, of having come from somewhere and of being able to go back, or on, somehow, some day or without hope"—"Text 8," p. 112) and delusions that something has interrupted the encompassing nothingness ("See what's happening here, where there's no one, where nothing happens, get something to happen here, someone to be here, then put an end to it, have silence, get into silence, or another sound, a sound of other voices than those of life and death, of lives and deaths everyone's but mine, get into my story in order to get out of it, no, that's all meaningless"—"Text 3," p. 89). In opposition to the unremitting and unchanging present of his existence, the narrator hypothesizes the inherently unknowable and unobtainable elsewhere. *There* becomes the multipurpose label for all the narrator's dreams of a different time or place. Like the bodies in *The Lost Ones* who seek escape from their cylinder through some niche or trapdoor, the voice imagines an escape via the powers of language and imagination to more conventional perceptions of time and space in which the beauties of the skies and the stars are once again visible: "And I have no doubts, I'd get there somehow, to the way out, sooner or later, if I could say, There's a way out there, there's a way out somewhere, the rest would come, the other words, sooner or later, and the power to get there, and the way to get there, and pass out, and see the beauties of the skies, and see the stars again" ("Texts 9," p. 121). But just as the lost ones will never find a trapdoor, so too the narrator will never escape his present condition. Even if he were to be translated into another time and place, his very existence would transform his place of escape into the same agonizing condition of a voice speaking in the present. There is no elsewhere: "You are there, there it is, where you are will never long be habitable. Go then, no, better stay, for where would you go, now that you know?" ("Text 2," p. 87).

The fusion of time and space into the archetypal present of a voice speaking focuses attention on the words the voice speaks. Although the worlds they project are fantastical and illusory, the words are the narrator's reality. They are the only things separating him from nonexistence: ". . . there is nothing but a voice murmuring a trace" ("Text 12," p. 137). Indeed, they are the narrator's life ("Text 6," p. 104) and "nothing will have changed" ("Text 2," p. 82) as long as they keep coming. Whereas the Unnamable sought to put an end to the words imposed on him by others, the voice in *Texts* no longer shuns words and their powers: ". . . I won't be afraid of the big words, any more, they are not big" ("Text 1," p. 78). Instead of urgently seeking an end, the narrator of "Text 2" calmly observes that the words are slowing down and "stopping too" (p. 82). Instead of insistently undercutting the validity of his stories, the narrator acknowledges their falsity and submits more readily to being their dupe: "Yes, no more denials, all is false, there is no one, it's understood, there is nothing, no more phrases, let us be dupes, dupes of every time and tense, until it's done, all past and done, and the voices cease, it's only voices, only lies" ("Text 3," p. 85). The lies no longer need be denounced: events no longer need be possible ("Text 5," p. 98). "Place" ("Text 1," p. 75), "others" ("Text 2," p. 82), and even the identity of the speaking self ("Text 3," p. 85) are dismissed as unimportant. Although the narrator occasionally may feel threatened by words—fearing he will disappear, "scattered by the everlasting words" ("Text 11," p. 127), or swallowed by "those little words" ("Text 8," p. 112), or buried by an avalanche of "wordshit" ("Text 9," p. 118)—he nonetheless accepts the arbitrary nature of language. It no longer matters if he can obtain a body by an act of will or people an empty world simply by speaking ("Text 3," pp. 85 and 89). He admits without hesitation that the answers to simple questions such as: "How long have I been here?" depend "on what is meant by here, and me, and being" ("Text 1," p. 76).

The narrator's, at least partial, acceptance of the limitations of language reflects the new attitude of *Texts* in general. Although they do not achieve the hesitant affirmation of works like *Enough*, they do avoid unmitigated negation. Contradiction is no longer the primary device for suggesting fluidity. *Texts* draws attention to the artificiality of positing statements only to deny them: "He has me say things saying it's not me, there's profundity for you, he has me who say nothing say it's not me" ("Text 4," p. 92). The danger of such immediate contradiction is that it creates a reverse reality by substituting a negative proposition for the original statement. *Texts* avoids the neatly dichotomized world of true and not-true by employing other techniques to intimate uncertainty. For example, the narrator may supply unexpected answers to leading and rhetorical questions. In the following passage instead of concluding that it does not matter how he describes himself, the narrator postulates that, in some inexplicable way, it does matter: "What matter how you describe yourself, here or elsewhere, fixed or mobile, without form or oblong like man, in the dark or the light of the heavens, I don't know, it seems to matter, it's not going to be easy" ("Text 3," p. 87). Similarly, instead of destroying all depictions of existence, *Texts* permits each of the thirteen vignettes to present its own version of how it is. None need be considered absolute, all-encompassing, or final. Consequently, none need be contradicted. Instead, each section comments upon and qualifies the others. Only by combining the thirteen discrete versions of how it is does the reader begin to realize the unspeakable void they intimate. Just as we learn about the speaker in "Text 4" not through description of who he is, but through descriptions of the stranger who he is not (pp. 91–92), so too we learn about the nothingness beneath the *Texts* not through contradictory descriptions of what the void is, but through depictions of the images which delimit it. Direct negation yields to a "new no" which admits us not to controverted reality, but to the absence that is nothingness itself: "No, something better must be found, a better reason, for this to stop, another word, a better idea, to put in the negative, a new no, to cancel all the others, all the old noes that buried me down here . . . yes, a new no, that none says twice, whose drop will fall and let me down, shadow and babble, to an absence less vain than inexistence" ("Text 11," pp. 130–31).

The "new no" approximates more closely the movement to nothingness because, although the texts are self-contained, they nonetheless reflect on, and interact with, each other. Perhaps more like the counterpoint of musical composition than the arrangement of conventional prose narrative, the moods and themes of the texts are interwoven into a densely textured pattern of rising and falling motifs. Neither hope nor despair is ever completely eliminated. Instead, *Texts* plays upon their emergence and resurgence. The acceptance, emphasized in "Text 2," of existence in the dark nothingness is counterbalanced by the concerns in "Text 3" of departing from that existence and resuming the previously renounced life above in the light. Similarly, the departures of "Text 3" are counteracted by the unanswerable questions which open "Text 4": "Where would I go, if I could go, who would I be, if I could be . . ." (p. 91). The "high hopes" which conclude "Text 6" (p. 105) are muted by the discouragement implicit in the queries of the narrator of "Text 7": "Did I try everything, ferret in every hold, secretly, silently, patiently, listening?" (p. 107). Although the narrator of "Text 9" reaffirms that there is a way out (pp. 117 and 121), his hope is silenced by the first words of "Text 10": "Give up . . ." (p. 123). In harmony with the themes of hope and despair are the motifs of location, movement, and sound. Evocations of the worldless, motionless, dark present are balanced by chords from the stories of life above in the light. After introducing the images of himself "down in the hole the centuries have dug" and the others "up above" (p. 76), the narrator of "Text 1" drifts into sleep. As if awakening from that sleep, the narrator of "Text 2" moves from dreamlike images of life above in the light to an acceptance of the present, an acceptance which will be reversed by "Text 3" and rephrased by "Text 4" into the recognition that the mistake is "to have wanted a story . . . whereas life alone is enough" (p. 93). This recognition is immediately countermanded by the stories of "Text 5" and the surrealistic images of "Text 6." "Text 7" returns to the strains of the present with the resolutions to stop searching elsewhere for himself and to lose no more time in hopeless pursuits because "that night is at hand and the time come for me too to begin" (p. 110). But the anticipated new beginning is replaced by the resurgence in "Text 8" of words spoken against the silence, "Only the words break the silence, all other sounds have ceased" (p. 111). The contrapuntal ebb and flow of words and silence, of here and there, of hope and despair produces the fluidity essential to nonrelational art without overwhelming *Texts* with direct negation and immediate contradiction.

In addition to intimating fluidity through counterpoint, the texts also suggest the void through their subtle progression. Silence and stasis gradually come to predominate the pieces. "Text 11" concludes with the narrator alone and stationary. While the narrator of "Text 12" begins with the antithetical assertion that it doesn't matter where he is going "so long as others are there" (p. 133), he too ends in solitude, "what a blessing it's all down the drain, nothing ever as much as begun, nothing ever but nothing and never, nothing ever but lifeless words" (p. 135). Against the mounting sense of nothingness are posited only the "lifeless" words which "Text 13" informs us are themselves slowing and stopping. In the last texts there are no resurging themes of hope or motion or life above in the light to counteract the decrescendo into the void. The images of silence and stasis themselves slow down and dwindle away until even "were there one day to be here, where there are no days, which is no place, born of the impossible voice the unmakable being, and a gleam of light, still all would be silent and empty and dark, as now, as soon now, when all will be ended, all said, it says, it murmurs" ("Text 13," p. 140).

The movement toward nothingness suggested by counterpoint and progression is further supported by the images the texts project. The images, like those in *How It Is*, are distinguished from both memories and stories. On the one hand, memories of life above in the light are dismissed as irrelevant. As the conclusion of *Texts* implies, even were a gleam of light to appear, it would change nothing, all would still be silent and empty and dark ("Text 13," p. 140). Life in the light reveals nothing of the essential condition of man: "To have suffered under that miserable light, what a blunder. It let nothing show, it would have gone out, nothing terrible, nothing showed, of the true affair . . ." ("Text 2," p. 82). Even a "good memory" of Mother Calvert creaming off the garbage is something the narrator wishes could be "wiped from knowledge" ("Text 2," p. 82). Mr. Joly "ringing the bells" ("Text 2," p. 83)—like Piers ("Text 2," p. 83) and the Grave brothers ("Text 2," p. 84)—is a rejected fragment from a barely recalled and now meaningless past. It is better to forget all that was "suffered under that miserable light [above]" ("Text 2," p. 82), better not to believe in that "ragbag" of former selves ("Text 6," p. 103). The most the narrator salvages from his past is the Proustian picture of himself looking in a mirror and seeing himself as a child of twelve looking into a mirror ("Text 6," pp. 103–04). Stories are equally suspect. Like memories of the past, fantasies of a future nanny named Bibby ("Text 3," p. 86) or a crony named Vincent ("Text 3," pp. 87–88) bring no comfort and must be abandoned. The narrator would be better off without a companion, "No, alone, I'd be better off alone, it would be quicker" ("Text 3," p. 88). Not bound to life above in the light by past experiences nor by future possibilities, the images nonetheless do borrow associations and connotations from a conventional, external world. Unlike the abstract and geometrical shapes of the residua, the images in texts refer to familiar and emotionally charged scenes of people waiting in rooms or embracing each other. Because these humanistic scenes are not constrained by, or explained in, the context of the narrator's past or future, they become metaphors for the way it is in general. In a world where words are inevitably false and alien, man becomes "a mere ventriloquist's dummy" ("Text 8," p. 113). Where time and space are so commingled that there is no way out, life is reduced to not stirring "hand or foot from the third class waiting-room of the South-Eastern Railway Terminus" ("Text 7," p. 108). Where identity is collective and "to be is to be guilty," one becomes at once clerk and scribe, "judge and party, witness and advocate" ("Text 5," p. 95) in a trial in which one neither understands what one hears, nor knows what one writes ("Text 5," p. 98). Where there is no past or future, man is left alone, "between two parting dreams, knowing none, known of none" ("Text 11," p. 131). Like the texts themselves, the images suggest the imageless void beneath their words. In order to understand the vivid yet apparently discontinuous scenes, the reader seeks for meanings in their arrangement and for associations beneath their given prose. Like the narrator of "Text 6," the reader wonders: "How are the intervals filled between these apparitions?" (p. 101). Attention is subtly shifted from the images to the intervals—to the void between texts and scenes. Moreover, as the reader recombines the images, he discovers in them a movement toward extinction and silence. The narrator moves from envisioning himself as both father and son, asking and answering his own questions and holding himself in his arms ("Text 1," p. 79), to a picture of dependence in which he is held and gradually suffocated by another's hands ("Text 10," pp. 123–

24), to an even gloomier portrait of isolation in which the narrator is a complete amputee, "no arms, no hands . . . amputated on all sides" ("Text 11," p. 129). The progression of the images and vignettes of *Texts for Nothing* is toward absorption in the void. By the end of the work the narrator has dwindled from the minimal position of being, like the speaker in "Gerontion," "a little dust in a little nook, stirred faintly this way and that by breath straying from the lost without" ("Text 6," p. 103) to the almost traceless instant when "there won't be any life, there won't have been any life, there will be silence, the air quite still that trembled once an instant, the tiny flurry of dust quite settled" ("Text 3," p. 137). The thirteen vignettes point to the moment when the dust will be quite settled and "there will be nothing where there was never anything" ("Text 13," p. 139). Only then will the sought-for nothingness be attained. Like a jigsaw puzzle of a dust-heap, the disintegration of *Texts for Nothing* is achieved only after the reader has recombined the pieces and colors of the texts into an image of the imageless "last images."

By counterpointing rather than contradicting his "last images," Beckett intimates a new attitude toward the uncertainty and fluidity of nonrelational art. Instead of exploring simply the fragmentation of external associations, *Texts* goes beneath their apparent diversity to the dualities of the universal narrator/narrated. Instead of examining the identity of that narrator primarily through negation, *Texts* proposes thirteen discrete images of him. Although these images never achieve even the tentative affirmation of *Enough*, they do provide uncontested, though provisional, postulations of the way it is. These postulations in turn are prevented from restoring the orders and meanings of relational art through their justaposition. Hope is counterbalanced by despair; memories of life above in the light by existence in the dark; language by silence. By recombining the disparate texts he is given, the reader of *Texts for Nothing* discerns neither total dissolution nor absolute cohesion, but rather the possibility that no relationships exist among the artist, his art, and external reality.

The "last images" of *Texts for Nothing* mark the end both of Beckett's most prolific period and of his emphasis upon fragmentation and tessellation. Although the dual processes continue to operate in all of Beckett's works, they are transformed and subdued by the conceptual shift which occurs in *How It Is*. Instead of fragmenting external orders, *How It Is* is content to explore the inner worlds of the imagination. Instead of attempting to locate the narrator/narrated amid the shards of former relationships, *How It Is* examines the hermetic worlds the narrator fabricates. The movement away from fragmentation of conventional associations and toward acceptance of arbitrary and artificial images is prefigured in *Texts* by the movement away from contradiction and toward counterpoint. Each of the thirteen texts remains an uncontested version of how it is, but none of the texts provides a complete image of existence: the fragments are accepted as adequate, but they still must be recombined to yield a vision of nonrelational art. All of the prose works written between 1944 and 1950 strive to create the uncertainty and fluidity of nonrelational art through the dual processes of fragmentation and tessellation. Like the narrator of the trilogy progressively stripping away layers of material reality in order to say himself, the pieces written during this period persistently shatter traditional associations of time, space, identity, and even language in an effort to attain the "nothingness" Watt discovers at Mr. Knott's house. Paradoxically, the more former patterns are broken apart, the more the works give rise to alternative interpretations. The difficulty of the pieces is not that they are fragmented, but rather that they provoke an agonizing surplus of possible reintegrations. Like Watt seeking to make sense of the picture in Erskine's room, the reader attempts to rearrange the fragments he is given into a more explicable picture. But just as Watt cannot provide an absolute explanation of the picture, so too the reader cannot restore the orders and certainties of earlier literatures. Semantic succor is denied both Watt and the reader: language cannot exorcise external events by labeling them nor can it provide them with signification through the imposition of symbols. The fragmentation of *Watt* invites tessellation, but the work insists upon the inviolability of the chasm between circumstance and signification. Whereas Watt is dismayed by the nonrelational void he encounters at Mr. Knott's house, Mercier and Camier not only accept the void but even delight in exploring its great formal brilliance. Just as they never stray far from Helen's apartment, so too their story never bridges the gap between word and world. The reconciliation of language and event is forestalled in Mercier and Camier by offsetting the witty dialogues with the futile quests they describe. The conventions which yield signification on the stage are countermanded by those that provide meaning in a novel. The forced and incompatible yoking of theatrical and novelistic techniques prevents fragments of former associations from fusing into symbols where none were intended. Having discovered the dissociation of word and world in *Watt* and having explored it in *Mercier and Camier*, Beckett moves beyond that dissociation in the four nouvelles to the universal substratum of the narrator/narrated. By fragmenting the external world even further, the nouvelles reduce it to its essential characteristics. As artificial diversities are shattered, formerly disparate characters, settings, times, and stories begin to blur and merge. Beyond the nothingness intuited by Watt is heard the archetypal voice of a storyteller telling his story. In examining the nature of the archetypal voice, the trilogy identifies the narrator with the processes of fragmentation and tessellation. Like the dual processes, the narrator/narrated is kinetic and noncorporeal. He exists in the dynamic tensions between antithetical impulses, between speaker and spoken, internal and external, fluid and fixed. Similarly, like the infinitely repeating patterns of the dual processes, the narrator never will be able to complete his quest. Although he consistently refines his self-definitions, the narrator never will be able to describe himself completely: another dimension will always be necessary to encompass both the speaker and his self-definition. Although he seeks the words that can put an end to words, the narrator discovers that speech is incapable of saying nothing and that fragmentation inevitably invites tessellation. Even in *Texts for Nothing* where the narration itself is broken into thirteen discrete sections, the impetus is toward reintegration. The reader discovers the nonrelational void, the "nothingness" promised in the title only by combining and counterpointing the disparate images. Beckett is the master of fragmentation, but his words demand concomitant efforts at tessellation. His works offer not the fragments Eliot shores against our ruin, nor the vision of unity Yeats projects for his Byzantine mosaic worker, but rather the fluidity and uncertainty of nonrelational art. The dual processes provide Beckett with new forms to express the possibility of a greater formlessness. Through fragmentation and tessellation, Beckett reveals that "the forms are many in which the unchanging seeks relief from its formlessness."

4. The voice and its words

In discussing Beckett's works it is frequently useful to divide his career into three segments: the early period of exploration in English extending from pieces like "Assumption" and "A Case in a Thousand" to Watt (1944), the middle period of French prose and the narrator/narrated beginning with Mercier and Camier and including How It Is (1946–60), and the later period of the enigmatic short pieces from Imagination Dead Imagine through the present (1965–   ). Useful as it otherwise may be, however, a tripartite division of the Beckettian canon obscures an important shift in the conceptual framework of Beckett's pieces. How It Is does not present simply a continuation of the techniques and themes developed in the trilogy. Instead the book marks a turning point in Samuel Beckett's career from an exploration of the limitations of the human mind and an emphasis upon definitions of the self, to an identification of the self with the voice and an acceptance, if not celebration, of the life of the imagination. Indeed, How It Is enables Beckett to surmount the attitude of disintegration L'Innommable once caused in him[1] by directing attention not to the divorce of the mind from the external world, but rather to the internal worlds the mind creates. Chaos is accommodated not by the creation of structures appropriate for an uncertain and fluid universe, but rather by the celebration of the artificiality of structure itself. How It Is reduces everything to a voice speaking in the eternal present creating its own universe. This interior focus in turn makes possible the highly self-conscious and arbitrary constructions of Beckett's recent fictions.

1

The works written prior to How It Is are concerned with the problems of a mind/body dualism. From Belacqua scoffing "at the idea of a sequitur from his body to his mind,"[2] to the Unnamable trying to say who he is even though there are no names or pronouns for him (p. 404), we see Beckett's characters trying to bridge the gap between the mind, which Murphy describes as a "large hollow sphere, hermetically closed to the universe without" (p. 107) and what Neary refers to as "the big blooming buzzing confusion" (p. 4) of the world. The problem for Beckett's characters, as for the post-Cartesian philosophers to whom Beckett frequently alludes, is that action, speech, identity, and thought become problematic once the mind is isolated from the material world. Ultimately, Murphy's quest to become immersed in the dark flux of the mind's third zone, "where he could love himself" (p. 7), is a self-destructive quest which can be accomplished only by annihilating that physical part of himself "which he hated" (p. 8). Watt's efforts to superimpose the rational constructions of his mind upon the irrational world he encounters meet with no greater success. No matter how many hypotheses he formulates, nor how many generations of "needy local men" he traces to guarantee the feeding of "two famished dogs" (pp. 91–117), Watt can never "penetrate the forces at play . . . or even perceive the forms they upheaved, or obtain the least useful information concerning himself, or Mr. Knott" (p. 117). Knott cannot be known: the rational mind, incapable of knowing the irrational, can only combine and permute its own limited elements. Those limitations are explored further in the trilogy as the first person narrator proffers a consciousness experiencing itself. From Molloy's inability to recall his name (p. 22) and Moran's contradiction of his own report (p. 176), to Malone's inventory of stories and possessions (pp. 181ff.), to the Unnamable's continuing effort to say the words that will put an end to words (p. 369), we see Beckett's successive narrators struggling to define themselves in relation to the external world and to the words they speak. Even after the Unnamable renounces foreign objects and "vice-existers" as terms in his self-definition, he is still forced to rely on a language learned from others (p. 314). The result is an infinitely repeating pattern in which some larger category is always necessary to encompass the speaker and his definition, to contain the perceiving mind and its self-perceptions.[3] While Beckett's early pieces portray a mind/body dichotomy, his works of the narrator/narrated investigate the restrictions that dichotomy imposes upon the mind.

The pieces written after *How It Is*, on the other hand, turn from an emphasis upon the mind's limitations to considerations of its imaginative constructions. References to, and comparisons with, an unreachable external reality are replaced by detailed descriptions of objects which exist only in the inner world of the mind's creations. Portrayals of a mind creating stories are omitted in favor of the deliquescent creations themselves. More-over, these creations often pay tribute to the imagination. *Imagination Dead Imagine* is based on a paradox: imagination is necessary to envision a state in which imagination is dead. Without imagination there is no mo-tion, no emotion, no voice, no thought, "no trace anywhere of life" (p. 63). The identification of color, sound, and even life with imagination is con-tinued in *Ping*, which catalogues what is finally over. Significantly, the last elements in this catalogue to be over are not the "heart breath" nor even the blue eyes, but the murmurs which are too indistinct to be quoted directly, too fleeting to be recorded. They belong to the world of the imagined, the "never seen," "invisible," "no trace." Yet it is precisely in these nonmaterial murmurs and their postulations of what is not that vi-tality persists. Like existence, the piece itself is over only after the final murmur has ended and the last "ping" has faded away. Just as the imagina-tive murmurs provide variety and vitality in *Ping*, so too those sentences associated with imaginary constructions provide mystery and meaning in *Lessness*.4 Four of the six groups of sentences Beckett wrote in compos-ing *Lessness* are relatively simple: they describe setting and body—the known or observable aspects of the present situation. The last groups of sentences, however, deal, not with given data, but with the imaginative and mental, postulating things that are not except in the mind, in dreams and figments and illusions. The mere mention of these illusions enriches the entire work by relieving the grey endlessness. By presenting figments and impossible futures, Beckett forces us to see what does not and can not exist in the "true refuge" except through the imagination.

Even if they do not describe the self-contained and fanciful construc-tions of *Imagination Dead Imagine*, *Ping*, and *Lessness*, Beckett's other later works embrace the imagination without lamenting its dissociation from material reality. For example, unlike the trilogy, *Fizzles* is not ob-sessed either with defining the narrator or with labeling, controlling, and hence divorcing him from his stories. Indeed, the narrator's identity and location are often difficult to determine. Sharp divisions between mind and world are blurred. The Unnamable's urgency to say his pensum and to find the correct words is gone. Instead, the words as stated are accepted as ade-quate, even if incomplete, depictions of the way it is. Everything "needed to be known" is known, imagined, and said: there is nothing beyond the world of the fiction: "Closed place. All needed to be known for say is known. There is nothing but what is said. Beyond what is said there is nothing. What goes on in the arena is not said. Did it need to be known it would be. No interest. Not for imagining" (p. 37). The sense of self-sufficiency suggested in *Fizzles* is central to *Enough*. As the title implies, the work is concerned with the moderate and the balanced. Even in a minimal world there can be too much—too much of silence, too much of speech, too much remembered, too much forgotten: "All that goes before forget. Too much at a time is too much. . . . Too much silence is too much" (p. 53). The piece deals with calm acceptance and the "eternally mild" (p. 59). Instead of the commitment to an unending pursuit of futile quests saying, "You must go on, I can't go on, I'll go on" (*The Unnamable*, p. 414); instead of the rebellious claim that "to be an artist is to fail, as no other dare fail";[5] instead of these, *Enough* hesitantly and tentatively proffers the reconciliation, calm acceptance, and perhaps even the affirmation of a narrator who feels it is enough to have spoken at all, of a narrator who can accept the inevitable failure of his quest saying, "Stony ground but not entirely. Given three or four lives I might have accomplished something" (p. 54). The piece, though a reduced and even minimal literature, is itself enough. When chaos cannot be captured, it is enough to have created an image that fleetingly gestures toward the void. When imagination is divorced from material reality, it is enough to have written words that wipe out everything but a sense of unity with the passing image (p. 60).

2

The transition from rebellious questing to tentative acceptance, from examination of the mind's limitations to exploration of its creations, from external definitions of the self to internal identifications with the imagination, is first expressed in *How It Is*.[6] By directing the narrator's attention to the self-creating powers of the voice and by eliminating external referents and efforts to locate oneself in opposition to an exterior order, Beckett frees both the voice and his fiction to consider earlier themes and subjects within a new framework. The more the voice must rely on its own words for both its existence and the wherewithal to endure, the more ambiguous its postulations become. Where everything is produced by and contained within a speaking voice, nothing need be ultimately affirmed or denied. *How It Is* is bound only by self-imposed limitations. Unencumbered by the problem of sequiturs between body and mind, the voice creates its own space, time, identity, and even style.

The shift in Beckett's framework begins with the reduction of everything to a voice speaking in an eternal present. Whereas *Molloy, Malone Dies*, and even *The Unnamable* contain vestigial characters with bits and scraps of a plot still clinging to them, *How It Is* reduces even those fragmentary characters and plots until there remain only the archetypal elements of the panting, the murmur, the dark, and the mud. Of these elements only the murmur in the mud has the capacity to differentiate, to individuate, to create. This imaginative murmur, then, is the source and substance of the universe—of the Pims and Boms, the sacks and tins, the memories and images. Only through our reading of the voice's whey of words does the narrator assume an identity or existence. Indeed, as the initial and final "stanzas" reveal, the book itself is literally a quotation of the voice's narration. Instead of a three-part division of eternity, we have the perpetual present formulation of a voice creating itself in the here and now. When the voice ceases, so does *How It Is* and our journey through its bizarre world ends.

The structure of *How It Is* intimates the overriding importance of our voice for that work. The presence or absence of the voice distinguishes the journey of part one from the abandon of part three (p. 21). Likewise, the couple of part two is subdivided by the momentous discovery that Pim "can speak then that's the main thing" (p. 56). Repeatedly the narrator anticipates the return of his voice (e.g., p. 60). If it is not with relief, at least it is without objection that he finds this voice "back at last in my mouth" (p. 106). Like Watt seeking to make a pillow of words, the narrator seeks solace in saying something, anything, to himself (p. 43). Just as the typography of *How It Is* consists of print and spaces, so too the universe consists of words and silences (p. 13). The narrator no longer searches for a "language meet for here" (p. 17); yet only through that language can he live (p. 129).

Although the importance of the voice is emphasized by the structure, its nature remains ambivalent, "this voice is truly changeable" (p. 15). Indeed, the voice freely contradicts and revises itself. The narrator asks a question, then denies his capability of asking such a question (pp. 92–93); he describes motions he makes to hear Pim's watch, then concludes that "all that beyond my strength" (p. 58); he posits a word, then retracts it as "too strong" (pp. 55, 115). Uncertainty increases as the voice points out its own faulty transmission. Not only do we depend on some less than assuring witness, but this witness himself depends on a less than definitive narration. Like Sam in *Watt*, the witness is trying to transcribe a story of which he hears only "bits and scraps" (p. 15) and "little blurts midget grammar" (p. 76) which come too fast and end too soon (p. 81). In spite of its ambiguity and uncertainty, however, the voice is consistent in its modes of operation. It remains loyal to the self-imposed limitations of the way the story is told. Reality is not really an issue. Phrases such as "it's one or the other" (p. 11), "I remember . . . or I forget" (p. 8), "It's not said or I don't hear" (p. 18) become refrains. Nothing, not even an ending, need be established irrevocably. The narrator may be engulfed in the mud, may be part of an unending cyclical progression, may be shat into the light. He may be the only figure who exists, or may be diffused into the great collapse of a million Pims and Boms. Unlike the trilogy characters, he may even die: "I am not dead to inexistence not irretrievably" (p. 69). The narrator's only self-imposed rule of order for dealing with permutations is that "justice" be maintained. This justice is itself nothing more than the preservation of symmetry. Every Bom must be a Pim for equivalent periods of time (p. 125). Every four yards to the north must be balanced by four yards to the south (p. 47). As in *The Lost Ones* and *Imagination Dead Imagine*, the narrator uses his mathematics to create verbal diagrams (p. 47). Ironically, in an uncertain world of undifferentiated mud, we know precisely how the narrator crawls—if he really does crawl. Likewise, the narrator's "dear figures" yield the percentage of words lost (if they are lost) (p. 95), and enable a contrast between Pim's "iso" buttocks (if Pim exists) and the narrator's own "ratio [of] four to one" (p. 37). The voice is thus consistently operating according to the abstract postulations of systems such as "mathematics astronomy and even physics" (p. 41), in an inconsistent world lacking the "history and geography" which gave time and place to mimetic novels.

The ambivalence of the voice is due not only to its uncertainty about the universe it postulates, but also to its ambiguous source. Although the narrator purports to be murmuring in the mud, at the same time he attributes the voice to some external person or thing which he is at best only quoting, "I say it as I hear it" (p. 7). As in *The Unnamable* there is a sense that the words are part of some pensum taught by and belonging to a "them" or "it" (p. 108). But there is no longer any urgency to define "who is speaking that's not said any more it must have ceased to be of interest" (p. 21). Nor are we concerned whether the narrator speaks from obligation, necessity, or desire; whether he uses his speech "freely" or not (p. 18). The narrator accepts without desperation the realization that his words can pass through him and beyond his control. Moreover, he uses the externality of the voice as the first premise in the proof of its divinity. If the voice is other and is the source of words, it may be the source of the murmurings of all Pims and Boms (p. 76). The voice is prime matter and prime mover. Like the Christian God it is creator and trinity, "the voice quaqua from which I get my life . . . of three things one" (p. 113). It is to this "voice quaqua the voice of us all" (p. 138) that the narrator assigns the "minimum of intelligence" required to validate his universe by hearing and noting our murmurings and by filling the "need of one not one of us an intelligence somewhere a love who all along the track at the right places according as we need them deposits our sacks" (pp. 137–38). The tasks are not too difficult since "to hear and note one of our murmurs is to hear and note them all" (p. 138). The external divinity not only creates us by giving us words, but it also confirms us by listening to us repeat them (p. 137). But, just as rationalists' proofs of God's existence led to agnosticism, so too the narrator's deduction leads to doubt. Given his world, it is unlikely that a voice as powerful and intelligent as his divinity would endure a system whereby it would hear its own story endlessly repeated. Since it is impossible to stop the cycle without causing injustice (p. 139), the voice would be forced rather to formulate a system eliminating himself as divinity and "admitting him to peace at least while rendering me in the same breath sole responsible for this unqualified murmur" (p. 144). The narrator has thus gone full circle. Beginning with a voice which he locates externally, he goes on to construct a universe over which such a voice would be the divine intelligence, only to end by acknowledging the errors of his system and his own responsibility for the voice.

Perhaps it is only in a Beckettian universe that a narrator can without contradiction assume responsibility for an external voice. The consistency, or at least compatibility of such claims is due to the paradoxical nature of the voice. It is both external and internal, universal and individual (p. 7). Internality is emphasized by the soundless voice of the journey (p. 18). No qualitative difference accrues between silent and audible murmurings, between "two cries one mute" (p. 48). The voice and its significance lie beyond mere vocalization. The essential and internal nature of the voice is also supported physiologically. Murmuring and panting are similar processes. An end will not come until both have stopped (pp. 104–05, 106). The voice, the pant, and even the fart are all defined by the same elementary description. Foreign matter is brought into the body, it is processed, waste products are expelled: inspiration, respiration, exhalation; ingestion, digestion, excretion. The application of voice to this pattern undercuts Western veneration of the mind. In the archetypal world of mud, dark, pant, and murmur, it is the murmur with its ability to invent that must bear the burdens normally associated with the mind, imagination, and thought. With embarrassing ease principles concerning human understanding can be plugged into the description—perception becomes foreign input, thought becomes processing, and ideas become mere waste products equivalent to the less inspiring and more earthy pant or fart. The voice, the pant, and the fart are the basic life process, are the hiss of air which bestows existence on the little that's left of the narrator:

> escape hiss it's air of the little that's left of the little whereby man continues standing laughing weeping and speaking his mind nothing physical the health is not in jeopardy a word from me and I am again I strain with open mouth so as not to lose a second a fart fraught with meaning issuing through the mouth no sound in the mud

> it comes the word we're talking of words I have some still it would seem at my disposal at this period one is enough aha signifying mamma impossible with open mouth it comes I let it at once or in extremis or between the two there is room to spare aha signifying mamma or some other thing some other sound barely audible signifying some other thing no matter the first to come and restore me to my dignity. (p. 26)

On another level the words restore the narrator to his dignity because they are that dignity. The voice creates the narrator, who in turn embodies that voice or, as the narrator says, "I personify it it personifies itself" (p. 112). He can have no desires beyond those the voice grants him (p. 12). He can make no judgments independent of the voice's evaluations (p. 37). He ceases to exist when the voice leaves him and returns to himself only when the voice returns to him (p. 95). Life is presented at its minimal point—"my life last state last version ill-said ill-heard ill-recaptured ill-murmured in the mud" (p. 7). Nevertheless, a certain dignity inheres in the resiliency and inevitability with which that ill-said continues to speak, to create itself and its fictitious words.

When the ill-said creates its fictitious worlds and material universe out of undifferentiated, soundless, and scentless mud (p. 25), attention no longer need be directed to the height of Cuchulain's statue[7] nor to the location of the Unnamable's jar. Geographic division becomes less important than the perception that the primeval mud (p. 11) is the protoplasm from which all else is derived and to which all things return. The mud is both "humanity restoring" drink and food (pp. 27, 28) and the excrement of billions (p. 52). Although the narrator imposes directions upon the vast plains of mud (p. 47), his compass references are only arbitrary divisions of a purposeless tack. The eastward movement is metaphorically meaningless. It cannot be a movement toward the sunrise with its conventional association of rebirth because birth, sunrise, and even the earth's rotation belong not to the mud, but to "life above in the light" (p. 123).

Nor can it be a journey toward death for "death [is] in the west as a rule" (p. 123). At best the journey from west to east, from left to right, is analogous to the motion of words across the printed page. The voice's geography belongs to its medium of words.

Likewise, objects depend on the voice's narration. The objects presented are purposely simple, few in number, grudgingly given, and rigidly controlled. Unlike the trilogy where characters, plots, and objects proliferate until they escape control, until for example, Malone does not know why his own character Sapo "was not expelled when he so richly deserved to be" (*Malone Dies*, p. 190), the objects here are contained and carefully labeled (pp. 8, 9, 11, 25). They never attain independent existence, but rather always remain subject to the voice's postulations. By revising his description of Pim's watch (p. 58), the narrator calls the materiality of that watch into question. The sack steadily depreciates from one of the early certainties (p. 8), to an incidental object, to one of the "not true" (p. 145). Indeed, the narrator is able to envision himself without sacks or other anomalous objects, "quite tiny," sustained only by the air and the mud (p. 17).

Paradoxically, these problematic objects bear a large burden of meaning. Having stripped away circumstantial reality and external association, Beckett thrusts enormous pressure on the few remaining objects. They must operate on a material level (sack as wet jute sack—p. 8), on a referential level (sack as penitential shirt—p. 36; as container of the world's howls and laughter—p. 38), on a symbolic level (sack as lover—p. 44; as body—p. 17), and on metaphysical and mythic levels. It is the necessity of replacing the sacks which calls into question the narrator's cyclical system and hypothetical divinity. His parallel claims that he will never let go of the sack (p. 10) nor of Pim (p. 55) and the parallel negations of the sack abandoned (pp. 46, 55) and Pim lost (p. 99) reveal the narrator's ultimate inefficacy. His burst sack and Pim's "not burst" sack raise the problems of justice and human understanding (p. 61). The deposition of sacks becomes a metaphor for the human condition and an image of how it is: ". . . we leave our sacks to those who do not need them we take their sacks from those who soon will need them . . ." (p. 111). Likewise, the tins of tunny tell us more about human existence than they do about the social and material reality of the narrator. They are less important in their function as containers of food than in their manipulability as objects to be counted, opened, thrown away, or returned to the sack half empty (p. 8). Significantly, the narrator never portrays himself doing anything so lifelike as eating the prawns or a crumb of mouldy tunny (p. 8). Instead, the tins are a crude measure of an approaching end when it will be possible to count them with one hand (p. 8). The narrator compares himself casting off empty tins to a dealer of cards and to "certain sowers of seed" (p. 11). Unlike the Biblical seed, the narrator's is hollow and exhausted, falling without hope or fertility in the random order of a card game. Even the narrator seeks no harvest from his tins but will, if he sometimes finds a tin, "make haste to throw [it] away again" (p. 11).

The quest for an end is itself undermined by the reduction of time to its most basic component. Past and future are irrelevant in a world without cause or effect. The three-part division of eternity (p. 24) is actually the three-part division of a stream of words uttered in the eternal present. Correlation between those three parts and those words is possible if part three is accepted as an accurate description of the present and the book is seen as a version of the traditional flashback. The viewpoint is that of a narrator who has already survived the journey and couple and is recounting them from his current abandoned position. Throughout, the first two stages are consistently referred to by the past tense, while the present is applied to the third, and the future is employed in conjecture about the fourth, "How it *was* I quote before Pim with Pim after Pim how it *is*" (p. 7, my emphasis). The narrator's decision to follow the "natural order" enables him, like Malone, to tally what he must say in order to make an end (p. 51). His sporadic knowledge of the entire cycle enables him to anticipate later stages. In the journey he predicts the discovery and loss of Pim (p. 20) and he knows that the difference between the silent journey and the abandon will be "words like now words not mine before Pim" (p. 21). The narrator's knowledge of the whole order allows—or causes—him to get "the various times mixed up in [his] head all the various times before during after vast tracts of time" (p. 107). Although the images belong to the journey (p. 10), they appear in the couple (pp. 85, 86, 88). Although numbers and "reckoning" are supposed to fade out after part one (p. 51), part three contains elaborate computations (pp. 114–42). The best indication that the whole must be spoken from the part three viewpoint is the existence of the narration itself. The book is dependent upon a voice which is "peculiar to part three or seven or eleven or fifteen so on" (p. 116). The speechless life in the couple can be portrayed only after speech has returned (p. 60). Moreover, existence is contingent upon the abandon: ". . . part three it's there I have my life" (p. 27). When the narrator seeks an end he does so in some future stage in which Bom would have come and been abandoned already. Bom would then be the abandoned voice using the present tense to tell of his own life in the couple, "ah if only all

past all in the past Bom come I gone and Bom on our life in common"
(p. 61).

Unlike the conventional flashback, however, the narration denies the validity of a past and the possibility of a future. As in *Happy Days*, once a
state is ended, it is as though it never existed. One "knows one's tormentor
only as long as it takes to suffer him and one's victim only as long as it
takes to enjoy him if as long" (p. 121). If there is "no more Pim [there]
never [was] any Pim" (p. 74). The narrator is displaced in time, cut off
from a causal world, denied an heroic past and a golden age (pp. 10, 54).
The lack of a future denies him any hope or goal (p. 143). He cannot deal
with questions such as what would happen if he were to lose the opener or
if the sack were finally empty (p. 9). Nor can he predict that no one will
ever come again to shine a light on him (p. 15). The present formulation
undercuts the narrator's entire metaphysics as he is forced to admit that
Pim never was and Bom never will be (pp. 86–87), that one cannot present
in three episodes "an affair which all things considered involves four" (p.
130). Pim's howl comes when asked how life is (pp. 96–98): the narrator's
scream comes when asked how it was (p. 144). This scream is "good" because it is proof of present life (p. 122). Yet, at the same time, the scream
is an acknowledgment that all descriptions of how it was are false. The
narrator is forced to return to the "vast stretch of time" (p. 7) of the
present with its only certainties of the mud, the dark, the pant, and the
murmur.

Before the vastness of the eternal present, any efforts to order or to
measure segments of time are as absurd and futile as having "Pim's timepiece . . . and nothing to time" (p. 40). In fact, all of the narrator's chrono-
metric devices are negated by his condition. The diminution of tins as a
crude measure of the approaching end is made ineffectual by the loss of
both the tins and the need for the tins. Likewise, the alarm-clocklike breath
bag (p. 19) becomes irrelevant when the narrator admits he no longer
sleeps (p. 40). Although he may, like Winnie, occasionally speak of time
in the "old style" of measurable units like days and weeks, the narrator
is aware that such units belong not to his vast, static world but to the
revolving world of life above in the light (p. 123). His world is one in
which time will not pass, in which waiting is too hopeful a word to describe
the present state. Even Belacqua is no longer indifferently waiting to live
through antepurgatory, but he has fallen over asleep, forgetting he is waiting and forgotten by those who have placed him there (p. 24).

In this timeless world, the narrator speaks to fill in the void, discussing
things and desires he no longer has in preference to not speaking at all

(pp. 12–13, 16, 18). The whole work becomes his effort to find the "there wherewith to beguile a moment of this vast season" (p. 91). Raising a hand, fluttering it, covering a face with it (p. 14), fluffing hair (p. 24), and drinking the mud (pp. 27–28) constitute the busy work and stage business that pass the time. Merely having gotten through a moment makes it a good moment. Consequently, all the good moments lie in the no longer accessible past (p. 10).

In this intensely insistent *now*, death and its counterfeit—sleep—assume importance as possible sources of relief. Death, never entirely ruled out (pp. 23, 69), is one of the things in which the narrator can perhaps believe (p. 21). Indeed, death pervades the work. The tins are described as being "hermetically under vacuum on their dead for ever sealed" (p. 92); the sack helps the narrator keep dying in a dying age (p. 17); the narrator is either born into death or dying at birth (p. 70); Krim and Kram cannot tell if the couple is alive or dead (p. 93). As in the trilogy the narrator posits words and stories to "keep busy otherwise death" (p. 81). Yet paradoxically, each story also seems to bring him closer to finishing what he must say in order to make an end (p. 109). The narrator seeks an end, but he is powerless to achieve one. Although suicide is a recurrent thought (pp. 40, 87), it does not seem to be a viable outlet, perhaps because the narrator is concerned about the family honor (pp. 83, 84), perhaps because he is unable to find a satisfactory method of ending his present condition (p. 63), or perhaps because he will not be freed, even in death, from the eternal present and the need to pass the time. Death is not the lowest level in an infinite, downward spiral (pp. 20–21). One slips lower and lower but nevertheless one continues to persist (p. 22), to endure "the same kingdom as before . . . the same it always was I have never left it it is boundless" (p. 43).

Just as death is portrayed as a desired but unattainable relief, so too sleep is made increasingly important and improbable. The narrator invents his breath bag to keep conscious track of the precious unconscious moments. He cannot simply sleep until rested, but must measure that sleep in half-hour intervals (p. 19). Sleeping with his tongue out is not only one of the narrator's resources (p. 28), it is the summation of his nights in the present formulation (p. 27). Life is the interval "from one sleep to the next" (p. 23), with value placed not on the intervals but on the sleeps. Sleep offers escape from "all the doing suffering failing bungling achieving" (p. 23) that compose the waking moments. It is hymned as the sole good which relieves the burning eyes, snuffs out the ruined body, and provides the little that the narrator still is with the hope and dream of other worlds and nonexistence (p. 36). But as sleep's significance mounts, so does the narrator's insomnia. Diminishing references to his naps terminate in the narrator's acknowledgment that he no longer does sleep (p. 40). The desire for the solace of sleep is raised to a religious appeal and then denied. Sleep is what one seeks for in vain, has no right to, does not deserve, and yet must pray for, "for prayer's sake when all fails" (p. 36).

Denied escape from the "vast season" of the present, the narrator explores the implications of his existence. Like a tree falling in an uninhabited forest, does a voice speaking in the eternal present need some "other" to hear its words and confirm its existence? As in *Film*, the narrator can examine the structural and dramatic convenience of Berkeley's dictum, *Esse est percipi* (to be is to be perceived), without attaching any "truth value" to the idea. The actual reality of a witness is less an issue than are the images and theories resulting from the narrator's felt need for one.

Like the presence or absence of a voice, the presence or absence of another is a major structural device. It is the fact of the couple rather than the role of tormentor or victim which is important: part four is unnecessary to our narration because it is essentially a repetition of part two (p. 131). The journey and the abandon are themselves defined in terms of the "other." The journey is a quest without hope and without the "all-important most important other inhabitant" (p. 13). Yet even in that solitude there remains the dream "of a little woman within my reach and dreaming too it's in the dream too of a little man within hers" (p. 13). Or, if that dream is too hopeful, there is an emergency dream of an alpaca llama in whose fleece one may huddle (p. 14). Part three presents not simply man alone, but man abandoned, rejected, and aware of his lack of the other. The need of another simply for its otherness manifests itself in the narrator's relationship with his sack. During the journey the sack is the only available other. By being an external object against which individuation may occur, the sack becomes the first sign of life (p. 8). More than a thing to be manipulated or an object to be possessed, the sack assumes almost sexual relationships with the narrator, who cradles and caresses it (p. 44), makes a pillow of it to lie "soft in my arms" (p. 46), murmurs endearments to it (p. 17). The narrator clings to the sack not from fear of losing it (p. 10) nor from expectation of any profit from it (p. 66), but because it admits of his own existence.

Like the sack, the narrator's people evolve out of his felt need for a witness. Long before they are named, Krim and Kram appear as listener and scribe. The narration technically cannot exist without their recording of the narrator's stream of words (p. 7). Their transcript is the book we hold and read. Yet Krim and Kram are unreliable witnesses. Not only do they "lose the nine-tenths" (p. 81) of what is being said, but their whole capacity for comprehension is made questionable by their inability to determine if the narrator and Pim are alive (p. 93), or to agree if their role permits affording the narrator relief (p. 82). Moreover, the narrator denies them an independent existence, even abandoning his own viewpoint in one scene to speak their thoughts (p. 81). At one point he tells us there is no witness, no scribe (p. 84). At another, like Watt dealing with the Lynch family, he postulates generations of Krims and Krams to insure continual observation (p. 80). Pim is similarly undermined. Pim is the necessary other. Only by feeling that Pim is there, can the narrator feel he himself is there still (p. 92). However, Pim's reality is questionable. Like Krim and Kram, Pim may be only a figment of the narration (p. 27). Not only does the narrator, as he says "efface myself behind my creatures when the fit takes me" (p. 52), but he quite blatantly assumes their names (p. 60) and lives (p. 72) and "plays" at being them (p. 57). The hope for another who will penetrate the voice's hermeticism is destroyed.

This failure of the "other" shatters the hope the narrator invests in his image of the couple. With a companion the narrator would have been a "more universal" man, another's words could have improved him, he realizes his injunctions could have been communicated by more humane means; but the companion (p. 67), the words (p. 69), and the realization (p. 90) all come "too late too late indisputably" (p. 69). The couple fails to attain certitude, purpose, affection, or vitality. The tragedy of this failure is magnified by the expectations the narrator holds for the conjunction. Not only is it to be the hoped-for end to solipsistic solitude, but it is also to be a source of consolation. The journey is less burdensome when placed in a series of similar sufferings (p. 48). The existence of one other increases the probable existence of a whole universe of others, "the moment there are two there were yes billions of us crawling" (p. 52). An endless progression of "billions of us" makes hearsay knowledge and communication possible (p. 119). Thus the failure of the couple destroys consolation, communication, and knowledge. No one knows another "either personally or otherwise" (p. 123). With the dissolution of the couple and the "other," inevitably comes the dissolution of the self: "at each instant each ceased and was there no more either for himself or for the other vast tracts of time" (p. 122).

Nothing so positive as the hopes from even an improbable couple is left unchallenged in the voice's world. The couple is simultaneously extolled and undermined. Communication and connection are desired and fled. The narrator desires no caller (p. 12) and prefers not to meet even himself. The discovery of Pim's voice which "makes us better acquainted" (p. 55) is the "hitch" that ends the "long peace" of the "beginnings of our life in common" (p. 55). Pim wants the narrator to leave him in peace (p. 98). When conceiving other worlds, the narrator imagines a more merciful one without a couple and thus without an abandonment or journey (p. 143). It is ambiguous whether Pim has been given to the narrator as a reward or as a punishment for his high morale: " . . . the morale at the outset before things got out of hand satisfactory ah the soul I had in those days the equanimity that's why they gave me a companion" (p. 25). Caught in the paradox of his system, the narrator needs the "other" to establish his own identity, yet finds life in the couple yields only false identity. There is no real conjunction and life in common is only an "orgy of false being" (p. 69).

By making the narrator's existence and identity dependent upon a voice whose nature is ambivalent, whose postulations are uncertain, and whose auditor is problematic, Beckett has diffused his work into an intangible, paradoxical vastness. He has gone beyond Proust and Joyce and the problems of temporal identity. As in *Ulysses*, identity is continuous and successive. The narrator is the same ancient voice throughout and he is three figures who cannot recall earlier stages. But Beckett destroys the perimeters of the self in space as well as in time. The narrator is not only the ancient external-internal voice, but he is also the spoken and the heard voice. His existence is contingent upon the other: no sharp divisions separate him from that other. The dispersion of identity yields ambiguous pronouns. The unnamed voice is called "he," "it," and even "I." Often the third person pronoun remains indefinite as "he" refers equally well to the narrator, Pim, Krim, Kram, Pam Prim, or Bom. The absence of individual boundaries results in the conjugation of names (pp. 114–15). In such a schema it is irrelevant whether the narrator is creating Pim or encountering one of a million non-individuated figures all identical to himself: ". . . in other words in simple words I quote on either I am alone and no further problem or else we are innumerable and no further problem either" (p. 124). Each figure is Everyman pursuing the same archetypal cycle through the "warmth of primeval mud impenetrable dark" (p. 11). In his career each plays both Pim's and Bom's role. In fact, there is no real difference between being Pim or Bom, between section two and four. Joy and sorrow, tormentor and victim, "I" and "he" all merge as identity is denied definitive borders and as existence is diffused into spoken and heard, Pim and Bom, I and Other.

Because everything in *How It Is* depends upon the diffuse, narrating voice, the form in which the voice creates its universe is as important as the content of that universe. In a world without past or future, cause or effect, there can be no subordination. The omnipresent now is experienced without punctuation and without the interlocking memories that made the well-made sentence possible. In such a universe the major concern is to pass the time while waiting for an end that will not come. The lack of hope removes urgency from the verbal games the voice plays with itself to fill in the void. But even in these games—even in enumerating what must be said to reach the last at last, in positing resources, or in asking oneself questions and providing the answers—the self-imposed limitations of the voice's universe must still be obeyed. In a world that has rejected traditional time, place, and identity, the voice can no longer ask how it got here, whence come its possessions, or even if it exists: ". . . how I got here no questions not known not said and the sack whence the sack and me if it's me no question impossible too weak no importance" (p. 7). Where everything, including identity, is ambiguous, pronouns become indefinite and names generic. Pim is victim: Bem is the tormentor already endured: Bom is the tormentor to come. Where nothing is certain, language itself begins to dissolve. Not only does the voice begin to contradict itself, but it also rejects its words as too strong (pp. 115, 127). Where there is no external order, all becomes a free-flowing mental construction. The lack of permanent and concrete connections is reflected in everything from the failure of the couple to communicate to the splitting apart of normal syntax groups. In a prose that intimates an entropic universe breaking down in the mud, there can be little imagery. The colors, gestures, near-metaphors, and almost-symbols that survive are few in number and sparingly used. Whereas earlier works are greatly concerned with the degenerating bodies of their characters, *How It Is* is almost amorphous. It is the voice which captures our interest. Its references to eyes, ears, hands, and heads are neither insisted upon nor pursued as physical realities. The body fades into surreality (p. 28). Even the eyes become strangely unseeing eyes. The important vision is mental rather than material. Hence the voice's need for two kinds of eyes: the blue to deal with the physical and "the others" at the back (p. 8) for the psychical.

Unlike the self-consciously artificial images of the later works, the images in *How It Is* are of "earth sky a few creatures in the light some still standing" (p. 8). The narrator may begin with himself alone, but his narration is irresistably drawn toward real or imaginary others: "The first is always me then the other" (p. 88). We see a woman worrying over a child (pp. 10–11), a boy praying at his mother's knees (p. 15), a boy and a girl walking hand in hand (pp. 29–31), a youth meeting Jesus in a vision (p. 45). The events Pim recalls are traumatic sunderings of relationships, when some bizarre and fatal accident breaks another's back. His wife Pam Prim falls or jumps from a window (pp. 76–78), his father falls when a scaffolding collapses (p. 78), his dog Skom Skum is run over by a dray (p. 85). The images not only portray recognizable interpersonal relationships, they also reflect other Beckettian works. The scene of the boy praying at his mother's knee (p. 15) is depicted in one of the photographs in *Film* and in the earliest known picture of Beckett himself.[8] A man sitting on the bed with his head in his hands (p. 21) appears in "The End" as does a figure in the stern of a boat seeking "an isle home at last" (p. 86).

Yet as familiar as the images initially appear, they are as different from the images of Beckett's earlier works as they are unlike the rotundas, boxes, and cylinders of the later pieces. Whereas the Unnamable's "delegates" tell him "about man," provide him with "the low-down on God," give him "courses on love, on intelligence," and teach him "to count, and even to reason" (*The Unnamable*, pp. 297–98), the voice's images do not create intellectual or emotional bonds between him and their "few creatures in the light" (p. 8). Although the narrator begins by saying he has only old dreams, things, and memories (p. 7), he quickly revises this statement. In a world without a definable past or sleep, there can be no memories nor any dreams. Therefore the narrator chooses to call the things he sometimes sees in the mud "images" (p. 11). Unlike memories, the images are impersonal and independent of an external reality. There is neither recall by the narrator of the life the images portray (p. 8), nor is there any question of, or even desire for, returning to such a life (p. 8). Moreover, the images cannot be controlled (p. 32). They come without warning or choice at irregular intervals (pp. 10, 15). In a rather strident passage the narrator compares the sudden emanation of images to an infant befouling his crib. "I pissed and shat another image in my crib never so clean since" (p. 9). He is unable to manipulate the figures in order to see them better. He cannot tell if the figure on the bed with his head in his hands is young or old (p. 18). Nor can he stop the couple when their images pass through him (p. 32). If he awaits their return, he waits in vain (p. 32). His viewpoint as an outsider is often limited and distorted: "... I watched him after my fashion from afar through my spy-glass sidelong in mirrors through windows at night ..." (p. 9). The distance between the narrator and his images, and the comparative happiness of the images, makes the narrator's own position more desolate. Although he may once have been a boy in the company of a little girl friend under the sky of April or May, he is so no longer. Although he responds to his impression that the couple is looking at him by trying to appear friendly and respectable (p. 29), the gesture is futile. When the scene ends he is still alone, unseen, in the mud: "I realize I'm still smiling there's no sense in that now been none for a long time now" (p. 31). His consciousness of the figure's improvement—"better than he was better than yesterday less ugly less stupid less cruel less dirty less old less wretched" (p. 9)—forces the narrator's recognition of his own steady decline from bad to worse (p. 9). The very relief offered by the images of "earth sky a few creatures in the light" (p. 8), makes the return to the mud that much more devastating, makes the losses of "the humanities I had" (p. 30) that much more noticeable.

The dissociation of the narrator from the images is compounded by the presence of Pim's images. Most of the images in part two ascribed to Pim can also be linked to the narrator. The narrator's brief reference to coming to "in hospital in the dark" (p. 22) is expanded by the image of Pam Prim's hospitalization (p. 77). The scene of the boy praying at his mother's knees (p. 15) reverberates in Pim's description of mamma (p. 78). The setting that leads into the narrator's vision of Jesus (p. 45) reappears in Pim's section. The narrator's concern with slipping and falling to lower levels is fulfilled in the falls that punctuate Pim's life and relationships. The similarities between the two sections invite us to borrow Pim's images to develop a prose context for the narrator. Isolation in the mud seems the end for one who "tried everything then gave up . . . never any good at anything" (p. 78), who "never knew anyone always ran fled elsewhere some other place" (p. 78), who sought only to "crawl about in corners and sleep" (p. 78) and to find the quickest, safest, darkest way home. The narrator's search for an end seems but a continuation of Pim's struggle to find a hole. The details leading up to such a quest, however, are only of secondary importance. We don't need to piece out the birth of love in the twenties nor its decline and the futile "effort to resuscitate" it (p. 82) in order to feel the decay and increasing solitude which inform the narration. In the mud such constructions are irrelevant. Everything results in the same voice seeking the same cancellation of itself. As the narrator more graphically says, ". . . what the fuck I quote does it matter who suffers . . . who makes to suffer who cries who to be left in peace in the dark the mud . . ." (p. 131–32). Just as it is unnecessary to determine if there is only one or three or millions of figures crawling in the mud, so too is it unimportant to distinguish among images or to fill in the gaps in the story they imply.

Like the images from life above in the light, the reduced and restricted imagery of How It Is offers both relief from, and a heightened awareness of, the barrenness and desolation of the narrator's world. This dual effect is particularly true of colors because they are used only in reference to the life above in the light. Blue belongs to the blue sky of a world where there is a possibility of beauty, happiness, and other people; a world where, rather than crawling face down in the mud, a boy can lift his eyes to the sky (p.

15) and a couple can walk with "heads high ... eyes open" (p. 29) through "glorious weather egg-blue sky and scamper of little clouds" (p. 29). These blue and white skies bring with them a sense of exhilaration, liberation, and expansion. They come to represent all that is lacking in a decaying world. They are linked with the fertility Pam Prim denies (p. 77), with a graceful, flowing movement antithetical to the halting crawl (p. 27), with the vision that is past of meeting Christ in a dream (p. 45). The colors are vibrant, startling, and solid. We see red tiled roofs (p. 15) and "emerald grass" bedecked with a colorful "dream of flowers" (p. 29). We are confronted by "blue of a sudden gold and green of the earth of a sudden in the mud" (p. 21). Hence, when the images dissolve, when there is "no more blue" (p. 106), when "the sky goes out the ashes darken" and we are returned to the mud (p. 32), then the absence of color is that much more noticeable, that much more decimating. In *How It Is* even an ambivalent color like white is still superior to the black of the mud. Although linked with the freedom of white clouds moving across blue skies, white is also associated with sterility. Surrounded by the white of the hospital Pam Prim begs Pim for "the holly ... for the berries anything a little colour a little green so much white the ivy anything" (p. 78). But, symptomatic of Pim's failure at life, he is unable to find any flowers except "marguerites from the latin pearl" (p. 77). Dying, Pam Prim forgives Pim for bringing marguerites, the flowers of tears and death, forgives him for being unable either to break the sterile white or to forestall the approaching impenetrable darkness.

The movement from vibrancy to pallor to "impenetrable dark" (p. 11) suggests the ultimate incommensurability of colors to the world of the mud, the dark, the pant, the murmur. A similar evocation and subsequent diminution occurs in Beckett's presentation of religious language without any religious underpinnings. God, Jesus, and heaven are neither believed nor denied: they are simply irrelevant. Just as in *Murphy* where the mental hospital which is shaped like a church without an altar, presents a Christian icon without its hope of salvation, so too here the religious imagery proffers symbols lacking completion and confirmation. The narrator is a distorted and parodic Christ-figure who understands everything but forgives, disapproves, and loves nothing (p. 41). Divine forgiving is replaced by an attitude that "divine forgetting [is] enough" (p. 79). Instead of seeking a world-without-end in God, the narrator seeks an absolute end. His passionate quest to be rid of himself, body, mind, and soul, elevates sleep's temporary surcease into a kind of mystical experience. Although heaven's existence is never belied, it is unimportant: sinking to the bottom, ascending to heaven, or not stirring, "half in the mud half out" (p. 104) all end in the same predicament "in any case" (p. 104). Likewise, a deity is not so much denied as it is unthinkably absurd. The narrator can conceive of no divinity—not even his intelligent ear—which would create and endure the present formulation. The concept of a god is simply another resource, a motif to help pass the time, an "old favorite" theme (p. 70). It is insignificant whether the narrator decides to "curse God or bless him" (p. 40). In either case he is only thinking of the return of his own voice. Although Pim intermittently believes in God (p. 97), mention of Him brings not solace but "desperation utter confusion" (p. 74). In a revision of the Cain and Abel story, Pim, the sometime-believer in God, is tortured by a narrator who, unable to kill Pim provokes instead, "in the mud [the] vile tears of [his] unbutcherable brother" (p. 74). Even the verse Pim's "mamma" recites with "muttering lips all the lower it's possible" (p. 78) is ironic in the context of *How It Is*:

> 15 . . . as for man, his days are as grass: as a flower of the field, so he flourisheth.
> 16 For the wind passeth over it, and it is gone; and the place thereof shall know it no more.
> 17 But the mercy of the *Lord* is from everlasting to everlasting upon them that fear him, and his righteousness unto children's children. . . .
> (Psalm 103)

In the mud man's days stretch from everlasting to everlasting without hope for an end, for mercy, for grass or flowers of the field or wind. The muttering lips are "possible," but the Psalm itself belongs to another world, another time.

In the mud it is the images which bear the consolation David found in God. They and not the Kingdom of Heaven lie beyond "the approaching veils" (p. 87). In fact, it is in the image of the boy sleeping in the sun (p. 45) that the closest approximation to a religious vision and affirmative experience occurs. The youth meets Jesus in "an image not for the eyes made of words not for the ears" (p. 45). The importance of that vision for the narrator is supported by its reappearance in two other passages. In the first the narrator tells Pim of his religious experience and "the feeling since then vast stretch of time that I'd find it again the blue cloak the pigeon the miracle he understood" (p. 70). But Pim's understanding is quickly negated by the narrator himself, "the childhood the belief the blue the miracles all lost never was" (p. 70). It is to this sense of loss which the final mention of the vision refers. The setting of the scene is repeated, "ten twelve years old sleeping in the sun at the foot of the wall" (p. 85), but this time the veils fall before the vision can come. That brief moment when a boy of ten or twelve dreamt of meeting Jesus contains all of the peace the world of the mud will ever know. Christ is not denied, but the possibility of reaching him is irrevocably past: "... what have I said no matter I've said something that's what was needed ... said it was me ten twelve years old sleeping in the sun in the dust to have a moment's peace I have it I had it. ..." (p. 86)

In an ambivalent world where everything, even the hopes of religion, can be reduced finally to a voice creating and correcting itself, a refrain of "something wrong there" is inevitable and natural. Inevitable because where nothing is certain, any statement must be only relatively true. Natural because where everything is self-consciously fictive, correction and revision can be flatly announced. Yet at the same time the refrain is disconcerting as it abruptly destroys any suspension of disbelief we may have willed. The prose demands that we, like the narrator, agonize over and experience the present formulation without the mediation of even the most minimal fictions. Moreover, we are required to draw upon our own resources to discern what is wrong and where. The errors themselves are significant in a work in which "my mistakes are my life" (p. 34). There are three or four basic categories our refrain labels as erroneous. It is used to negate any statements implying a continuity with the past, a predictable future, or a possibility of change. The narrator can say neither that he has steadily gone from bad to worse (p. 9), nor that he crawls toward a ditch which will never come (p. 16), nor that one day he and Pim will travel together (p. 57). The refrain is also appended to any statements granting credence to other bodies or objects. It is wrong to speak of Pim's timepiece (p. 40), of Krim's knowledge of the couple (p. 93), or of the couple itself as "two little old men" (p. 54). We are uncertain one body exists let alone others. A voice may be posited, but a choir of such voices must be undercut (p. 107). The narrator knows only himself, not "[him] who is coming towards me and [him] who is going from me" (p. 116). References to the narrator's own body are themselves problematic. Although the hand controls a large amount of the book's imagery, its activities are repeatedly crippled by the refrain. Unsure whether or not the hand is really disintegrating, whether or not the thumb has dropped off (p. 28), we have no assurance that the fingers and thumb do hold a sack (p. 34), that the hand does flesh Pim's buttocks (p. 37) or feel his cheek (p. 56), that a hand ever descends on an arse for the first time (p. 121), or even that the hands exist and can be seen lying "tense in the mud" (p. 43). Finally, the refrain contradicts statements the narrator makes about his own cyclic theory. Unable to determine ultimately if there is eternal recurrence or eternal presence, he finds fault with both systems. In a cyclic world it is incorrect to call anything a first or last member, to say that a clinking tin is the "first respite very first from the silence of this black sap" (pp. 24–25). Likewise, in a cyclic world one is not simultaneously Pim and Bom and the roles should not be equated in the conjugation of their names (p. 115). The "inevitable number 777777" (p. 140) cannot be, at the same time, Bom to 777778 and Pim for 777776. But, if the world is an eternally present now, one cannot alternate roles and be "now Bom now Pim" (p. 115). Everything must stem from the essential present of the abandoned where the narrator has a voice with which to create the other parts. It is difficult to imagine any other formulation (p. 129): it is impossible to depict any other order (pp. 116–17). *How It Is* is only a voice speaking in the present and creating a universe of Pims and Boms, sacks and tins, voiced and voiceless. Any statement which tries to ignore or circumvent this essential fact will naturally have "something wrong there" and will inevitably be undermined by the refrain. The prose style of the narration insists upon our facing "how it is present formulation" (p. 129).

Every element in *How It Is* from typography to time, from "objects" to "others," derives from a voice narrating itself. The imaginary worlds the voice creates assume the ambivalence and uncertainty surrounding that voice. Although everything depends upon a stream of words, the source of those words is ambiguously external and internal just as identity is indistinctly I and Other. Existence and continuation are the present act of speaking. Time is only the now against which words are spoken. The already-mentioned and not-yet-said fade into irrelevance. Murphy's concerns for mimetic details, like the Unnamable's desires for self-definition, are replaced by a voice speaking in the eternal present. Instead of examining the limitations of the mind/body dichotomy, the work explores the fluid universe of the mind and its imagination. The murmurs in the mud mark a shift from exterior orders to internal fabrications. Just as the speaker and his narration intimate the way it is for us, so too the voice and its words suggest how it is in Beckett's canon.

5. Residual fiction

". . . soon there will be nothing where there was never anything, last images." [1]

Samuel Beckett's residual fictions [2] are logical extensions of the essential Beckettian literary experience. The artist and his need to create confront the fact that there is nothing to create, nothing with which nor from which to create, no power and no desire to create. In the pieces written during the 1960s, however, Beckett rejects both the narrating "self" and the fluid forms of earlier works. In their place he creates rigid structures that mathematically and scientifically describes fantastic objects, people, and images. No longer content to suggest the chaos through the postulations of a voice creating itself, Beckett develops deceptively objective analyses of highly articulated structures. Paradoxically, the very artifice of these carefully constructed structures points toward their underlying structural meaninglessness, while the arbitrariness beneath their order gestures toward a more fundamental absence of order. The pieces are images of the abyss, structures enclosing the void. Although Beckett's works have always demanded the reader be engaged in the interrelationship of structure and content, in the later pieces the burden of interpretation is placed increasingly upon the reader. It is he and not the artist who attributes meaning to the inexplicable; he and not the artist who must manipulate the given structures in order to understand an implicit content.

If an art is honestly to accommodate the possibility of nonrelation among the artist, his art, and an external reality, that art must call into question even implicitly personal, ordered, and meaningful relationships. If the narrator of the trilogy does not actually invite our identification, nonetheless he does postulate a "self," a being separate from the chaos, a "figure" imposing order on Neary's "ground." The speaker returns to the works, the connotations, associations, and correspondences which had been stripped from plot and character. The impersonal is thus made personal and the orderless, ordered. The residual fictions, on the other hand, strive for a more objective pose. The self begins to dissolve into the impersonal, "omniscient" voices of *Imagination Dead Imagine, Ping,* and *Lessness.* The pieces analytically deal with the imaginary. Despite their starkness, the images of Beckett's previous fictions are associated still with a material world. Although the tins and openers of *How It Is* exist only as the voice's postulations, nevertheless they are reminiscent of conventional objects. Conversely, the more recent images are fantastical; the white figures and cylindrical worlds are imaginative constructions. While the nature of language prevents Beckett from totally escaping an external structure, the fantasies free him from pre-established implications and innuendoes. Like the second zone of Murphy's mind, the images are of forms without parallel in another mode. Though art cannot attain the formlessness of the dark zone, it can at least avoid the mimetic parallels of the light. The resulting works of the half-light compose a new type of intellectual novel. The burden of meaning is thrust upon the reader. *Lessness* presents a randomly arranged collection of words, images, and sentences which the reader must organize. It is the reader who must manipulate the collection in order to glimpse the inexplicable lying beyond art.

The objective pose evokes a simple, declarative prose. Instead of the scintillating and amazingly long sentences of the early works, we are given brief and elliptical ones. Instead of the fluid phrasing of *The Unnamable* in which one idea imperceptibly flows into the next, we are presented with choppy, almost unrelated sentences. The absence of transitions emphasizes the fragmentary nature of the world described. The words themselves are precise, unencumbered by unintentional connotations. The prose admits no more than its surface statements allow. Fluidity pointing to chaos is replaced by rigidity enclosing a void. The pieces are exceptionally brief in order to limit their worlds. The fantasy must not become too real or too familiar lest a new "reality" and order be substituted for the old. A new attitude toward art is suggested. Obscurity and confusion come not from omission as in *How It Is,* nor from excessive addition as in "Text," but from the inability of the mind to retain an objective image, "no question now of ever finding again that white speck lost in whiteness" (*Imagination Dead Imagine*). Protestations of impotence or mastery disappear as the persona analytically states as best he can, what he can. It is for the reader to notice the absences those observations entail. Cumulative "symbols" and mantic meanings are replaced by an ordering device similar to that in music.

Repetition and refrain supplant conventional manners of meaning. Words, like notes, are arranged mathematically and effect us subliminally. Moreover, like notes, not chords, each word strives to strike only one meaning, strives to be "pure," not connotative; scientific, not emotional. But the words, and the images, break down. Without reneging on his own postulations and rules, Beckett's latest pieces accomplish what the earliest pieces unsuccessfully attempted: they offer a structure that is self-disintegrating. The printed texts provide the scenario for the reader's efforts to create meaning. Ultimately, however, the reader is forced to return to the text, to the residual structure which provocatively refuses to mean.

1

The self-destruction of the analytic prose of *Imagination Dead Imagine*[3] (*Imagination Morte Imaginez*—1966) offers a glimpse into the realms beyond analysis, beyond the residue. As the title implies, the piece is based on a paradox: imagination is necessary to envision a state in which imagination is dead. The essential situation is thus briefly and simply described, yet that situation is itself paradoxical if not impossible, ambivalent if not unclear. The imperative mood in both title and work demands involvement, but we do not know from whom. The second person remains unspecified and could refer equally well to us, to the persona, or to some unidentified other: "No trace anywhere of life, you say, pah, no difficulty there, imagination not dead yet, yes, dead, good, imagination dead imagine" (p. 63). Unlike the assuring interventions of the eighteenth century, which carefully led us from one scene to the next while explaining how each came about, the persona's injunctions, "go in," "Go back out" (p. 63), add to our confusion. Who is to go? Go in where? How? Go back out to what? Explanatory transitions are deliberately omitted. The rotunda is treated simultaneously as an object to be entered and as a mental fabric woven from imagination. Perception of the piece as an imaginary fabric undercuts the need for scientific precision. When all is fantasy, the narrating "self," like the verifying witness, is irrelevant. Instead of a speaker with whom we might identify, we have a voice moving through his descriptions like a camera, zooming in for a closeup of the unblinking eye, panning the rotunda's floor, dropping back for a panoramic shot of the "plain rotunda, all white in the whiteness" (p. 63). Issues of identity are supplanted by the impersonal and objective. The piece evokes diagrams and tabulations.

But the scientific, objective pose increasingly breaks down. Like the elaborate time structure in *Murphy*, the mathematical precision of *Imagi-*

nation Dead Imagine is only an overlay. As we read we realize that the rational numbers are only crude estimates made under adverse conditions:

> Wait *more or less* long. . . . *More or less long,* for there may intervene . . .
> pauses of *varying* length. . . . [pp. 63–64] . . . the sighting of the little fabric
> quite as much a *matter of chance.* . . . left eyes which at *incalculable in-*
> *tervals.* . . . *In this agitated light,* its great white calm now so rare and
> brief, *inspection is not easy.* [p. 65; here and elsewhere all emphasis in
> passages from *Imagination Dead Imagine* is mine.]

Metaphoric terms and colored words seep into the analytic language:

> . . . solid throughout, a ring *as in the imagination* the ring of bone. (p. 63)
> *Piercing* pale blue the effect is striking. (p. 65)

The voice's objectivity merges with subjectivity as fact and observation
yield to assumption and opinion:

> . . . the bodies *seem* whole and in fairly good condition, *to judge by the*
> *surfaces exposed to view.* The two faces too, *assuming* the two sides of a
> piece, *seem* to want nothing essential. (p. 66)

Apparent contradictions are not explained, "No way in, go in . . ." (p. 63).
Although the rotunda's dimensions make it too small to hold three bodies,
and although the whole is described as solid, we "go in" to view the two
figures lying on the floor. Much of our information about the rotunda is
based on our experience of it. The experience itself is made problematic by
man's tendency to adapt to all situations. Habituation deadens our powers of observation, turning "such variations of rise and fall" into "countless
rhythms" (p. 64). Things which initially strike us as strange may soon pass
unnoticed: "The extremes . . . are perfectly stable, which in the case of the
temperature may seem strange, in the beginning" (p. 64). Even language
seems to be vitiated by experience. Notice for example, how the following
sentence runs down and trails off into prepositional phrases and the passive
voice after its initial, direct observation: "Between their absolute stillness,
and the convulsive light the contrast is striking, in the beginning, for one
who still remembers having been struck by the contrary" (p. 66). Experience, moreover, makes everything, even eternity, relative. Our analytic prose
is itself coming apart. The failure of the diagrammatic and precise intimates
the underlying, nebulous flux. Not the image but its dissolution, not the
object but its breakdown, contain whatever "meaning" there is. As Beckett
says in *Dream of Fair to Middling Women:* "The experience of my reader

shall be between the phrases, in the silence, communicated by the intervals, not the terms of the statement...."⁴

Just as we may become too habituated to the rotunda to be struck by the contrary, so too we are in danger of becoming too accustomed to Beckett's images. The pieces can gesture only briefly to an instant of dissolution, before the concrete structures of language erect new systems of order. To postpone the influx of meaning the voice uses negative propositions to describe the rotunda. We learn not what it is, but what it is not: "Islands, waters, azure, verdure, one glimpse and vanished, endlessly, omit. Till all white in the whiteness of the rotunda" (p. 63). Not what we can say happens, but what we cannot say happens:

> Leave them there, sweating and icy, there is better elsewhere. No, life ends and no, there is nothing elsewhere, and no question now of ever finding again that white speck lost in whiteness, to see if they still lie still in the stress of that storm, or a worse storm, or in the black dark for good, or the great whiteness unchanging, and if not what they are doing. (p. 66)

Similarly, the voice suggests meanings without directly postulating them. The fetal positions of the figures imply, but never assert, a womb-like structure. While the rotunda may have when rapped a tomb-like ring, "as in the imagination the ring of bone" (p. 63), the figures' misting of a mirror (p. 65) belies any sepulchral readings. Although the presence of both a male and a female figure suggests an androgynous nature for the rotunda, and although those figures assume a reversed yin and yang position,⁵ nonetheless the figures remain distinct and reversed. They have not yet become the sketchy, sexless, and single figure in *Ping*. The variations of life are reduced to rhythmic repetition. Not only are there fewer sets to be permuted than in previous works, but those sets are reduced from powers of action (Murphy's biscuits) and methods of arrangement (Molloy's sucking stones) to mere presence or absence of heat and light (p. 64). Beckett's image of life is coming closer to the cyclic rhythm of respiration dramatized in *Breath* (1966). Imagination is gone, but traces of life remain in unblinking eyes, slightly sweating bodies, and a misted mirror. Language too strives to be minimal. Although no one word is rejected as too strong, the whole is told from a discredited viewpoint: "Rediscovered *miraculously* after what absence in perfect voids it [the rotunda] is *no longer quite the same, from this point of view, but there is no other*" (p. 65). Concrete meanings are avoided as sentences are made fragmentary and disjointed: "Only murmur ah, no more, in this silence, and at the same instant for the eye of the prey the infinitesimal shudder instantaneously suppressed" (p. 66). The resulting ambiguous syntax admits diverse, though not infinite, interpretations. For Brian Finney the "ah" of the above passage is murmured, almost experimentally, by the reader to break the silence the couple seeks,[6] while for Ruby Cohn the "ah" is a sign of life performed by the figures and noted by whomever the "eye of prey" represents.[7] The burden of selecting an interpretation from the implied possibilities rests on the reader because a deceptively analytic prose refuses to assume absolute meanings, because a highly articulated structure is made to imply a more fundamental absence of relationship.

2

Ping[8] (Bing—1966) continues Beckett's rigid reductions. The recondite, allusive, and foreign language of Beckett's earliest pieces is replaced by a few simple and common words repeated and rearranged. Complex, interrelated sentences and self-conscious structures yield to simple and even fragmentary phrases dealing with imaginary worlds. The "narrator/ narrated" disappears as an impersonal voice dispassionately pronounces phrases. Not only "I" but also "he" and "she" are gone. Even the personal observations, opinions, assumptions, and occasional poetic phrases of Imagination Dead Imagine have been eliminated. The depersonalized, computerlike voice of Ping focuses attention on its words, not on itself. Moreover, the words are themselves less emphatic, less concrete. The image can no longer be objectively analyzed and measured. The diagrammatic language of Imagination Dead Imagine is restricted to a box, "white one yard by two" (p. 69), containing a fixed and featureless figure. Instead of entering a cylinder almost at will and observing its inhabitants, we are confined to a box in which everything keeps fading and disappearing in the shining "white on white invisible" (p. 70). But in spite of its reductions in language, character, plot, and narrator, Ping remains a surprisingly dramatic piece. Ping is the drama of the interaction between reader and form.

Though apparently simpler than preceding works, Ping is one of Beckett's more difficult works to read. The common words, arranged and rearranged into recurring phrases, compel the reader to become a "fellow-writer, rearranging the words on paper in order to see the significance of repetition, permutation, combination, or singularity."[9] In this verbless work it is the reader who performs the action. Ping invites tabulations and computation. In her own effort to "see the significance" Ruby Cohn reveals that the English text contains 1,030 words—of which 120 are permuted—gathered into seventy sentences, punctuated only by periods, and printed as an unbroken block on the page. In this unbroken block "white" appears some ninety times while "ping" occurs thirty-four times—nine times followed by "elsewhere," seven times by "murmur(s)," four times by "silence," twice by "a nature," twice by "not alone," once by "image," once by a "meaning." The simple words describe a simple, minimal world of "only just almost never." No longer does Beckett need to call any word too strong, for he has created phrases that take away more than they give. When we read "that much memory almost never" (p. 71), our dominant impression is of memory's absence, not of its feeble persistence. In a similar fashion the negation of "over"—"white colour alone unover" (p. 71)—emphasizes not continuation, but termination. Being over becomes the positive state, and definition is through negative proposition, through reference to what no longer exists. *Ping* deals not with what is enough, but with ephemeral and fading velleities. Measurements are replaced by qualifying phrases and fleeting moments: "perhaps a nature" (p. 70), "brief murmurs" (p. 69), "one second" (p. 69). Like the image of "blue and white in the wind" (p. 70), like the figure, indeed like the box itself, all of which disappear into whiteness almost before they have been glimpsed, *Ping* fades and dissolves almost before we can read it. The reader is left with a shape that gestures toward shapelessness, and with phrases that suggest but never mean.

The verbless, unbroken block of words that constitutes *Ping* is given movement and shape by the intermittent and enigmatic "pings" which begin and interrupt sentences. The word "ping" itself is meaningless: it is a nonsense word, a short, quick ringing sound like that of a rifle bullet, a sound so instantaneous as to be almost as if it never were. Indeed, Beckett's revisions[10] show a movement toward briefer, more ephemeral sounds from "paf" to "hop" to "bing." In the English text Beckett alters even the voiced "b" of "bing" to the voiceless and hence even slighter "p" of "ping." The sound, like the light in *Play*, seems to control the flow of words, to mark the movement of thoughts. It indicates the points where the mind skips or changes focus: Beckett has magnified the stream of consciousness until he can actually show the infinitesimally brief moments in which the mind, as it were, blinks. The precise nature of the "pings," however, remains ambivalent. We never know, for instance, whether an external interruption, or an internal hesitation causes the jumps. Although they may alter our focus slightly, the "pings" never take us outside the box. The most we know is that the figure is within a box and that there is a soundless but unknowable elsewhere. Like stage directions or time signatures, the "pings" control the meter and rhythm of the piece, separating the phrases into longer and shorter groups. Whereas many of Beckett's other works emphasize time as unending cycle or an eternal present of waiting, *Ping* reduces time to the fleeting "one second perhaps" (p. 70) and to memories so dissipated and remote as to be almost nonexistent. The passage of time itself is dramatized as the increasing frequency of the "pings" parallels the increasing fragmentation at the end of the piece.

While "ping" remains an individual and distinct sound, most words in the piece are grouped in phrases. We read in blocks of words: adjective plus noun, adverb plus verb form, "Light heat/white floor/one square yard/never seen" (p. 69, my divisions). Unlike the early works in which the word was the unit of meaning, meaning in *Ping* resides in the phrase and its permutations, in variations within repetitions. If the words may be likened to notes and the phrases to chords, then the phrases themselves are grouped into themes. Descriptions of the body are counterpointed by those of the box. Occasionally a new motif may appear such as the scarred and torn flesh, but for the most part the piece recombines elements elaborating its initial chords, "All known all white" (p. 69). Even other colors are accompanied by the pervasive whiteness—"light grey almost white" (p. 69). In such a work meaning becomes rhythmical, cumulative, associational.

The movement and drama of the piece comes from the reader's involvement with the musical motifs of the permuted phrases. Gradually descriptions of setting and figure make the initial propositions intelligible. Everything is known; everything is white. Within that known white everything of a one yard by two, rectangular white box of some light and heat is fixed a bare, elemental body, itself unable to perceive the box, mistaking shining white walls for a shining white infinity: "Planes meeting invisible one only shining white infinite but that known not" (p. 70). We have lost not only the dual figures of *Imagination Dead Imagine*, but also the precision with which they were described. Our new figure is shapeless and sexless. Like a ragdoll its legs, toes, and seamlike mouth appear "joined like sewn." Slowly the figure becomes, if not more lifelike, at least more distinct. Repeated occurrence draws the basic outline of a "bare white body fixed" with "hands hanging," "Palms front," "head haught," "White feet," "heels together right angle." A single mention sketches in other details, "mouth white," "heart breath," "nose ears," "nails fallen white," "long hair fallen white." No longer is life revealed in a slightly sweating body or a misted mirror. Even "heart breath" seems to be negated by its following phrase, "no sound" (p. 70). If not already over, the circulatory and respiratory systems are so reduced as to be imperceptible and soundless. The body's life signs are restricted to barely tinged flesh, "given rose only just" (p. 69), and fading eyes, "Eyes alone unover given blue light blue almost white" (p. 69). These pale blue eyes provide the major contrast to the overwhelming whiteness. They are the only objects not yet over:

Bare white body fixed only the eyes only just (p. 69)

Only the eyes only just light blue almost white (p. 69)

Eyes alone unover given blue light blue almost white (p. 69)

Only the eyes only just light blue almost white fixed front (p. 69)

Eye holes light blue alone unover given blue light blue almost white only colour fixed front (p. 70)

Only the eyes given blue light blue almost white fixed front only colour alone unover (p. 70)

Only the eyes given blue fixed front light blue almost white only colour alone unover. (p. 71)

Notice in the above examples how a slight alteration in the order of the phrases, along with the introduction of phrases previously associated with another part of the text (that is, the movement from the "bare white body fixed" to the eyes "fixed front"), slowly increases our understanding and enables the voice to present longer, more complicated sentences. The incremental effect allows the voice to present its fullest, most sustained depiction of the figure: "Bare white one yard fixed ping fixed elsewhere no sound legs joined like sewn heels together right angle hands hanging palms front. Head haught eye holes light blue almost white fixed front silence within" (p. 71). Ironically, it is after this summary in which the figure is most clearly described that the whiteness begins to take over completely. The expanded portrait is abruptly pulled apart and contracted, while the blue of the eyes is suddenly removed from the familiar phrases: ". . . eye holes light blue almost white last colour ping white over. Ping fixed last elsewhere legs joined like sewn heels together right angle hands hanging palms front. Head haught eyes white invisible fixed front over" (p. 71). The work, beginning in stark whiteness, gradually teases life and variety into its world only to deny those possibilities and thus heighten its barrenness.

The movement toward sterility is reflected in the treatment of image and sound. The "pings" guide us through a world whose silence is broken neither by sounds from within the box ("silence within," p. 69) nor by external noises ("elsewhere no sound," p. 70). Yet, just as a fading blue somehow persists in a world of whiteness, so too brief and almost imperceptible murmurs exist in a world of stillness: "Brief murmur only just almost never all known" (p. 69). More minimal than even the "ah" of *Imagination Dead Imagine*, the murmurs are too indistinct to be quoted directly, too fleeting to be recorded—"murmur only just almost never one second perhaps" (p. 70). The low, infrequent murmurs, like the rapid, glancing "pings," underscore rather than interrupt the overwhelming silence. Like setting and figure, the murmurs are "always the same all known" (p. 69). Yet precisely these murmurs, the least tangible elements in an already ephemeral world, offer the most vibrant passages in *Ping*. They both relieve and emphasize the starkness by suggesting and recalling what no longer is present. In a world that increasingly approaches absolute zero, vitality persists in the murmurs and their postulations of what is not. Imagination is not yet dead; life still adheres to our reduced figure; "perhaps [there is] a way out" (p. 69), "perhaps a nature" (p. 70), "perhaps a meaning" (p. 70), "perhaps [the figure is] not alone" (p. 69). Although the figure does not experience escape, externality, order, or even an "other," he never discounts them. In fact his murmured memories imply that a meaning, a more colorful nature, and even another figure were once available to him. Just enough memory remains to recall dimly a different order; just enough is left from that "afar flash of time" (p. 71) to highlight the present stillness: "Ping murmur only just almost never one second perhaps a meaning that much memory almost never" (p. 70). The images that can be recalled are drastically reduced from those scenes that lightened Pim's world. The "fine image fine I mean in movement and colour blue and white of clouds in the wind" (*How It Is*, p. 27) becomes the sporadic and shrinking: "Ping perhaps a nature one second with image same time a little less blue and white in the wind" (p. 70). Moreover, with each recurrence the image dwindles as rearrangement of the phrases shifts emphasis from the image itself ("blue and white in the wind"), to its unchanging character ("with image always the same time a little less," p. 71), to its transitory nature ("Ping image only just almost never one second light time blue and white in the wind," p. 71). Indeed, by the last mention of the image the blue and white have disappeared altogether: "Ping perhaps not alone one second with image same time a little less dim eye black and white half closed long lashes imploring that much memory almost never" (p. 71).

Significantly, the image, "blue and white in the wind," disappears when the provocative black and white eye is first clearly discerned. This second eye is thus implicitly linked to the images, memories, and murmurs. It is part of the imaginary world with which the figure decorates his encompassing white box. Yet, the description of the eye remains apart from the other murmurings. Although its appearance is anticipated by two sentences postulating "black" ("traces alone unover given black light grey almost white on white"), this eye does not really evolve from permuted phrases. Similarly, though dim, unlustrous, and half-closed, this black and white eye does not really belong in a world of fading pastels and overwhelming whiteness. While the figure is at best only roughly outlined, the black and white eye is presented in fine detail. Instead of reducing the eye to "eye holes light blue almost white fixed front" (p. 71), we are given a close-up of the eye "half closed long lashes imploring" (p. 71). "Imploring" stands out from the impersonal, unemotional prose in which *Ping* is written. Like the eyes which haunt Krapp (*Krapp's Last Tape*) and Croak (*Words and Music*), the imploring eye suggests other worlds of emotion, character, and plot. Suddenly the figure's rather wistful murmur, "perhaps not alone," becomes desperately significant. Was he alone in that past he can hardly remember? Is he alone now? Are those "grey blurs" and "traces alone unover" the shadowy and fading outlines of another figure? The questions go unanswered. While our figure feels there might be a meaning, *Ping* refuses to dictate one. Murmurs, memories, and blurring traces alike offer "signs [with] no meaning" (p. 69). It is the reader, cursed as in *Enough* by "the art of combining," who attempts to order the phrases and trace a meaning.

Although the reader may try to find a meaning, may try to read "white scars invisible same white as flesh torn of old given rose only just" (p. 71) as a symbol for suffering and sacrificed mankind, *Ping* is deliberately made too ephemeral and elusive to bear even an emblematic meaning. Like the "pings" and the murmurs which disappear into silence almost before they have been heard, like the image and the box which fade into whiteness almost before they have been glimpsed, *Ping* dissolves into formlessness almost before it has been read. The reader's manipulation of Beckett's phrases yields not a discourse about that fleeting instant when absolute zero is finally achieved, but a dramatization of that moment. Minimal life of "only just almost never" is used to gesture toward the void of "henceforth never" (p. 72) lying just beyond life and art. Not only must we slowly and painstakingly come to an understanding of the little we have been given, but more devastatingly, we are forced to see the rapid dissolution of even that little. We are thrust into the end by the abbreviation of phrases and body, by the fragmentation of time, by the increase in white. *Ping* is the drama, not of the "fixed elsewhere," nor even of the "white infinite," but of the "one second perhaps": it is a drama of the approaching end in which everything is presented to heighten our perception of that end. *Ping* becomes a catalogue of what is finally over. Consistent with Beckett's other works, the last element in this catalogue to be alone unover, is not the "heart breath" nor even the blue eyes, but the murmur. Just as in *How It Is* where the important vision comes not from the blue eyes but the others at the back of the head; so too here life is associated with the murmured, with the imagined, with the "never seen," "invisible," "no trace." Moreover, it is not simply a murmur, but the murmur of perhaps another that is the last thought to evaporate before all is over: "Head haught eyes white fixed front old ping last murmur one second perhaps not alone eye unlustrous black and white half closed long lashes imploring ping silence ping over" (p. 72). When even the murmur has ended and the last "ping" faded away, the piece is over. Like the box which keeps disappearing into the "shining white infinite but that known not" (p. 72), *Ping* creates an image of that which is imageless.

3

By thrusting on us the burden of creating order and meaning, the residua demand a new critical response. Not only are conventional analyses inadequate to explain the pieces, but even traditional literary terms seem inappropriate. Instead of comparing the works to novels and short stories, we are forced to find parallels in music and drama, or, as H. Porter Abbott does, in a new species of poetry. Beckett is dealing not simply in words and sounds, but in words and sounds whose real impact is subliminal or preconscious. He is striving to create, through the medium and limitations of language, an art that can use those limitations to suggest that which lies beyond language. Whereas *music, drama,* and *poetry* all suggest an art that is ordered and coherent, an art that yields an encompassing and unified vision, the residua increasingly insist upon being taken apart and analyzed. In order to come to terms with the pieces, we must read them not as a whole, nor even as paragraphs or sentences, but rather as permuted phrases and repeated words. They deal not with order, but with the arbitrariness of order; not with fiction, but with assumptions masked by fiction. *Lessness*[11] (*Sans*—1969) takes the antiliterary tendency of the residua even further. In order to read the work at all the reader must reverse Beckett's creative process and break the piece back down into groups of sentences and into permuted phrases within those groups. No longer content with satirizing, negating, or dissipating his own forms, Beckett creates a work that insists upon being unmade.

Beckett's method of composition in *Lessness* is, at best, disconcerting. He wrote sixty sentences, each belonging to one of six groups, each group consisting of ten sentences. Next he randomly drew the individual sentences from a container to yield the order of the first half of the piece. By mixing the sentences and again drawing them randomly, Beckett established the order for the last half of the piece in which each of the sixty sentences is repeated. To determine the paragraphing, Beckett wrote, as Cohn explains, ". . . the number 3 on four separate pieces of paper, the number 4 on six pieces of paper, the number 5 on four pieces, the number 6 on six pieces, and the number 7 on four pieces of paper. Again drawing randomly, he ordered the sentences into paragraphs according to the number drawn. . . ."[12]

The very idea of an art work ordered by chance is unsettling. Even after classical conceptions of perfection, harmony, and balance had made way to admit arts of imperfection, discord, and imbalance, the artist's purpose and control were still jealously guarded. Beckett, on the other hand, yields a portion of his control to the laws of probability and permutation. Art is implicitly consigned to the mathematician and computer programer. J. M. Coetzee even resorts to a Univac 1106 to deal with *Lessness*.[13] His results verify mathematically what the reader suspects: no significant linguistic principle orders the arrangement of phrases, sentences, or paragraphs. In fact the paragraph is not even a "different *kind* of structural element from the sentence." Component parts instead are arranged and rearranged according to combinatorial mathematical rules.

Although disturbing, the "rule-governedness" of *Lessness* is purposeful and deliberate. Like all literary works, *Lessness* is based on assumptions, but its assumptions are mathematical. Instead of pretending that some inherent ordering process—be it thematic, chronological, associative, or symbolic—controls the displacement of words, *Lessness* is openly the product of chance. Meaning is dependent on the random arrangements of a finite set. The piece could continue until all possible permutations of the sixty sentences had been presented, but nothing would have been changed or added. A single repetition is sufficient to suggest that all of the millions of possible reorderings are equally authoritative, equally meaningless. Just as mathematics is a mental construction which is completely knowable because it is completely abstract, so too the concept of order is an arbitrary abstraction which originates and exists only in man's mind. By structuring *Lessness* upon the admittedly arbitrary rules of combinational mathematics, Beckett reminds us of the equally arbitrary rules of all systems and languages. Moreover, if man is, as post-Cartesian philosophers suggest, solipsistic, then the most valid systems are the completely imaginary. Ordering devices which depend on external authority are problematic. By pretending to an authority they don't have, such systems, like the box in *Ping*, enclose our minds so deceptively that we are unaware they are enclosed. The rule-governed, random order of *Lessness* frees us from the encircling assumptions inherent in language and literature—frees us, like the little body in a world of ruins fallen open, to face the endless, issueless, true refuge of nonorder.

In spite of its random arrangement *Lessness* is provocatively resonant. We are tempted to find purpose in the disposition of sentences as, for example, the initial paragraphs establish setting and situation before introducing either the "little body" or a past or a future. Similarly, the last paragraph seems to conclude the whole work appropriately. It is hard not to feel that the final sentence is a deliberate and conscious climax. Even critics who are aware of Beckett's method of composition are enticed into interpretation by the powerful ending. The impact of *Lessness* resides somewhere between mathematics and art. Though organized randomly, the piece suggests meanings beyond the rules of probability. J. M. Coetzee's computer analysis itself concludes not with the statistical but with the interpretative: "The residue of the fiction is then *not* the final disposition of the fragments but the motions of the consciousness that disposes them according to the rules we have traced, and no doubt to others we have failed to trace." [14] *Lessness* is random but significance still adheres to it.

Since the order is random and since no new arrangements will change the work significantly, the reader must look to the sentences for any vestiges of meaning. The sentences, like those in *Ping*, are composed of repeated and permuted phrases dealing predominately with a setting and a body, but also postulating an imaginative realm of dreams and future possibilities. Instead of interrupting "pings," pauses are indicated by white space and paragraphs. But along with the "pings" the sense of movement and dramatization has disappeared from the prose. Although *Lessness* has greater variety than *Ping*—more nouns, more directional adverbs, more images— and although it frees the body from a container and reinstates verbs, *Lessness* is a more static work. It deals with the unending rather than the dwindling, with the unchanging rather than the dissipating. Unlike the fragmented sentences in *Ping*, which combine phrases of setting and body with those of murmur and memory, each sentence in "Lessness" is homogeneous. In fact, the sentences can be divided thematically into groups or families.[15] Although the themes may be elusive, the divisions seem fairly clear. For example, Ruby Cohn and Martin Esslin find different significances and hence different labels for similar groups:[16]

Ruby Cohn

(1) the ruins as "true refuge"
(2) the endless gray of earth and sky
(3) the little body
(4) the space "all gone from mind"
(5) past tense combined with "never"
(6) future tenses of active verbs and the figment sentence, "Figment dawn dispeller of figments and the other called dusk"

Martin Esslin

(1) the ruins
(2) the vastness of earth and sky
(3) the little body
(4) the fact that the enclosed space is now forgotten—"all gone from mind"
(5) a denial of past and future
(6) an affirmation of past and future

The first four families elicit fairly consistent titles. The last two groups, however, give rise to discrepancies not simply because they lack identifying refrains such as "the little body" or "all gone from mind," but more importantly because their essential character remains ambivalent. To Cohn the distinction between the two groups is one of tense, whereas to Esslin the difference is one of assertion. The lack of agreement is significant for it emphasizes the qualitative differences between sentences of the first four groups and those of the last two. The first groups describe setting and body—the known or observable aspects of the present situation. They present the rules and limitations under which *Lessness* must operate. The last groups, on the other hand, are less clear, less precise, and more enigmatic because they deal not with given data, but with the imaginative and mental, with daydreams and figments. Like the murmurs in *Ping*, they contain much of the mystery and vitality of the work. The tensions in *Less-*

ness are reflections of the tensions between these two types of groups, between the imaginative and the given.

"Ruins true refuge long last towards which so many false time out of mind" (1,i:21,i). The initial sentence of *Lessness* introduces the first group of sentences, those characterized by the appearance of the phrase "true refuge." This group describes the situation of *Lessness* without any mention of the little body. The four walls of a container, such as the one in *Ping*, have fallen open into scattered ruins, thus revealing at long last an ash grey, soundless, and issueless true refuge. All of the sentences in the group repeat and rearrange the same small set of ideas and phrases. Moreover, many of these ideas and phrases—such as the greyness, the soundlessness, and the "fallen open" endlessness—are picked up and repeated in other groups until the dominant impression is of a world so blank and so minimal as to be an image of nothingness, of nonbeing. The fluctuations of light and dark in *Imagination Dead Imagine* and even *Ping's* shining white infinite are reduced to a pervasive and passive grey. Beckett introduces into this nondescript grey a tenuous sense of affirmation. The four walls have fallen not "over" into destruction, but "open" into rebirth and freedom. The ruins are "issueless." The description captures our attention not simply because "issueless" appears independently rather than in a phrase, but also because "issueless" remains ambivalent. It suggests simultaneously that the ruins are without progeny, without egress, and without points of question, dispute, or decision. The issueless true refuge offers no means of escape, yet it also offers no matters for contention. A refuge that is "true" exists when man stops trying to escape formlessness through artificial containers and accepts the grey endlessness, when man ceases to tell himself stories to pass the time until there is an end to passing time and accepts the unchanging and eternal present as the only possible endlessness.

"All sides endlessness earth sky as one no sound no stir" (1,ii:22,vi). The second sentence of *Lessness* introduces a second group of sentences. This group expands our understanding of the situation by describing the setting in more detail. Although there is no refrain appearing in all of the sentences, each sentence mentions either the greyness or the endlessness or both. Thus this group continues the image of nothingness begun in the "true refuge" section. The sentences are developed not so much by repeated phrases as by similar phrasing. Grey is applied to every aspect of setting: "Same grey all sides earth sky body ruins" (6,vi:13,ii), "Earth sand same grey as the air sky ruins body fine ash grey sand" (9,iii:17,vi). The grey endlessness is brought into perspective by the introduction of the "little body only upright" (6,iv:22,ii). But this body is presented here only as an

aspect of setting. Like the earth and the sky it too is grey, it too is without
sound or stir: "no sound not a breath" (6,vi:13,ii), "no stir not a breath"
(8,iv:15,ii). The body's sole significance seems to be that it is the only
thing upright in the "flatness endless" (9,v:16,iii).

It is a third group that the body takes on what minimal shape it has.
In contrast to the ragdoll figure of *Ping* with its mouth, legs, and toes
"joined like sewn," the little body of *Lessness* is rigid and blocklike:
"Little body ash grey locked rigid" (4,iii:24,ii), "Legs a single block arms
fast to sides" (7,ii:23,i). The body becomes the only untoppled column in
the midst of ruins. Its contours have been eroded and "overrun" (8,ii:24,iii).
Its features, like those of a weather worn statue, are barely defined: ". . . grey
face features slit and little holes two pale blue" (3,ii:20,vii), ". . . grey smooth
no relief a few holes" (7,iv:18,ii), ". . . grey face features overrun two pale
blue" (12,v:18,i). Although the slitlike holes are too indistinct to be called
eyes, their pale blue persists. In fact, were it not for this pale blue and the
"heart breath," we would mistake the immobile figure for part of the ruins.
Though diminutive in size and significance, nonetheless the "little" body is
still there, still alive, and still the "only upright."

While the third group describes the appearance of the "little body," the
next family of sentences defines the body's intellectual capacities through
negative proposition. The sentences increase the stillness by offering a litany
of what is now "all gone from mind." The body has lost the powers of
reasoning—"calm eye light of reason all gone from mind" (12,vi:21,iii and
8,v:19,iii)—and of observation and sensual perception—"Face to calm eye
touch close all calm all white all gone from mind" (12,i:23,v). Images
from Beckett's other works, particularly *Ping*, are rejected. The "mighty
light," the "sheer white," the "four square" walls, and the "blank planes"
are all gone. The true refuge is not in a circumscribed "little void," but in
the vast unending. Contrasts rather than repetitions link this group of sentences to the other groups. The phrases speak of what no longer exists, of
"white," not "grey"; of "blank planes," not "fallen open four walls over
backwards"; of "calm eye," not "little holes"; and of "little void" not "all
sides endlessness." *Ping* offered an infinitesimal world on the verge of
nonexistence: *Lessness* rejects even that world. Now "all [is] gone from
mind."

Whereas the fourth group describes what no longer exists even in the
mind, a fifth group postulates the things that are not except in the mind,
except in dreams and figments: "Never but this changelessness dream the
passing hour" (2,v:16,v). This group is the richest of the six sections. Although some repetition and some phrases from other groups are incorpo-

rated, these links from "reality" are always set in opposition to the figments and dreams. Emphasis is not upon the "silences" and the "grey air timeless," but rather upon the imagined laughter, cries, and passing light which fail to mask the silent vastness:

> Never but silences such that in imagination this wild laughter these cries (10,iii:18,vi).

> Never was but grey air timeless no sound figment the passing light (2, iii:16,vi).

The mind divides endlessness into dreams of "the passing hour" (2,v:16,v) and of "the days and nights made of dreams of other nights better days" (7,vi:18,iii). In imagination the eternal present can be ignored momentarily by the "happy" illusion that there can be an end, that there is "only one time to serve" (6,ii:20,vi). These illusions of a passing time are, however, consistently labeled as illusions, dreams, and figments. In the timeless "true refuge" of nonbeing human time is one of the broken containers, one of the scattered ruins which have fallen over backwards. The mere mention of these scattered ruins—of passing time, of days and night, of light, of wild laughter and cries—enriches both this group and the entire work by relieving the grey endlessness. Similarly, the ambiguous syntax and unusual word choice of the section add to its elusive charm. The sentences seem to mean more than they say. For example, the negation "never but" elicits at least two responses. As implied by Cohn's description of this group—"past tenses combined with never"—the figments of passing time never were anything other than dreams. The figment light never existed outside the imagination. On the other hand, Esslin's description—"a denial of past and future"—suggests that the phrase not only negates the reality of the figments in the past but also denies any present or future possibilities. The present contains nothing except one "changeless dream." Even murmurs and other imaginings are excluded. Ambivalences are compounded as a negating phrase appears in only nine of the ten sentences. An almost imperceptible hope adheres to that tenth sentence, the sentence which so tantalizingly and provocatively concludes *Lessness*: "Figment dawn dispeller of figments and the other called dusk" (10,iv:24,iv). The sentence is lovely, moving, and enigmatic. A similarly striking but elusive image occurs in the sentence, "Never but imagined the blue in the wild imagining the blue celeste of poesy" (12,ii:21,ii). The archaic and obsolete words draw attention to themselves, making the "blue celeste of poesy" more vibrantly present than other dreams, than even the given grey endlessness.

The heavenly power of imagination persists even amid the scattered ruins; its images and sounds, its dreams and figments add an inexplicable, perhaps subliminal, layer of meaning to the world of *Lessness*.

The final group of sentences, like the dream and figment section, is rich in possibilities and variations. It contains no identifying phrase and few repetitions. Instead, the section deals with future possibilities, with the return of a diverse world in which man can act and speak. This future man is distinct from his present counterpart. Unlike the "little body" that blends into the ruins, future man is made strangely personal by the return to the pronoun "he" and by his ability to distinguish himself from his environment through motion. It is the hypothetical figure of the future—not the present figure with "legs a single block"—who will take a step in the sand, who will "live again the space of a step" (7,vii:17,ii). Whereas the "little body" has become so petrified that it no longer murmurs "ah," the future man's power of motion returns to him traces of plot and suggestions of heroic action. In spite of everything he will move "one step more," "he will make it":

> In the sand no hold one step more in the endlessness he will make it (6,vi:14,iii).

> One step more in the ruins in the sand on his back in the endlessness he will make it (7,v:18,v).

> One step more one alone all alone in the sand no hold he will make it (9,vii:22,iii).

Like Job, he will be able to "curse God again as in the blessed days" (3,i: 23,iv). The future is a return to past possibilities. When viewed from the scattered ruins, the limitations endured by the characters of the trilogy and *How It Is* suddenly become hoped-for blessings. To be able to walk, crawl, live again, and turn one's face to "the open sky the passing deluge" (3,i: 23,iv), become affirmative actions. Emphasis is on what can again be done "as in the blessed days." Man can stir again, his heart will beat again, the privilege of being rained on will return again. Even the return of unhappiness is a blessed relief, "Old love new love as in the blessed days unhappiness will reign again" (9,ii:20,iii). The days and nights only dreamt of in the fifth section will come to pass: "He will live again the space of a step it will be day and night again over him the endlessness" (7,vii:17,ii). Man will be returned to the image that haunts Beckett's works "of blue the passing cloud" (4,iv:15,iii). But in this subtly cyclic work, the return again to diversity and action is also an implicit return to the false refuge of imagined days and mental categories. The future possibilities are undercut by the recurring image of man with something over him again:

It will be day and night again over him . . . (11,iii:14,iv).

He will go on his back face to the sky open again over him the ruins the sand the endlessness (11,i:17,v).

Passing days and passing light will again enclose man. He will be on his back, face to the sky, underneath the passing deluge, below the passing cloud. The return to order and action is a return to false containers. By presenting the impossible future Beckett forces us to see what does not and can not be in the "true refuge."

By thus breaking *Lessness* down into sentences and phrases, by re-grouping the components, and by analyzing the resulting families of sentences, the reader is able to envision the "true refuge." Meaning and interpretation depend on the reader's involvement, depend on his manipulation of the moving yet enigmatic sentences. Just as *Lessness* deals with the tensions between being and nonbeing, between temporal and eternal, between imagined orders and the given endlessness; so too the piece exists between composition and decomposition, between form and formlessness. Beckett encloses his perception of order fallen open into the true refuge of nonorder, in an order which is itself so arbitrary that it begins to unravel. Instead of creating new containers, Beckett creates in *Lessness* an art that seeks to be unmade, an art that pushes the assumptions of language and literature over backward to admit the chaos "long last towards which so many false time out of mind."

In his latest works Beckett successfully accomplishes what his earliest pieces failed to do: he creates structures that disintegrate without belying their own assumptions. He develops an art that accommodates the mess without turning it into another kind of absolute order. Although Beckett never rejects imagination nor totally discards the body, he moves away from the Joycean kind of art which can do, can know, art which reflects in its carefully controlled and interconnected images an external world. Instead of a scintillating, print-oriented, and traditional art, Beckett offers, first, the spoken narration of an impotent narrator struggling with language and then impersonal and abstract images expressed in simple yet elliptic words and phrases. Characters and narrators are replaced by the objective, analytic prose of a mind in dialogue with itself. External references yield to arbitrary and fantastical images which dissolve almost before we have finished reading. The pieces are difficult not because too much has been included, nor because too much has been omitted, but rather because they present images of an underlying void. We can glimpse nothingness only momentarily before we inevitably begin fabricating our own orders to cover the void. The residua create from fiction, poetry, drama, music, and mathematics a new genre which demands the reader's intellectual involvement, yet also relies on subliminal responses, on sound and pattern, to effect meaning. Paradoxically the pieces use deceptively objective analyses of highly articulated shapes to enclose a more basic shapelessness and a more fundamental absence of order. Beckett uses the limitations of language and literature to capture the essence of the void by implication and exclusion: he expresses the chaos by avoiding it. He evolves in his short works a style that adheres ever more rigidly to the need to create in the face of nothingness. His pieces move from parodic stories to serious, though fleeting, glimpses into the true refuge of endlessness. The study of Samuel Beckett's residual fiction is the study of a journey to the self-dissipating image: ". . . soon there will be nothing where there was never anything, last images."

6. A sense of sufficiency

In "Literature of Exhaustion" John Barth observes almost enviously of Beckett and his work: ". . . for Beckett, at this point in his career, to cease to create altogether would be fairly meaningful: his crowning work, his 'last word.' What a convenient corner to paint yourself into! 'And now I shall finish,' the valet Arsene says in *Watt*, 'and you will hear my voice no more.' Only the silence *Molloy* speaks of, 'of which the universe is made.' " [1] Such a silence would be itself a statement about the impossibility of speech. But more than a decade after Barth's essay (1967) Beckett continues to publish, continues to avoid the convenient corner of exhausted silence. Many of Beckett's recent pieces do not even manifest the earlier desire to have done with speech altogether. Instead, the pieces reflect the narrator's calm acceptance of a gradually increasing quiet. Tranquillity replaces the Unnamable's urgency; adequacy relieves Malone's failures; imperturbability supersedes Moran's impatience and Molloy's indifference. The new mood reflects a new response toward art. Beckett accepts both the impossibility of a nonrelational art and the improbability of a relational one. Instead of denying the associations of traditional narratives, Beckett allows them to commingle with, but not supplant, the uncertainty and fluidity of nonrelational art. He employs conventions without being enslaved by their assumptions. Memories may be restored without confirming a correspondence to the past. Allusions may reappear without providing external meanings. Other figures return, but not love; a complete body, but not significant, physical action; naturalistic settings, but not anthropomorphic order; language games, but not Apollonian control and knowledge. It no longer is necessary to deny, explode, or implode the external worlds of association, nor to celebrate the hermetic and artificial worlds of the imagination. The two realms can be interleaved and permuted. The desire for pure and absolute structures yields before a sense of sufficiency. When fail-

ure is no longer inevitable and success not yet obtainable, it is enough to
have spoken at all. Beckett no longer seeks the impossible: his art does not
have to *be* the formless, dark zone of Murphy's mind. It is enough to reconcile but not reunite an impotent speaker with a fluid, uncertain universe.

1

A sense of sufficiency is dependent upon a delicate balance of nonrelational abstractions and traditional associations. But reconciliation without
capitulation is difficult to achieve. In *From an Abandoned Work*,[2] for example, the tensions between relation and nonrelation, between order and
disorder, produce not a harmoniously intertwined work, but rather a disjointed and contradictory one. Conventional assumptions underpin, or
from a Beckettian point of view undermine the piece. Everything is too
solidly given, too easily explained, and tentative affirmation topples into
absolute, but useless assertion.

Written in English, after *Texts for Nothing* failed to extract Beckett
from an attitude of disintegration[3] and before *How It Is* had announced its
celebration of the inner worlds of imagination, *From an Abandoned Work*
is quite literally a fragment from an aborted novel. "According to Mr.
Beckett, the fragment results from an attempt to return to fiction in English,
in 1954 or 1955. Asked why it ends abruptly, he had replied that 'there was
just no more to be said.' "[4] The work is abandoned not simply because it
has nothing more to say, however, but also because it has found no legiti-
mate way of saying it. Instead of evoking a new relationship between the
speaking voice and its creations, Beckett's return to English also returns
him to the structures and certainties of earlier literatures. Instead of either
the abstract images of the residua or the disembodied voice of *How It Is*,
From an Abandoned Work proffers the theatrical associations of a dramatic
monologue.[5] As in the dramatic monologue, the narrator is knowable,
though odd: he is himself consistent, though our perceptions of him may
alter gradually. He loves "all things still and rooted" (p. 39), detests things
mobile (p. 39), is affected strongly by white (p. 41), mutters to himself
"all day long" (p. 43), and is a "very slow walker," but "one of the fastest
runners the world has ever seen" over a short distance of five to ten yards
(p. 42). We are confidants of his opinions (p. 39), doubts (p. 40), and resolutions (p. 40). Although we may find his applications of them questionable, the narrator possesses familiar values. He assumes conventional literary postures. In "pain and weakness" (p. 43) he looks back on his youth,
back to the time when he had "piercing sight" (p. 40) and a "great mem-

ory" (p. 42). The format is that of a flashback made disjointed by the filter of our narrator's dim consciousness and imperfect sense of art. Not only does the narrator have a past, but unlike other Beckettian figures, he can remember much of that past, from the three days he selects to tell us about, to the day he told his father about Milton's cosmology (p. 42), even to a half forgotten fact about "a ton of worms in an acre" (p. 45). As the narrator describes past events, he incidentally and unconsciously reveals more about himself. Although he will not go out of his way to avoid the distasteful, and although he values tenacity of purpose, he himself wanders about aimlessly: ". . . I have never in my life been on my way anywhere, but simply on my way" (p. 39). He possesses a great memory but "no thought" (p. 42). He "never loved anyone" (p. 42), "never talked to anyone" (p. 43). He denies his mother has any affection for him (p. 40), refuses to acknowledge her imploring gestures (pp. 43–44), desires to continue cursing her from hell (p. 44). Moreover, the narrator suffers from uncontrollable rages (pp. 41–42) and an abnormal mental condition: "I was mad of course and still am, but harmless, I passed for harmless, that's a good one. Not of course that I was really mad, just strange, a little strange, and with every passing year a little stranger, there can be fewer stranger creatures going about than me at the present day" (p. 44). Random remarks have already begun to suggest a hypothetical prose context when the narrator himself suggests that he, at least metaphorically, killed one or both of his parents: "My father, did I kill him too as well as my mother, perhaps in a way I did, but I can't go into that now, much too old and weak" (p. 44). Although the narrator's memory fails at this crucial point and we never know if he did kill his father or anyone else (p. 45), the guilt and the psychological motivations remain. Plots are possible; actions, explicable; characters, manipulable.

Again, as in the traditional dramatic monologue, *From an Abandoned Work* assumes that memory is viable and that situation and setting are stable. The resulting diversity of things and people, actions and memories, prevents the narrator from confronting the possibility of a primal and uncertain universe. Vitality seeps into the discourse as horses, butterflies, and stoats replace jars, pencils, and notebooks. Specific details lend authenticity and variety to the nonself. The addition of colors makes the woman waving in the window seem concrete (p. 40): she is a particle from reality, not simply a "mental" figment. Similarly, whereas the figure in *How It Is* will have to endure the present aided only by the mud, the murmur, the dark, and the pant, the narrator of *From an Abandoned Work* has memories and motion to entertain him. Like Beckett's other characters, the narrator talks of waiting for time to pass and seeks an end that "cannot be far off now" (p. 45). Like them he has to "get through somehow" (p. 46) the hundreds and thousands of similar "unremarkable" days. Like them he speaks of death as an ongoing process (p. 43) and envisions his "reward" as a refuge from the succession of days into a timeless time, into "a long unbroken time without before or after, light or dark, from or towards or at" (p. 19). But unlike other Beckettian figures, the narrator is spared confrontation with the eternal void. Our sense is not of trying to pass the time, but of time passing. Although the narrator may have to live through successive unremarkable days, our impression is of his ability in narrating to "move on in time skipping hundreds and even thousands of days" (p. 46). While he may refer often to death, such thoughts are, as the narrator admits, not his. They come out of habit and without conviction, "the old thoughts born with me and grown with me and kept under" (p. 43). The narrator's frequent interruptions of himself to return to the thread of his story, also return him from the eternal present to the linear order of "plot."

The narrator's ability to create a linear "plot"—to control his language and fashion his story—distinguishes him further from Beckett's other figures. His voice is not merely the voice of a man speaking in order to exist; it is also the voice of an artist creating a story, selecting what material and what days to include, deciding what shall not be said again (p. 47) and what does not sound right (p. 46). Whereas the Unnamable battles with his words, the narrator of *From an Abandoned Work* plays with his. Words have been his only loves (p. 48). He obtains pleasure from manipulating them: he enjoys speaking foreign words (p. 41), rhyming simple words (pp. 42 and 45), and reversing common words (p. 48). The chaos is mitigated by the narrator's ability to fashion his own order.

Indeed, were it not for a few passages reasserting uncertainty, the chaos not only would be mitigated, but would be circumvented altogether, and *From an Abandoned Work* would fit easily into the traditions of Apollonian literature. Beckett attempts to forestall the triumph of conventional orders by qualifying his narrator's control. The narrator may select his days, but they still do not yield a coherent plot. He may describe others, but he doesn't know their motivations (p. 40). He plays with his words, but sometimes they appear unbidden (p. 46). The narrator's qualified control of his words intimates a deeper contradiction in the nature of the narrator himself. On one hand, his words are meant to be spoken. As in many of Beckett's works, the narrator is a compulsive talker, even suffering a sore throat caused by his incessant mutterings (p. 43). He revises his story and contradicts himself, not in the fashion of a man writing a story, but rather in that of a man speaking to himself. Instead of crossing out lines or deleting passages, the narrator retains what he has said and explains it (pp. 43–44), or comments on its validity (pp. 45, 48). Yet on the other hand, the voice intends its words for print: "Now is there nothing to add to this day with the white horse and white mother in the window, please read again my descriptions of these, before I move on in time . . ." (pp. 45–46). The narrator can move on in time, but he is incapable of clarifying whether he is speaking or writing. His condition remains vague. Unable to accept the limitations his story imposes on him, the narrator increasingly loses control of it until he is forced to abandon it altogether.

The curious tensions in *From an Abandoned Work* between spoken and printed, between love of "all things still and rooted" (p. 39) and the power to move, between a narrator who can and cannot create, all indicate a work that is the result of, rather than the resolution to, the problems of reconciling the narrator's memories and a fluid universe. The return to English is a return to people and objects which are too solidly present, too diverse, too powerful, too easily explained. Suggestions of plot and psychological motivation overwhelm delicate ambivalences. Trappings from the external world obscure internal fluctuations. Unable to construct a manner of speaking consistent with its content, *From an Abandoned Work* is left with nothing more to say.

2

Whereas Apollonian assumptions overwhelm *From an Abandoned Work*, those assumptions are themselves subverted in *The Lost Ones* (*Le Dépeupleur*).[6] Just as the highly articulated forms of the residua gesture to a more fundamental absence of structure, so too the carefully fabricated associations of *The Lost Ones* indicate a more basic disorder. Like the residua, *The Lost Ones* presents an artificial image diagrammatically described. But unlike the residua, that description concentrates less upon the cylinder itself, than upon the rules that enable the bodies to persist within it. Instead of one or two amorphous, androgynous, and anonymous figures, *The Lost Ones* present bodies "of either sex and all ages from old age to infancy" (p. 30). The image of single, elemental figure is replaced by an image of a whole society. *The Lost Ones* is Beckett's version of the social novel: it is what the novel of manners must be in a meaningless, fluctuant world.

The traditional novel of manners deals with man's relationship to man in the context of a society. Because the manners of that society determine the behavior of the characters, those manners and that society are usually portrayed realistically and in detail. In his book on the novel of manners James W. Tuttleton defines the novel of manners as:

... a novel in which the manners, social customs, folkways, conventions, traditions, and mores of a given social group at a given time and place play a dominant role in the lives of fictional characters, exert control over their thought and behavior, and constitute a determinant upon the actions in which they are engaged, and in which these manners and customs are detailed realistically—with, in fact, a premium upon the exactness of their representation.[7]

In *The Lost Ones* Beckett explores the underlying assumptions of the novel of manners by pursuing them to their logical ends. He creates an image of society in which the thought and behavior of the members is not only controlled but even supplanted by the "manners, social customs, folkways, conventions, traditions, and mores" of the cylinder. Whereas the bodies remain relatively indistinct and impersonal, referred to only as "bodies" or lost "ones," the rules for the use of ladders are described in detail. Whereas the purpose of the quest is undefined, the methods of the search are explicitly detailed. Beckett turns the novel of manners, with its "premium upon the exactness of . . . representation," into a coldly analytic report. Instead of a narrator whose wisdom, control, and compassion reflect the structures of a universe in which characters can and do form meaningful relationships, Beckett's narrator reflects the disinterested precision of a scientist describing the physical properties of a gaseous system. The motion of the bodies about their closed system—affected by the presence of others yet isolated from them—suggests a human equivalent to Brownian movement. The scientific analogy becomes increasingly significant when the narrator reveals that the bodies are slowly languishing; they, like molecules, are approaching absolute zero. *The Lost Ones* thus offers another Beckettian image of the imperceptibly yet inexorably approaching end. This time, however, the image is not simply of a single figure on the edge of nothingness, but rather of a whole society moving, unwittingly, toward the abyss.

Like the narrators of the great nineteenth-century social novels, Beckett's narrator is external, omniscient, omnipotent. He is superior to, and hence distinct from, the lost bodies. Unlike a mere visitor to the cylinder, he perceives the gradual and fluctuant death of the bodies (p. 18). Like one "in the secret of the gods" (p. 19), he knows of the desultory decline of religious persuasions. Although the beginning of the cylinder is "unthinkable" and its end is unimaginable, the narrator thinks of, imagines, and describes both beginning and end. He postulates what will happen "over a long enough period of time [to the] eyes blue for preference" (p. 39). He knows what the floor of the cylinder would look like if it were "suitably lit from above" (p. 29). While the narrator is distinct from the bodies, he is also one of the initiated. He can see with eyes other than those of flesh to distinguish between vanquished and sedentary (p. 31), to note the clear-cut zones of the cylinder, "imaginary frontiers invisible to the eye of flesh" (p. 43). Furthermore, the narrator's powers of perception separate him from us. If it were not for the narrator, we would draw false conclusions about the cylinder. We are like the "intelligence" which would be tempted to assume bodies must progress in stages from one type to the next (p. 33).

Although our narrator adopts the posture of knowledge and power of the nineteenth-century narrator, he is placed nonetheless in a world that is neither knowable nor controllable. The assumptions beneath his Apollonian omniscience and omnipotence are put in a context that makes them irrelevant. Our narrator's scientific precision cannot penetrate the interpersonal nor the subjective. He must deal with life in terms of physical laws, not human responses. While the effect of the cylinder's climate "on the soul is not to be underestimated" (p. 52), the narrator prefers to explain the effect on the skin. His knowledge is restricted to that which can be observed and measured. Moreover, even that knowledge is undermined by errors ("That is not quite accurate"—pp. 16–17), estimations ("ten seconds or thereabouts"—p. 17), and revisions ("from time immemorial rumor has it or better still the notion is abroad"—p. 17). The self-conscious narrator qualifies his own story by drawing attention to its peculiarities ("this at first sight is strange"—p. 21) and to the limitations of his language ("the ladders themselves seem rather to shed than to receive light with this slight reserve that light is not the word"—p. 40). In spite of his claims that answers to questions he poses are "clear and easy to give [it] only remains to dare" (p. 52), the narrator never does dare to answer those questions or many others. Even in the simple world of the cylinder, "All has not been told and never shall be" (p. 51).

"All" cannot be told because the devices and assumptions of a novel of manners are undermined by the persistance of a nonrelational context. The distinctions between that context and those of earlier literatures are strikingly illustrated by a comparison of *The Lost Ones* and the source of its French title, "L'Isolement." Lamartine's work deals with isolation. The poet, lamenting the death of his beloved, finds himself isolated. His grief and his loss leave him indifferent to and unmoved by his surroundings. Natural scenes which had once been sources of beauty and joy have become part of an empty and vain world. Instead of individual suffering, however,

The Lost Ones presents isolated man in a society of isolated men. The loneliness and solipsism expressed in *How It Is* are shown to be the universal condition. Society is composed of figures who are simultaneously Pim and Bom, victim and victimizer, coupled and abandoned. Bodies are acquainted only "in theory." Even man and wife are strangers who may pass without recognition or acknowledgment (pp. 35–36). Whereas another person made the world come alive for Lamartine, for the lost bodies the Other is a source of torment. As in Beckett's *Film*, the eyes of others are felt as "some old abomination" (p. 54). Lamartine hopes to find a resolution to his grief some place beyond the edges of the universe where, having cast off the spoils of the earth, he will be reunited with his beloved. But for the lost ones there is no hope. As we learn in the first three sentences, both search and flight are in vain: "Abode where lost bodies roam each searching for its lost one. Vast enough for search to be in vain. Narrow enough for flight to be in vain" (p. 7). The bodies must endure the hellish vibrations of light and temperature as long as any among them continues to search. For them there will be no resolution, neither beyond the cylinder nor after the questing ends. In fact, the bodies, incapable of perceiving the gradual depreciation of the cylinder, are denied even the hope of an end. For such beings there is only the absolute zero of total isolation and total indifference to both their surroundings and themselves.

In such an indifferent and entropic world the manners of a society become simply structures the inhabitants create to hide the underlying chaos from themselves. "All" has not been told in Beckett's novel of manners precisely because the work analyzes structures which are themselves artificial overlays. Through his distillation of the techniques of the social novel Beckett is able to expose the vanity of imposing any structures on an abyss. The cylindrical world reflects our world; its simple rules and objects are images of our own more complex but equally artificial orders. The zones of the floor mimic our reliance on geographical divisions. The happy few who hold the missing rungs (p. 10) suggest our concern with material possessions. Similarly the types of bodies and their roles and privileges become archetypes of our social castes and classes. The vanquished may be stepped on, but the sedentary, "morbidly susceptible to the least want of consideration" (p. 28), must be stepped over.

Perhaps the most disconcerting of the cylinder's archetypes are those of religion and law. The myths of the cylinder promise a way out, an escape from the world of meaningless quests. Although these myths are dying out, they will never be disproved. Indeed, the myths are so cunningly devised that they can't be refuted. Since none exists who can retain a "perfect mental image of the entire system" of tunnels (p. 12), none can ever prove that there is not a "secret passage branching from one of the tunnels" (p. 18). Likewise, since the bodies will never join together in the "instant of fraternity" necessary to explore the hub of the ceiling (p. 21), the ceiling "where for amateurs of myth lies hidden a way out to earth and sky" (p. 21) will remain "inviolable." We know, as the bodies do not, that they will never find a passage out. They hope to escape into a world resembling ours: they seek a passage "leading in the words of the poet [cf. Dante] to nature's sanctuaries . . . giving access to a flue at the end of which the sun and other stars would still be shining" (p. 18). In a similar fashion, our religions postulate a passage to yet another, better realm. Escape through the trap-door is but one myth in the infinite progression of myths man embraces to obscure his present condition.

The use and transport of ladders presents the myth of law. The laws themselves are simple, logical, and consistent. They are based on a few basic precepts: the ladders may be mounted by no more than one body at a time (p. 22), they may be moved in one direction only (p. 27), descent takes precedence over ascent (p. 23). From these arbitrary limitations Beckett, in a parody of the teleological argument, creates a harmonious system in which "all is for the best" (p. 42) and in which every object is functional (p. 23). In fact harmony becomes a major motif. The rule for movement between the cylinder's zone is "one example among a thousand of the harmony that reigns in the cylinder between order and license" (p. 44). Tolerance tempers discipline (p. 49). Just as scientific laws explain random molecular motion, so too the cylinder's laws seem to give meaning to a purposeless search; seem to harmonize order and license, discipline and tolerance, artifice and abyss. The laws are designed to forestall anarchy (pp. 22, 26, 27).

But the futility of the laws soon becomes evident. The laws which are arranged to insure that all is for the best are only a thin veneer masking the underlying lawlessness. The harmony is repeatedly broken by outbursts of violence. Initially the real violence of the cylinder is only obliquely implied. Encased in a passage focusing on the cylinder's silence is the suggestion that perhaps all is not for the best: "The only sounds worthy of the name result from the manipulation of the ladders or the thud of bodies striking against one another or of one against itself as when in a sudden fury it beats its breast" (p. 9). Why are the bodies striking against one another? Why would a body "in a sudden fury" beat its own breast? Although the narrator ignores these questions, discord begins to destroy the harmony. Unexplained references to violence proliferate. The happy few who possess the missing rungs use them "mainly for attack and self-defense [while their] solitary attempts to brain themselves culminate at the best in brief losses of consciousness" (p. 10). It is the sedentary "whose acts of violence most disrupt the cylinder's quiet" (p. 14), whose outbursts of fury may "throw the entire cylinder into a ferment" (p. 29). Those who threaten the facade of harmony by entering the climber's area without authorization, by leaving the queue early, or by traveling in the wrong direction are met with violent opposition. The need for violent enforcement emphasizes rather than alters the ultimate futility of legislated order. The cylinder tends naturally to discord and entropy. Just as the lulls heighten the stillness of the vanquished, making "that which is normally theirs seem risible in comparison" (p. 37), so too the underlying chaos makes even the simplest systems of order and law seem risible in comparison. We are left with an image of archetypes coming undone.

Ironically, Beckett's concrete portrayal of the cylinder with its exact and detailed descriptions evokes a sense of disintegration, impotence, and uncertainty. Like the hollow core of a cylinder, the center of Beckett's work is inexplicable. The diagrammatic novel of manners has controlled the Apollonian impulse, but the quest which informs the customs of the cylinder remains enigmatic. Like the artist who, having nothing to express and nothing with which nor from which to express, is nonetheless obligated to express, the bodies are compelled to search without hope or purpose. Each one independently searches for "its lost one," but that lost one is neither another body ("If they recognize each other it does not appear. Whatever it is they are searching for it is not that," p. 36) nor the self ("None looks within himself where none can be," p. 30). Yet whatever it is that is sought, the need to seek is itself so great "that no place may be left unsearched" (pp. 50–51). Even those who have abandoned the quest may suddenly search again, the sedentary may climb again (pp. 13–14), the eyes of the vanquished may "search afresh" (p. 32). In fact, everything in the cylinder is subject to a diminishing recurrence. The closed system of the cylinder is committed to a downward spiraling course. In one of the few similies of his late period Beckett compares the cylinder's course to a gradually diminishing heap of sand: "Even so a great heap of sand sheltered from the wind lessened by three grains every second year and every following increased by two if this notion is maintained" (p. 32). It is the image of the infinitely, infinitesimally approaching end, this notion of the bodies as always "darkward bound" (p. 20), that shapes *The Lost Ones*. The cylinder, and the work itself, cohere only "if this notion is maintained." But the very repetition of the phrase "if this notion is maintained" (pp. 32, 39, 60) draws attention to the tenuous, hypothetical nature of the work. Placement of the refrain at the end of *The Lost Ones* calls the entire book into question: "So much roughly speaking for the last state of the cylinder and of this little people of searchers one first of whom if a man in some unthinkable past for the first time bowed his head if this notion is maintained" (pp. 62–63). What happens to the cylindrical world if this notion is *not* maintained?

In many ways the primary function of the final section of *The Lost Ones* is to make the whole work problematic and thereby restore the humanity of associations to Beckett's residual novel of manners. Although Beckett had written the first fourteen sections by 1966, it was not until 1970 that he was able to write the final paragraph. The differences between these two portions of the book suggest that Beckett sought to counterbalance the analytic statements of his initial paragraphs with a conclusion which would return mystery and uncertainty to the cylinder and to *The Lost Ones*. Having negated Apollonian assumptions, he sought to mitigate the impersonality of his residual abstractions. The prose of the first fourteen paragraphs is neither ambiguous nor elliptical. It describes a cylinder that can be measured, inspected, and tested. The narrator speaks as a scientist about a controlled and knowable system. Although he admits pathos may exist in the cylinder, he does so through inversion and negation: "And the thinking being coldly intent on all these data and evidences could scarcely escape at the close of his analysis the mistaken conclusion that instead of speaking of the vanquished with the slight taint of pathos attaching to the term it would be more correct to speak of the blind and leave it at that" (p. 39). The effect is to emphasize not the pathos but rather the mistaken conclusions of "the thinking being coldly intent on all these data and evidences."

The fifteenth section, on the other hand, is more personal and ambiguous. The sentences become longer, the adjectives and adverbs more elusive, the syntax more ambivalent. Connotative and emotional words replace facts and figures. Characters are no longer simply "bodies": they are referred to as "this little people of searchers" (p. 63). The cold, impersonal distance between narrator and cylinder breaks down. Instead of analytically announcing the end of the cylinder, the narrator dramatizes the final hush (p. 62). We are pulled back from the scientific world of statement and measurement to the Beckettian realm of maybe and perhaps. We are left once again on the edge of the abyss, peering into "those calm wastes" of unseeing eyes. Like Murphy, we are left behind, specks in the vast unseen: lost bodies, each searching for its lost one.

3

The reconciliation implicit in the last section of *The Lost Ones* between the residual and the personal, between Apollonian assumptions and non-relational uncertainty is more clearly and completely depicted in *Fizzles* (1976).[8] In that collection of eight pieces, elements of traditional narratives are restored to the prose without reasserting, as in *From an Abandoned Work*, conventional meanings. At the same time the fluidity of nonrelational art is postulated without evoking, as in *The Lost Ones*, a primarily analytic prose. The resulting balance increases the ambiguities of Beckett's works by enabling the narrator to embrace without preference both types of art. Instead of battering against the walls of the impenetrable or flinging himself into the abyss of subjective-objective dichotomies, the narrator accepts impure structures and incomplete answers as adequate, if not accurate, responses. Instead of denigrating the intuitive and negating the personal, the narrator accepts an increasingly affective tone. Urgency and abstraction yield to a pervading sense of sufficiency.

Perhaps the best way to intimate the new tone of *Fizzles* is to contrast that work with the trilogy. The contrast is particularly useful because of the number of places in which *Fizzles* duplicates only imperfectly the earlier work. Like the voice(s) of the trilogy, the voice(s) of *Fizzles* struggles with pronouns, questions identity, and objects to the Berkelian perception which will cause self-conscious existence. Just as Worm refuses to come out of his dark cave into the light of cognition, so too the narrator of "Fizzle 2" has Horn report at night because he can "bear everything bar being seen" ("Fizzle 2," p. 19). But unlike Worm, the narrator ultimately will acknowledge others and thus be forced to admit his own perceivability, i.e., his own existence: "I'll let myself be seen before I'm done. I'll call out, if there is a knock, Come in!" ("Fizzle 2," p. 20). Just as the Unnamable tries to identify himself with a speaking voice rather than a physical body, so too the narrator in "Fizzles 3 and 4" distinguishes between the "he" that is born and moves and the "I" inside ("Fizzle 3," p. 27). But unlike the disembodied voice in *The Unnamable*, the figure in "Fizzle 1" can also accept and even caress his body, ". . . the clothes, singlet and trousers . . . and finally . . . the hands as now and then they pass back and forth, over all those parts of the body they can reach without fatigue" ("Fizzle 1," pp. 11–12). Just as the narrator of the trilogy fails to find an acceptable name or pronoun, so too the speaker in *Fizzles* talks of *Murphy, I,* and *he.* But unlike the Unnamable, instead of berating a language that can provide no pronoun for the essence of being, the narrator of *Fizzles* accepts the words available to him. The isolation and alienation inherent in being unspeakable dissipate before a willingness to include even the reader in the flow of words. The narrator is willing to speak of *we* and *us*: "These allusions to now, to before and after, and all such yet to come, that *we* may feel ourselves in time" ("Fizzle 2," p. 20, my emphasis). Similarly, instead of protesting against foreign authorities and inexplicable pensums, the narrator in *Fizzles* accepts responsibility for his actions and tasks. Although it may be better had he never returned from the journey, the narrator will nonetheless attempt to "elucidate" it as a lesson for himself: "I thought I had made my last journey, the one I must now try once more to elucidate, that it may be a lesson to me, the one from which it were better I had never returned" ("Fizzle 2," pp. 21–22). Even that elucidation is less urgent, less shrill, less agonized than the Unnamable's. While in its quest for an end to questing the trilogy progressively strips away external orders and increasingly immobilizes the narrator until Molloy's crutches have yielded to Malone's bed and the Unnamable's jar, *Fizzles* accepts without objection the resurgence of both journey and mobility. The protagonist in "Fizzle 2" not only accepts exile from the refuge of his bed, but even trains for the journey he must undertake. "For I have taken to getting up again. I thought I had made my last journey. . . . But the feeling gains on me that I must undertake another. So I have taken to getting up again and making a few steps in the room, holding on to the bars of the bed" ("Fizzle 2," pp. 21–22). The "heroic" isolation and doomed failures of the Unnamable are replaced by a figure that accepts without hope of attainment the quest for a grail that may never have existed.

The new mood in *Fizzles* is the result of Beckett's ability to balance fluidity and uncertainty with intimations of an external world, a recoverable past, and a controllable language. The Cartesian schism between body and mind, which in some fashion has plagued all of Beckett's narratives from the early "Assumption" through the most recent pieces, is present in *Fizzles*. But here, instead of agonizing over the dichotomy or denying the physical world, Beckett accepts the possible duality without asserting any viable relationship between body and mind. Specificity can be applied to descriptions of an exterior order without granting any credence to that order. The narrator can talk of an eastern window, a wicker chair, or a beech tree ("Fizzle 2") without being committed to their reality. Details do not necessitate sentimentality nor grant priority. The pathetic fallacy is avoided as sunsets are described in emotionless, colorless passages: "Or anywhere any ope staring at nothing just failing light quite still till dark . . ." ("Fizzle 7," p. 49). Romantic correspondences are averted as contact does not initiate meditation or identification. Figures can pull themselves up by the boughs of trees without being absorbed by them ("Fizzle 6," p. 43). Unlike the voice of *How It Is* which is the source of all images and objects, the narrator of *Fizzles* discriminates between images developing in inner and in outer space: "It is in outer space, not to be confused with the other, that such images develop" ("Fizzle 2," p. 21). Boundaries may be allowed, the troublesome physicality of the body may be acknowledged—even counted as a blessing ("Fizzle 1," pp. 9–10)—but identity is not made less problematic nor motion more comprehensible thereby. Although the figure in "Fizzle 7" can move from chair to window and back, the return of motion does not break the stillness of his life. The idea of physical death can be reintroduced, but the concept does not carry with it assurances of termination. No longer worrying about existence as the space of an opening door, the narrator can adopt the voice of an aged man seeking reintegration of his dust and the earth: "Old earth, no more lies, I've seen you, it was me, with my other's ravening eyes, too late. You'll be on me, it will be me, it will be us, it was never us. It won't be long now, perhaps not tomorrow, nor the day after, but too late. Not long now, how I gaze on you, and what refusal, how you refuse me, you so refused" ("Fizzle 6," 43). Although he seeks reintegration, the narrator observes without hysteria that the earth now refuses him. The dwindling may never be completed. Questions about mortality go unanswered despite Beckett's adoption of more conventional postulations. No longer struggling to avoid solutions, Beckett's *Fizzles* accepts the absence of answers.

The rapprochement of man and world is accompanied by a reconciliation of man and memory. Although memory is never substantiated, indeed it is characteristically undercut by phrases such as "the dung litter of laughable memory" ("Fizzle 8," p. 58), its restoration provides the figures in *Fizzles* with the possibilities of a recoverable past, a distinguishable identity, and a hypothetical happiness. Instead of the eternal present of *How It Is* in which all that goes before is forgotten, the barefoot, bareheaded character in "Fizzle 1" has "a number of memories" and "a little past" to entertain him on his journey. Although it is fragile and limited—unable to go back beyond that first instant when the figure suddenly knew he had ventured forth again—memory is nonetheless available. Because events can be recalled, a history can take shape, "studded with occasions passing rightly or wrongly for outstanding" ("Fizzle 1," p. 13). The monotony of existence is relieved and "enriched" by the ability to remember and to categorize the "summits" and the "minima" of existence: "So with one thing and another little by little his history takes shape, and even changes shape, as new maxima and minima tend to cast into the shade, and toward oblivion, those momentarily glorified, and as fresh elements and motifs . . . in view of their importance, contribute to enrich it" ("Fizzle 1," pp. 14–15). Memory is returned, but it is not made absolute. Like Beckett's universe, memory itself is being reshaped continuously: new maxima and new minima preclude certainty and fixity. The figure may have a history, but like the dark zone of Murphy's mind, it is perpetually forming and reforming. The ambivalence of memory permits Beckett to suggest past moments of happiness, love, and loss without verifying or sentimentalizing them. Whereas *How It Is* rejects images of life above in the light, "Fizzle 6" incorporates those images in the narrator's serenade to the earth.

> For an instant I see the sky, the different skies, then they turn to faces, agonies, loves, the different loves, happiness too, yes, there was that too, unhappily. Moments of life, of mine too, among others, no denying, all said and done. Happiness, what happiness, but what deaths, what loves. I knew at the time, it was too late then. Ah to love at your last and see them at theirs, the last minute loved ones, and be happy, why ah, uncalled for. ("Fizzles 6," p. 44)

Memories are possible, but the past is not allowed to overwhelm or relieve the present. The narrator reverts from thoughts of former happiness to awareness of his present isolation: "No but now, now, simply stay still, standing before a window, one hand on the wall, the other clutching your shirt, and see the sky, a long gaze" ("Fizzle 6," p. 44). Memory may postulate a prior love, but the hypothesis goes untested and the happiness is never felt.

As is the case with memory and an external word, so too the language of *Fizzles* reintroduces Apollonian elements without reproducing omniscience and omnipotence. Conventional punctuation and sentences appear, but not conventional arguments and orders. The narrator asserts more control over his language, but his stories do not attain greater certainty. While the mantic meanings and scintillating word games of the earliest prose never emerge, the narrator can nonetheless play with his words, altering for example "flora and fauna" or "narrow straits" into more Beckettian propositions:

Walls and ground, if not of stone, are no less hard, to the touch, and wet. The former, certain days, he stops to lick. The fauna, if any, is silent. ("Fizzle 1," p. 11)

In any case little by little his history takes shape, with if not exactly its good days and bad, at least studded with occasions passing rightly or wrongly for outstanding, such as the straitest narrow, the loudest fall, the most lingering collapse, the steepest descent. . . . ("Fizzle 1," p. 13)

Neologisms and foreign words are absent, but the prose may still sport an occasional archaic phrase ("a reminder of bedlam nature," "Fizzle 5," p. 38). The narrator's qualified ability to manipulate his words is accompanied by a vocabulary of acceptance and ephemerality. To the narrator of *Fizzles*, change may be "gentle" ("Fizzle 1," p. 13); memories, "fragile" ("Fizzle 1," pp. 12 and 13); and a lingering dawn, "magical" ("Fizzle 8," p. 55). Sufficiency, if not control, tempers the narrator's monologue. While the movement of the figure at the end of "Fizzle 7" may be "impossible to fol-low let alone describe," the narrator can both follow and describe it ade-quately. Instead of battling against the unknowable, the narrator of "Fizzle 5" asserts that everything that needs to be known is known: "Closed place. All needed to be known for say is known. There is nothing but what is said. Beyond what is said there is nothing. What goes on in the arena is not said. Did it need to be known it would be. No interest. Not for imagining" ("Fiz-zle 5," p. 37). Similarly, the speaker of "Fizzles 3 and 4" admits at least partial control of, and responsibility for his words and images. It is the internal "I" who provides his physical counterpart with the names, places, and faces that will cause him to love again, lose again: ". . . I'm still inside, the same, I'll put faces in his head, names, places, churn them all up to-gether, all he needs to end, phantoms to flee, last phantoms to flee and to pursue, he'll confuse his mother with whores, his father with a roadman named Balfe. I'll feed him an old curdog, a mangy old curdog, that he may love again, lose again, ruinstrewn land, little panic steps" ("Fizzle 3," p. 27). Just as the restoration of names and faces does not prohibit the loss of love, the return of partial control does not guarantee a meaningful conclusion. A conventional end never comes because the imagination fab-ricates enough memory to keep one trodding the ruinstrewn land with little panic steps. As the narrator of "Fizzle 4" explains, "he" will never rest: even when there is nothing left in "his" head, the speaker will feed it all it needs to go on: ". . . he'll get up and go on, badly because of me, he can't stay still anymore, because of me, he can't go on any more, because of me, there's nothing left in his head, I'll feed it all it needs" ("Fizzle 4," p. 20). Even the conclusions the narrator wants to fabricate never appear and "Fizzle 1," for example, terminates with the promise of a story that is never told. Much like the Unnamable's inability to avoid the words of others, the narrator's ability to manipulate his own language leads not to assurance and fixity but to the paradoxical proposition of going on when one can't go on.

The possibilities, though not probabilities, of an external world, recoverable past, and controllable language make the given, isolated, and uncertain condition of *Fizzles* more poignant. Despite an apparently expanding range of possibilities, the figures are ultimately no more knowledgeable or powerful than their predecessors. Their failures, because no longer assured and inevitable, are more painful. Sympathetic imagination enables Keats to identify with a nightingale. Similarly, merely by raising his eyes the speaker in "Fizzle 3" can merge with a hedge: ". . . he has only to raise his eyes, open his eyes, raise his eyes, he merges in the hedge, afar a bird, a moment past he grasps and is fled . . ." ("Fizzle 3," p. 26). But the moment passes before the speaker can consider its import, before he is led to ask Keats's question, "Do I wake or sleep?" The moment passes, but the imagination is not awakened and the transcendent vision is never glimpsed. In a parallel movement the figures in the *Fizzles* are spared the shocking oscillations of light and temperature that assault the bodies in *The Lost Ones*. Instead of a fatal alteration from the present foul air to "the other, the true life-giving," the narrator of "Fizzle 1" postulates a gentle and gradual change. But even as he raises the possibility of a benign change, the narrator undermines its salutary effect by suggesting that such an alteration would be too gradual to be noticed. Perhaps even now the air is less foul, but if so the narrator is unaware of its improvement ("Fizzle 1," p. 13). Because relationships are not denied absolutely, because transcendent vision and salutary change can be conceived, their failure to materialize is felt all the more keenly.

Perhaps the image which best exemplifies the poignancy inherent in positing sufficiency rather than certainty is the pervasive image of a leaden dawn: "There in the end all at once or by degrees there dawns and magic lingers a leaden dawn" ("Fizzle 8," pp. 55–56). While the sun never actually rises in "Fizzle 1," the possibility of a dawn lingers without contradiction; "And all may yet grow light, at any moment, first dimly and then—how can one say?—then more and more . . ." ("Fizzle 1," p. 9). In an unusual expression of judgment the narrator goes so far as to suggest that the figure in "Fizzle 1" was wrong perhaps to give up trying "to pierce the gloom. For he might well have succeeded, in the end, up to a point" ("Fizzle 1," p.

9). Whereas *Lessness* dismisses such allusions to passing time as containers that prevent man from attaining the true refuge of fallen open endlessness, *Fizzles* focuses on sunrises and sunsets, on changing rather than changeless time. The figures in "Fizzles 6 and 7" are defined by their responses to the greying light. The narrator of "Fizzle 7" is present to us only at the "close of a dark day" as he watches the sun shine out at last and go down ("Fizzle 7," p. 47). The narrator of "Fizzle 6," in an astonishing passage, admits shame for his inability to endure as do the cockchafers and darkness, admits shame for his controversion through an artificial lamp of the natural dwindling of light.

> It's a cockchafer year, next year there won't be any, nor the year after. . . . Three years in the earth . . . then guzzle guzzle, ten days long, a fortnight, and always the flight at nightfall. To the river perhaps, they head for the river. I turn on the light, then off, ashamed, stand at gaze before the window, the windows, going from one to another, leaning on the furniture. ("Fizzle 6," pp. 43–44)

The persistence of a leaden light restores man to guilt, not to grace. Like the elements of relational art which appear in the prose without any corollary meanings, the possibility of a dawn arises in *Fizzles* without any attendant hope, illumination, or signification. The light is leaden. But even a leaden light suggests alternatives to the dark flux, and its persistence serves as a reminder of the daylight that does not come. The persistence of Apollonian associations, even unsubstantiated ones, suggests, but never guarantees, an alternative to a nonrelational universe.

Unlike the voices of the trilogy and *How It Is*, the narrator of *Fizzles* speaks not in terms of a darkness, but of less light, "just less light still when less did not seem possible" ("Fizzle 7," p. 49). His concern is not to pierce the impenetrable and posit absolute answers, but "increasingly to spare [himself] needless fatigue" ("Fizzle 1," p. 9) for "it matters little in any case" ("Fizzle 1," pp. 10 and 11). He no longer tries to force an ending; instead he will "leave it so" ("Fizzle 7," p. 51) and talk impassively of ending "yet again" ("Fizzle 8," p. 55). Although his narrations repeat familiar Beckettian themes and styles, his mood reflects a new and growing serenity and tranquillity. Beckett is able to restore the possibilities of external worlds, tentative memories, and a controlled language without also restoring Apollonian certainty, absolutes, or order. The struggle to avoid meaning is replaced with an acceptance of nonmeaning. Unlike the artist mentioned in *Endgame* who saw only ashes when confronted with a field of wheat, the figures of *Fizzles* look indifferently on ashes and wheat alike. The resulting vision makes Beckett's pieces perhaps more attractive as acceptance and reconciliation bring his works closer to the worlds in which we must daily live.

4

In noting the new mood of Beckett's pieces, John Pilling speaks of "an art of success" whose new aesthetic "is advertised in the first sentence of *Enough*: 'All that goes before forget.' The new 'art and craft' is much less elaborate and much more rudimentary than the old. Whereas Molloy believed that it was the role of objects to restore silence, the speakers of the residua and fizzles believe that the role of objects is to inspire speech and render speech itself an object of disinterested contemplation."[9] While "sufficiency" rather than "success" is perhaps a more useful term for an art that continues to deny itself unqualified knowledge, unquestioned assertion, and unambiguous resolutions, Pilling is quite right in observing that the first clear articulation of a disinterested acceptance of objects and speech occurs in *Enough* (*Assez*—1966).[10] As its title might suggest, *Enough* is a hymn of adequacy and acceptance. Moreover, its reconciliation of relational and nonrelational elements enables *Enough* to structure itself on the possibility, raised by the last section of *The Lost Ones* and by the dawn imagery of *Fizzles*, of a more personal, emotional prose. Instead of the individual figures in *Fizzles* or the society of isolated beings in *The Lost Ones*, *Enough* presents a speaker who is identified by his relation to another being. His life in the couple may be over now, but the narrator is defined primarily by that previous association. Though drastically reduced and modified from traditional narratives, man's relationship to man is at the center of the work.

In *Enough*, as in *How It Is*, the presence or absence of another figure is one of the dominant structural devices. The couple marks what the narrator considers his life: "It is then I shall have lived then or never" (p. 57). Everything prior to the meeting of the narrator and his bent figure is forgotten or dismissed, "All that goes before forget" (p. 53). Similarly, the moment when the couple comes to an end is repeatedly before us, expanded upon, explained, and revised (pp. 53, 55, 57, 58). The entire "story" is structured upon the tensions between now and then, between the speaker's present act of narration and his previous life in common. While most other Beckettian narrators speak in order to make time pass, in order to survive the present and initiate the future, the narrator of *Enough* speaks in order to come to terms with the past. Both present and future are engulfed by the past until even the weather is meaningful only in relation to the past: "I don't know what the weather is now. But in my life it was eternally mild" (p. 59). Although the past can not be relived, it can be revived in the narrator's stories and while he neither excludes the possibility of actually finding his companion again (p. 58), nor counts on it unduly (p. 59), our narrator does contrive his words to evoke at least the sensation of the other's presence. The piece can end and enough will have been said only when the present has been transcended and the two are together again (p. 60).

Despite its thematic and structural importance, the couple are open to diverse interpretation. We never know who or what the narrator and his companion are. They may be simply two figures traveling through what appears to be a post atomic-war landscape of mounds and craters (p. 58) and mild, windless days, overcome by "sudden pelting downpours" (p. 59). In their strange world the only other living things are stemless flowers "flush with the ground" (p. 59). All that was upright has been bent down or swept away (p. 59) until it survives only in the memories and murmurs of the old companion: "He murmured of things that for him were no more and for me could not have been. The wind in the overground stems. The shade and shelter of the forests" (p. 60). But even on this literal level the couple is ambiguous in the English text. Although the sex of the companion is known from his first appearance, "I did all *he* desired" (p. 53, my emphasis), the narrator's sex is never revealed. Like T. S. Eliot's Tiresias, an "old man with wrinkled dugs," our narrator is an everyman perceiving, foretelling, and foresuffering all.

On another level the couple may be taken to represent the dichotomy of mind and body. The companion, whose physical appearance is sketched in from his misshapen figure to his bloodshot blue eyes (p. 56), assumes the role of body. It is he who decides when the couple shall halt or move (pp. 56–57), he who speaks (p. 55), he who takes the narrator by the hand (p. 54), he who controls movement even in sleep (p. 59). Just as the mind is subject to the body's sensations and desires, so too the narrator is dependent on his companion for all his knowledge (p. 54) and desires: "I only had the desires he manifested" (p. 53). But even on this level, even if the companion is taken to be the narrator's body, the hermeticism and isolation of the purely mental are broken.

On yet another level the relationship of the couple may be taken as a parable of Beckett's own art. Beckett the narrator breaks from the older generation of relational artists. Raised and educated by traditional literatures which have taught him all he knows (p. 54), the narrator discovers that their conventions and associations, like his cotton gloves, have become "rather tight" (p. 54). He is unlike the older generation which could, by fastening its eyes upon the ground out of "love of the earth and the flowers' thousand scents and hues" (p. 57), still assume correspondences, still speak of storms and shade and shelter (pp. 59 and 60). His minimalist prose, again like his cotton gloves, sharpens shapes by simplifying them (p. 54). He cannot conjure from windswept craters a world of Apollonian diversity, possibility, and certainty. But he no longer rejects that world either. Now he accepts without protests its existence for his predecessors whom he is coming slowly to resemble. He and the old companion have suffered the same needs and satisfactions (p. 53). Just as the bent-figure "wished everything [he said] to be heard" (p. 55) and would wait for the narrator to position himself to hear it (p. 55), so too our narrator seems to want his words recorded and will pause to give the pen time to note" (p. 53). He shares with more conventional artists the same desire to communicate and the same restrictions of language. No longer of a different generation (pp. 53–54), our aging narrator envisions his affinities with the earlier literatures. Although they sought truth's flowers in different places, both sought for the flowers, both trod them down with equal step: "I see the flowers at my feet and it's the others I see. Those we trod down with equal step. It is true they are the same" (p. 56). Although Beckett sought a shape for the possibility of nonrelation, he, like the Apollonian, sought for it in structures and forms. Each type of artist gathered materials from the ground he trod: each created art from the world he perceived.

In a variation of this parable the companion represents a previous, more verbal Beckett from whom the present, almost silent author seeks inspiration (or at least the wherewithal for creation). The ten years of travel together (i.e., the period in which the narrator shall have lived, if ever—p. 57) becomes Beckett's most prolific period (1946–56). In such a reading the narrator's final evocation of the earlier Beckett's hand is manifested literally as the words of *Enough* emerge and the silence Barth speaks of is broken. Once again Beckett fashions, from ambiguities about the narrator's physical location, metaphors that almost mean and interpretations that never crystallize. Associations with an external world and with others are accepted and reconciled to postulations of uncertainty.

Whatever the couple is taken to represent, there is a sufficiency and adequacy expressed about it. Instead of the defiance and determination of the man who claimed that "to be an artist is to fail, as no other dare fail," [11] of the man who committed characters to the unending pursuit of futile quests saying, "you must go on, I can't go on, I'll go on," [12] *Enough* hesitantly and tentatively proffers the reconciliation, calm acceptance, and perhaps even the affirmation of a man who feels it is enough to have spoken at all, of a man who can accept the inevitable failure of his quest saying, "Stony ground but not entirely. Given three or four lives I might have accomplished something" (p. 54). As the title suggests, the work is concerned with the sufficient, the moderate, and the balanced. Even in a minimal world there can be too much—too much of silence, too much of speech, too much remembered, too much forgotten: "All that goes before forget. Too much at a time is too much. . . . Too much silence is too much" (p. 53). The piece, like the weather, deals not with the extremes of storms, but with calm acceptance and the "eternally mild. As if the earth had come to rest in spring" (p. 59). There are questions one sees but never asks (p. 53). Desires are no longer manifested (p. 53). Reasoning is a sedative rather than a tool of investigation: "It is with this reasoning I calm myself when brought up short by all I know" (p. 58). Emphasis is on the unity and sameness beneath the diversity and flux: "And he often added that the sky seemed much the same" (p. 58). Parts are fused, "anatomy is a whole" (p. 55), past and present join. Entropy is expressed in images, not of decay, but of a spreading peace and calm: "We lived on flowers. So much for sustenance. He halted and without having to stoop caught up a handful of petals. Then moved munching on. They had on the whole a calming action. We were on the whole calm. More and more. All was" (p. 60). The present situation is accepted. Although inexplicable ("I could tell you more about radishes"—p. 60), "man's destiny" is reconcilable. It is enough to have departed momentarily, enough to have spoken at all against the passing time, enough to have invoked the old companion's presence. The piece, although a reduced and even minimal literature, is itself enough. When chaos cannot be captured, it is enough to have created an image that fleetingly gestures toward the void. When art must fail, it is enough to have tried. When it requires three or four lives to accomplish anything, it is enough to have written words that wipe out everything but a sense of unity with the passing image: "Now I'll wipe out everything but the flowers. No more rain. No more mounds. Nothing but the two of us dragging through the flowers. Enough my old breast feels his old hand" (p. 60). The piece is finished. No more words are necessary for the narrator or the story: what has been said has been enough.

5

Although no more words are necessary for the narrator of Enough, Beckett's new mood of adequacy does not lead to the silence Barth predicted in

"Literature of Exhaustion." Acceptance of both the impossibility of a non-relational art and the improbability of a relational one leads not to a frustrated impasse but rather to increasingly tranquil depictions of reconciliation. For example, two of Beckett's recent publications, "Sounds" and "Still 3," [13] present not pictures of stasis and despair, exhaustion and finality, but rather images of silence and stillness, serenity and tranquillity. A sense of sufficiency produces increasingly calm shapes to accommodate an uncertain and fluid universe.

The mood of "Sounds" and "Still 3" suggests the quiet of an ephemeral world passing peacefully away at its moment of extinction. Serenity is possible because the pieces are indifferent to the distinctions between internal and external realms which troubled earlier narrators. The figure in "Sounds" listens equally for the noise of the lightest leaf or for the sighs of his own breath. His postures intimate both Belacquaesque isolation, as he sits with his head in his hands, and exterior connections, as he stands embracing a tree. Even his speech patterns mix once mutually exclusive worlds. The wind is described in terms of the self and its mutterings: the wind makes "no more sound than a ghost or mutter [of] old words once got by heart . . ." (p. 156). It is no longer necessary to denounce associations or to seek absolute answers. Peace comes as the agonized questions that informed earlier quests fade away: "No not yet not listening again in vain quite yet while the dim questions fade where been how long how it was" (p. 156). Even the language of "Sounds" and "Still 3" reflects a greater sense of harmony and evokes a more mellow music than before. Contradiction, interjection, and interruption yield to longer cadences and more sustained phrases. Negation itself contributes to the spreading calm by silencing the diversions that would destroy the dream: "Or if none hour after hour no sound of any kind then he having been dreamt away let himself be dreamt away to where none at any time away from here where none come none pass to where no sound to listen for none of any kind" ("Sounds," p. 155).

Although the pieces are without urgency, they are not without energy. Although Beckett accepts the impossibility of finding a shape for nonrelation, he does not abandon the quest. "Sounds" and "Still 3" are serene but not static. Just enough imagination persists to keep the narration going. Almost inaudible sounds recur just frequently enough to keep the silence from being absolute: ". . . suddenly some sound room or loft low and brief never twice the same to wonder over a moment . . ." ("Sounds," p. 156). Barely perceptible images appear just often enough to forestall the growing darkness. There is enough movement, even in a minimalist world, to sustain Beckett's narratives. Instead of an impasse the pieces project a tranquil diminishing. Instead of falling into Barth's exhausted silence, the pieces drift softly to rest. As in Valéry's "The Spinner," which ends at the same moment its drowsy spinner nods into sleep, Beckett's pieces tranquilly blend into the spreading calm: "Leave it so then this stillest night till now of all quite still head in hand as shown listening trying listening for a sound or dreamt away try dreamt away where no such thing no more than ghosts make nothing to listen for no such thing as a sound" ("Sounds," p. 156). "Size as seen in the life at say arm's length sudden white black all about no known expression eyes its at last not looking lids,[14] the ones no expression marble still so long then out" ("Still 3," p. 157). There are no more sounds or images to disturb the peace, and an impotent speaker has been reconciled to an ambiguous universe.

Reconciliation leads not to an exhausted silence but to images of serenity. Urgency, not artistry, disappears as Beckett commingles relational and non-relational worlds. No longer insisting on pure and absolute structures, Beckett is freed from the necessities of either exploding external associations or examining only internal ones. He no longer seeks the impossible: his art does not have to *be* the chaos. It is enough if he can return to Apollonian conventions without reasserting their assumptions; enough if he can make a residual prose more subjective without restoring order and certainty. A sense of sufficiency predominates, enabling Beckett to create new shapes to accommodate the uncertain and fluid human condition. And that in itself is enough.

Notes

1. The shape of ideas

1. Samuel Beckett, quoted by Harold Hobsen, "Samuel Beckett: Dramatist of the Year," *International Theatre Annual* (London, 1956), 1: 153.

2. Jean-Jacques Mayoux made a similar observation: "It is his [Beckett's] particular mission to go to the furthest limits of what is human and show us that it still is human." Quoted in "Samuel Beckett and Universal Parody," *Samuel Beckett: A Collection of Critical Essays*, ed. Martin Esslin (Englewood Cliffs, N.J.: Prentice-Hall, 1965), p. 79.

3. Although "A Poetics of Indigence" anticipates some of the points made in my first chapter, *Accommodating the Chaos: Samuel Beckett's Nonrelational Art* was written before the publication of James Knowlson's and John Pilling's *Frescoes of the Skull: The Late Prose and Drama of Samuel Beckett* (London: John Calder, 1979; New York: Grove Press, 1980).

4. Samuel Beckett, *Murphy* (New York: Grove Press, 1957), p. 65.

5. Samuel Beckett, "Three Dialogues," quoted in *Samuel Beckett: A Collection of Critical Essays*, p. 21.

6. D. H. Lawrence, "Poetry of the Present [1918]," in *The Complete Poems of D. H. Lawrence*, ed. Vivian de Sola Pinto and Warren Roberts (New York: Viking, 1964), 1:182.

7. D. H. Lawrence, *Complete Poems*, p. 182.

8. Israel Shenker, "Moody Man of Letters: A Portrait of Samuel Beckett, Author of the Puzzling *Waiting for Godot*." *New York Times*, 6 May 1956, Section 2, p. 3. Deirdre Bair points out in *Samuel Beckett: A Biography* (New York: Harcourt Brace Jovanovich, 1978), p. 651, fn. 22, that it is problematic whether the idea and phrasing in this interview are Beckett's or Shenker's. Bair quotes a letter to her from Shenker which says "that he had been careful not to say anywhere in the article that he had actually interviewed Beckett, but had used an obvious literary device in order to write it as one long quotation of Beckett's speech and thought."

9. Samuel Beckett, *Proust* (New York: Grove Press, 1931), p. 61.

10. Samuel Beckett, *The Unnamable* in *Three Novels by Samuel Beckett* (New York: Grove Press, 1965), p. 414.

11. Samuel Beckett in an interview with Tom F. Driver, "Beckett by the Madeleine," *Columbia University Forum* 4 (Summer 1961): 23.

12. Samuel Beckett, quoted by Alan Schneider in "Beckett's Letters on 'Endgame': Extracts from His Correspondence with Director Alan Schneider," *Village Voice*, 19 March 1958, p. 15.

13. Samuel Beckett in an interview with John Gruen, "Samuel Beckett Talks about Beckett," *Vogue* 154 (Dec. 1969): 210.

14. Samuel Beckett, "Dante . . . Bruno . Vico . . Joyce," *Our Exagmination Round His Factification for Incamination of Work in Progress* (Paris: Shakespeare and Company, 1929), p. 14.

15. Beckett to Driver, p. 23.

16. Beckett to Gruen, p. 210.

17. Hugh Kenner in *A Reader's Guide to Samuel Beckett* (New York: Farrar, Straus & Giroux, 1973), p. 94, says, "Molloy in Beckett's first venture is a new kind of character, what he once called in a letter 'the narrator/narrated.' "

18. "Poetry Is Vertical," quoted by Sighle Kennedy in *Murphy's Bed* (Lewisburg, Pa.: Bucknell University Press, 1971), p. 304.

19. Beckett to Shenker, p. 1.

2. The unwilling apollonian

1. Beckett to Gruen, p. 210.

2. Beckett to Shenker, p. 3.

3. Beckett, "Dante . . . Bruno . Vico . . Joyce," pp. 13, 15, 12.

4. James Joyce, quoted by Hugh Kenner in *Flaubert, Joyce and Beckett: The Stoic Comedians* (Boston: Beacon Press, 1962), p. 31.

5. Beckett, "Dante . . . Bruno . Vico . . Joyce," p. 15.

6. Samuel Beckett, "Text," *New Review* 2 (April 1932): 57. This piece, which is an extract from the unpublished *Dream of Fair to Middling Women* (1932), has been reprinted by Ruby Cohn in *Samuel Beckett: The Comic Gamut* (New Brunswick, N.J., Rutgers University Press, 1962), p. 308.

7. Samuel Beckett, "Assumption," *transition* (Paris) 16–17 (June 1929): 268–71; Beckett, "Sedendo et Quiesciendo," *transition* 21 (March 1932): 13–20 (like "Text," this piece is an extract from the unpublished *Dream of Fair to Middling Women*: portions of this piece also appear in "Draff," the last story in *More Pricks Than Kicks*); Beckett, "A Case in a Thousand," *The Bookman* 86 (Aug. 1934): 241–42.

8. Samuel Beckett, *More Pricks Than Kicks* (New York: Grove Press, 1972). Portions of this work originate in the unpublished *Dream of Fair to Middling Women*.

9. Cohn, *The Comic Gamut*, p. 22.

10. "Still the author's intent is serious. 'A Case in a Thousand,' along with *More Pricks Than Kicks*, can be viewed as part of a necessary demolition work."
"I have been primarily concerned to show that much of the bad writing is bad for a purpose: that the well-read incompetent was indeed a calculated guise. This is, quite simply, the best way to explain the sheer variety of failure which we have observed in *More Pricks*." H. Porter Abbott, *The Fiction of Samuel Beckett: Form and Effect*, Perspectives in Criticism, No. 22 (Berkeley: University of California Press, 1973), pp. 21 and 35.

11. "Because his [Belacqua's] life is finite he is able to toy with the notion of physical reality, and he boasts of having achieved mental freedom. In this respect he is *de mauvaise foi* in his claims, and his anguish remains strictly intellectual, for he can always end his discontent—either by resuming a normal life among his fellowmen, or by committing suicide. His distress is self-imposed even though unjustifiable; his attitude is hypocritical because he can choose an alternative to his condition. He exists within a system that provides him with safety margins: the reality of physical life on the one hand, and that of death on the other. The essential difference then between his predicament and that of Beckett's ageless bums rests on a temporal basis." Raymond Federman, *Journey to Chaos: Samuel Beckett's Early Fiction* (Berkeley: University of California Press, 1965), p. 43.

12. Beckett's self-conscious comments in *More Pricks Than Kicks* range from the subtleties of an implicit comparison (e.g., in "Walking Out" Belacqua, having been beaten up for his voyeurism, is unable to imitate the narrator of "Love and Lethe" and tiptoe silently away from the scene of the "inevitable nuptials"), to acknowledgment of the story as printed matter ("We know something of Belacqua, but Ruby Tough is a stranger

to these pages," p. 87, or ". . . even the most captious reader must acknowledge . . . the versimilitude of what we hope to relate in the not too distant future," p. 89), to overt references to other parts of the collection ("Alba Perdue, it may be remembered, was the nice little girl in 'A Wet Night,' " p. 127).

13. Samuel Beckett, *Murphy* (New York: Grove Press, 1957).

14. Heraclitus, quoted by Hippolytus, *Heraclitus: The Cosmic Fragments*, ed. G. S. Kirk (Cambridge: University Press, 1954), p. 105.

15. Heraclitus, quoted by Plutarch, *The Cosmic Fragments*, p. 135.

16. John Fletcher, *The Novels of Samuel Beckett* (New York: Barnes & Noble, 1964), p. 220.

17. Heraclitus, quoted by Hippolytus, *The Cosmic Fragments*, p. 88.

18. Alain Robbe-Grillet, *For a New Novel: Essays on Fiction* (New York: Grove Press, 1965), p. 27.

19. Robbe-Grillet, *For a New Novel*, p. 148.

20. Sighle Kennedy in *Murphy's Bed* unveils an elaborate and complex system showing Murphy's simultaneous movements through mythological, astrological, and scientific time.

21. Kennedy, *Murphy's Bed*, p. 250.

3. Fragmentation and tessellation

1. T. S. Eliot, *The Waste Land* in *The Complete Poems and Plays*, 1909–1950 (New York: Harcourt, Brace and World, 1971), p. 50.

2. W. B. Yeats, *A Vision* (New York: Collier Books, 1975), pp. 279–80.

3. Samuel Beckett, *Malone Dies*, in *Three Novels by Samuel Beckett* (New York: Grove Press, 1965), p. 197.

4. "I think perhaps I have freed myself from certain formal concepts. Perhaps, like the composer Schönberg or the painter Kandinsky, I have turned toward an abstract language. Unlike them, however, I have tried not to concretize the abstraction—not to give it yet another formal context." Beckett to Gruen, p. 210.

5. Samuel Beckett, *Watt* (New York: Grove Press, 1959), p. 128.

6. Samuel Beckett, *Watt*, French translation, British copy (marked) from which translation was made, six notebooks of translation, corrected typescript by author and corrected proofs are held by the Special Collections of the Ohio State University Library, Columbus, Ohio.

7. Samuel Beckett, *Mercier and Camier* (New York: Grove Press, 1974). The original French *Le Voyage de Mercier et Camier autour du Pot dans les Bosquets de Bondy* was written in 1946 but remained unpublished until 1970 except for the following excerpts which are noted by Federman and Fletcher in *A Bibliography*, pp. 71 and 85: "Mercier et Camier (Extrait)," Annales publiées trimestriellement par la Faculté des Lettres et Sciences Humaines de Toulouse (n.s.), I, fasc. 3 (Nov. 1965), Littératures XII: Études et Documents, XIXe–XXe siecles, pp. 153–54. Another extract appeared in *Le Monde*, *Supplément au Numero* 7157, 17 Jan. 1968, p. v. "Madden" and "The Umbrella," trans. Hugh Kenner assisted by Raymond Federman, *Spectrum* 4 (Winter 1960): 3–11.

8. Federman, *Journey to Chaos*, p. 145.

9. Cohn, *The Comic Gamut*, p. 97.

10. Abbott, *Form and Effect*, p. 76.

11. Colin Duckworth, "The Making of Godot," in *The Casebook on 'Waiting for Godot*,' ed. Ruby Cohn (New York: Grove Press, 1967), pp. 91–92, observes that *Mercier and Camier* is an Ur-*Godot* exhibiting many coincidences of style and theme in: "the setting of the play; the origins and meaning of the tree; Godot; the rendezvous and the theme of waiting; the creation of the characters and the relationships between them; the perfection of the dialogue and suppression of certain precise details to be found in the manuscript."

12. Vivian Mercier, "The Uneventful Event," *Irish Times*, 18 Feb. 1956, p. 6.

13. The similarities of the dialogue of Mercier and Camier to that of Vladimir and Estragon are demonstrated in the following excerpts taken from *Mercier and Camier*, p. 86, and from Samuel Beckett, *Waiting for Godot* (New York: Grove Press, 1954), p. 40:

> "If we have nothing to say, said Camier, let us say nothing.
> We have things to say, said Mercier.
> Then why don't we say them? said Camier.
> We can't, said Mercier.
> Then let us be silent, said Camier.
> But we try, said Mercier.
> We have got clear without mishap, said Camier, and unscathed.
> What did I tell you? said Mercier. Continue.
> We advance painfully—
> Painfully! cried Mercier.
> Laboriously . . . laboriously through the dark streets . . . (*Mercier and Camier*)

> "Estragon: In the meantime let us try and converse calmly, since we are incapable
>   of keeping silent.
> Vladimir: You're right, we're inexhaustible.
> Estragon: It's so we won't think.
> Vladimir: We have that excuse.
> Estragon: It's so we won't hear.
> Vladimir: We have our reasons.
> Estragon: All the dead voices.
> Vladimir: They make a noise like wings.
> Estragon: Like leaves.
> Vladimir: Like sand.
> Estragon: Like leaves." (*Waiting for Godot*)

14. Although the mysterious Quin is mentioned in several of Beckett's works, he never actually appears in any. As J. M. Coetzee points out, however, "The name given to the ur-Knott through draft A and part of draft B is James Quin" ("The Manuscript Revisions of Beckett's *Watt*," *Journal of Modern Literature* 2, no. 4 (Nov. 1972): 476.

15. Samuel Beckett, "The Expelled," in *Stories and Texts for Nothing* (New York: Grove Press, 1967), pp. 9–25; "The Calmative," in *Stories and Texts for Nothing*, pp. 27–46; "The End," in *Stories and Texts for Nothing*, pp. 47–72; "First Love," in *First Love and Other Shorts* (New York: Grove Press, 1974), pp. 9–36. Although written in 1946, the four stories suffered many delays between composition, translation, and publication. "Le Calmant" and "La Fin" were not available until 1955 when they, along with "L'Expulse" (first printed in *Fontaine* X, Dec. 1946–Jan. 1947) and *Textes pour rien*, were released in a single volume, *Nouvelles et Textes pour rien*. "Premier Amour" was not released for publication in French until 1970 and in English until 1972.

16. Cohn, *The Comic Gamut*, p. 114.

17. Samuel Beckett, *Molloy*, in *Three Novels by Samuel Beckett*, pp. 7–176; *Malone Dies* in *Three Novels*, pp. 179–288; *The Unnamable* in *Three Novels*, pp. 291–414.

18. V. A. Kolve, "Religious Language in *Waiting for Godot*," *The Centennial Review* 11, no. 1 (Winter 1967).

19. Hugh Kenner, *Samuel Beckett: A Critical Study*, New Edition (Berkeley: University of California Press, 1968), p. 63.

20. For a more detailed account of Beckett's games with the names of his characters, see Cohn, *The Comic Gamut*, chapter 6.

21. Dieter Wellershoff, "Failure of an Attempt at De-Mythologization: Samuel Beckett's Novels," in Esslin, *A Collection of Critical Essays*, p. 97.

22. For a further list of similarities, see especially Ludovic Janvier, "*Molloy*" in *Twentieth Century Interpretations of Molloy, Malone Dies, The Unnamable*, ed. J. D. O'Hara (Englewood Cliffs, N.J.: Prentice-Hall, 1970) and David Hayman, "*Molloy* or the Quest for Meaninglessness: A Global Interpretation," in *Samuel Beckett Now*, ed. Melvin J. Friedman (Chicago: University of Chicago Press, 1970).

23. David H. Helsa, *The Shape of Chaos: An Interpretation of the Art of Samuel Beckett* (Minneapolis: University of Minnesota Press, 1971), chapter 4.

24. John Fletcher, "Interpreting *Molloy*," in Friedman, *Samuel Beckett Now.*

25. G. C. Barnard, *Samuel Beckett: A New Approach: A Study of the Novels and Plays* (New York: Dodd, Mead, 1970), chapters 3 and 4.

26. Hayman, "*Molloy* or the Quest for Meaninglessness," in Friedman, *Samuel Beckett Now.*

27. Janvier, "*Molloy*," in *Twentieth Century Interpretations*, p. 54.

28. Beckett to Shenker, "Moody Man of Letters," p. 3.

29. Samuel Beckett, *Texts for Nothing* in *Stories and Texts for Nothing* (New York: Grove Press, 1967), Text 4, p. 92.

30. According to Federman and Fletcher, A *Bibliography*, p. 63, Texts 3, 6, and 10 were published as "Trois Textes pour rien," in *Lettres Nouvelles* 1 (May 1953): 267–77. Text 11 was first published as "Encore un pour rien. Texte inédit de Samuel Beckett," in *Arts-Spectacles* 418 (3–9 July 1953): 5. Texts 1 and 12 were first published as "Deux Textes pour rien," in *Monde Nouveau/Paru* 10 (May–June, 1955): 144–49. Texts 4, 8, and 13 were reprinted in *Monologues de Minuit*, ed. Ruby Cohn and Lily Parker (New York: Macmillan, 1965), pp. 117–32.

4. The voice and its words

1. In the Shenker interview (pp. 1, 3), after describing *L'Innommable* as a work of "complete disintegration," Beckett confides: "The very last thing I wrote—*Textes pour rien*—was an attempt to get out of the attitude of disintegration, but it failed."

2. Beckett, *More Pricks Than Kicks*, p. 29. Other Beckett works referred to in this chapter and cited parenthetically will be to the following Grove Press Editions: *Watt* (1959), *Murphy* (1957), *Three Novels by Samuel Beckett: Molloy, Malone Dies, The Unnamable* (1965), *Fizzles* (1976), and *Imagination Dead Imagine, Ping*, and *Enough* in *First Love and Other Shorts* (1974).

3. Beckett's infinitely repeating pattern is often observed; for example, see also Hugh Kenner's *Samuel Beckett: A Critical Study* (Berkeley: University of California Press, 1968), David H. Helsa's *The Shape of Chaos: An Interpretation of the Art of Samuel Beckett* (Minneapolis: The University of Minnesota Press, 1971), and the articles, especially those of David H. Helsa and Edouard Morot-Sir, in *Samuel Beckett and the Art of Rhetoric* (Chapel Hill: North Carolina Studies in the Romance Languages and Literatures, 1976).

4. Samuel Beckett, *Lessness*, New Statesman 79 (1 May 1970): 635.

5. Beckett, "Three Dialogues," p. 21.

6. Samuel Beckett, *How It Is* (New York: Grove Press, 1964).

7. In his article, "The Thirties," in *Beckett at 60* (London: Calder and Boyars, 1967) A. J. Leventhal recalls receiving an urgent postcard from Beckett requesting that he "measure the height from the ground of Cuchulain's arse"—referring to the statue in the Dublin General Post Office. As Leventhal points out, Beckett needed this information to be certain Neary actually could "dash his head against [Cuchulain's] buttocks, such as they are" (*Murphy*, p. 42).

8. This photograph is reproduced in *Beckett at 60: A Festschrift* (London: Calder and Boyars, 1967), facing page 24 and in Bair, A *Biography*, facing page 114.

5. Residual fiction

1. Samuel Beckett, *Texts for Nothing* in *Stories and Texts for Nothing* (New York: Grove Press, 1967), p. 139.

2. The term "residual fiction" is derived from *Residua*, Beckett's translation of *Têtes-*

Mortes (literally, a chemical residue), a work published in 1967 by Éditions de Minuit containing the French versions of *Imagination Dead Imagine*, *Ping*, *Enough*, and *From an Abandoned Work*. Because they are stylistically and thematically disparate from the other residua, *From an Abandoned Work* and *Enough* will be considered in chapter 6.

In response to a questionnaire sent him by Brian Finney quoted by Finney in *'Since How It Is': A Study of Samuel Beckett's Later Fiction* (London: Covent Garden Press, 1972), p. 10, Beckett said of the Residua: "They are residual (1) Severally, even when that does not appear of which each is all that remains and (2) In relation to whole body of previous work."

3. Samuel Beckett, *Imagination Dead Imagine*, in *First Love and Other Shorts* (New York: Grove Press, 1974).

4. Samuel Beckett, *Dream of Fair to Middling Women*, quoted by Lawrence E. Harvey in *Samuel Beckett: Poet and Critic* (Princeton, N.J.: Princeton University Press, 1970), p. 342.

5. Abbott, *Form and Effect*, p. 147.

6. Finney, p. 26.

7. Ruby Cohn, *Back to Beckett* (Princeton, N.J.: Princeton University Press, 1973), pp. 249–50.

8. Samuel Beckett, *Ping*, in *First Love and Other Shorts*.

9. Cohn, *Back to Beckett*, p. 251.

10. Raymond Federman and John Fletcher, "Appendix II," in *Samuel Beckett, His Works and His Critics: An Essay in Bibliography* (Berkeley: University of California Press, 1970), reprint all ten typescript drafts of *Bing* followed by Beckett's own English translation, *Ping*.

11. Beckett, *Lessness*, New Statesman 19 (1 May 1970): 635. *Lessness* presents an endless, issueless, grey world of "ruins true refuge" in which the only upright object is an immobile, blocklike figure.

12. Cohn, *Back to Beckett*, p. 265.

13. J. M. Coetzee, "Samuel Beckett's *Lessness*: An Exercise in Decomposition," *Computers and the Humanities* 7 (March 1973).

14. Coetzee, p. 198.

15. The sentences may be divided into the following groups:

(1) "ruins true refuge"

Paragraph 1, sentence i (21,i) 8,i (17,i)

1,iv	(13,iii)	8,iii	(23,ii)
2,i	(16,iii)	8,vi	(20,v)
4,v	(16,iv)	10,i	(20,i)
7,i	(22,i)	11,iv	(19,i)

(2) grey, endlessness

1,ii	(22,vi)	6,vi	(13,ii)
2,iv	(14,i)	8,iv	(15,ii)
5,i	(15,iv)	9,iii	(17,vi)
5,iii	(20,iv)	9,v	(16,ii)
6,iv	(22,ii)	11,ii	(14,ii)

(3) "little body"

1,iii	(17,iv)	7,ii	(23,i)
3,ii	(20,vii)	7,iv	(18,ii)
4,iii	(24,ii)	8,ii	(24,iii)
5,ii	(13,i)	9,i	(24,iv)
6,iii	(24,i)	12,v	(18,i)

(4) "all gone from mind"

2,ii	(19,v)	9,vi	(17,iii)
3,iii	(23,iii)	10,iii	(20,ii)
4,ii	(17,vii)	12,i	(23,v)
8,v	(19,iii)	12,iii	(16,i)
9,iv	(22,v)	12,vi	(21,iii)

(5) dreams and figments of imagination

2,iii	(16,vi)	7,vi	(18,iii)
2,v	(16,v)	10,ii	(18,vi)
4,i	(15,i)	10,iv	(24,iv)
6,ii	(20,vi)	12,ii	(21,ii)
7,iii	(19,iv)	12,iv	(19,ii)

(6) things "he" will do and experience

3,i	(23,iv)	7,vii	(17,ii)
4,iv	(15,iii)	9,ii	(20,iii)
6,i	(18,iv)	9,vii	(22,iii)
6,v	(14,iii)	11,i	(17,v)
7,v	(18,v)	11,iii	(14,iv)

16. Ruby Cohn's list is taken from *Back to Beckett*, p. 265. Martin Esslin's list is from his Introduction to the BBC Radio 3 production of *Lessness* (25 Feb. 1971) and is quoted by Finney, pp. 39–40.

6. A sense of sufficiency

1. John Barth, "Literature of Exhaustion," *The Atlantic*, 220, no. 2 (Aug. 1967), 31.

2. Samuel Beckett, *From an Abandoned Work*, in *First Love and Other Shorts*, pp. 39–49. Although *From an Abandoned Work* and *Enough* were both published with the residua in *Têtes-Mortes*, their style and themes align them more persuasively with the works expressing a sense of sufficiency.

3. Shenker (pp. 2–3) quotes Beckett as saying: "At the end of my work there's nothing but dust—the nameable. In the last book 'L'Innommable'—there's complete disintegration. No 'I,' no 'have,' no 'being.' No nominative, no accusative, no verb. There's no way to go on.

"The very last thing I wrote—'Textes pour Rien'—was an attempt to get out of the attitude of disintegration, but it failed."

4. Raymond Federman and John Fletcher, *Samuel Beckett: His Works and His Critics: An Essay in Bibliography* (Berkeley: University of California Press, 1970), p. 28.

5. *From an Abandoned Work* lends itself to production. According to Federman and Fletcher's *Bibliography* (p. 28) the work was first broadcast on the B.B.C. Third Program, 14 Dec. 1957, and had its American premier at Santa Barbara, 24 Feb. 1965. The piece is perhaps best known through Jack MacGowran's inclusion of it in *Beginning to End*, a dramatic production of excerpts from several of Beckett's pieces.

6. Samuel Beckett, *The Lost Ones* (New York: Grove Press, 1972).

7. John W. Tuttleton, *The Novel of Manners in America* (Chapel Hill: University of North Carolina Press, 1972), p. 10.

8. Samuel Beckett, *Fizzles* (New York: Grove Press, 1976). Although the precise dates of composition are not clear, "Fizzles 1 through 6" seem to have been written in French ca. 1960 and translated into English in 1973–74. "Fizzle 7" was written in English in 1972. "Fizzle 8" was written in French and translated in 1975.

9. John Pilling, "The Significance of Beckett's *Still*," *Essays in Criticism*, 28, no. 2 (April 1978): 145.

10. Samuel Beckett, *Enough* in *First Love and Other Shorts*, pp. 51–60.

11. Beckett, "Three Dialogues," p. 21.

12. Beckett, *The Unnamable*, p. 414.

13. "Sounds" and "Still 3" are reprinted in the Appendix to Pilling's essay, "The Significance of Beckett's *Still*," *Essays in Criticism*, 28, no. 2 (April 1978): 155–57.

14. In Pilling's text of "Still 3" the phrase reads "not looking lips," but in a letter to me dated 17 Sept. 1979, John Pilling says, "I think my text of 'Still 3' is incorrect in the next to last line—sense, and the eagle eye of Susan Briezna, suggests that 'lips' should be 'lids.' "

Selected bibliography

Abbott, H. Porter. *The Fiction of Samuel Beckett: Form and Effect*. Perspectives in Criticism, no. 22. Berkeley: University of California Press, 1973.
———. "A Grammar for Being Elsewhere." *Journal of Modern Literature* 6, no. 1 (Feb. 1977): 39–46.
Admussen, Richard L. *The Samuel Beckett Manuscripts: A Study*. Boston: G. K. Hall and Co., 1979.
Bair, Deidre. *Samuel Beckett: A Biography*. New York: Harcourt, Brace, Jovanovich, 1978.
Barge, Laura. " 'Coloured Images' in the 'Black Dark': Samuel Beckett's Later Fiction." *Publications of the Modern Language Association* 92, no. 2 (March 1977): 273–84.
———. "Life and Death in Beckett's Four Stories." *South Atlantic Quarterly*, 76, no. 3 (Summer 1977): 332–47.
Barnard, G. C. *Samuel Beckett: A New Approach: A Study of the Novels and Plays*. New York: Dodd, Mead and Company, 1970.
Barth, John. "The Literature of Exhaustion." *The Atlantic* 220, no. 2 (Aug. 1967): 29–34.
Beckett, Samuel. "Act Without Words I and II." In *Krapp's Last Tape and Other Dramatic Pieces*. New York: Grove Press, 1960. Pp. 123–41.
———. "All Strange Away." *Journal of Beckett Studies*, no. 3 (Summer 1978): 1–9.
———. *All That Fall*. In *Krapp's Last Tape and Other Dramatic Pieces*. New York: Grove Press, 1960. Pp. 29–91.
———. "Assumption." *Transition* 16–17 (June 1929): 268–71.
———. *Breath*. In *First Love and Other Shorts*. New York: Grove Press, 1974. Pp. 89–91.
———. "The Calmative." In *Stories and Texts for Nothing*. New York: Grove Press, 1967. Pp. 27–46.
———. *Cascando*. In *Cascando and Other Short Dramatic Pieces*. New York: Grove Press, 1968. Pp. 7–19.
———. "A Case in a Thousand." *The Bookman* 86 (Aug. 1934): 241–42.
———. *Collected Poems in English and French*. New York: Grove Press, 1977.

————. *Come and Go.* In *Cascando and Other Short Dramatic Pieces.* New York: Grove Press, 1968. Pp. 65–71.

————. *Company.* New York: Grove Press, 1980.

————. "Dante . . . Bruno . Vico . . Joyce." *Our Exagmination Round His Factification for Incamination of Work in Progress.* Paris: Shakespeare and Company, 1929. Pp. 3–22.

————. *Eh Joe.* In *Cascando and Other Short Dramatic Pieces.* New York: Grove Press, 1968. Pp. 33–41.

————. *Embers.* In *Krapp's Last Tape and Other Dramatic Pieces.* New York: Grove Press, 1960. Pp. 93–121.

————. "The End." In *Stories and Texts for Nothing.* New York: Grove Press, 1967. Pp. 47–72.

————. *Endgame.* New York: Grove Press, 1958.

————. *Enough.* In *First Love and Other Shorts.* New York: Grove Press, 1974. Pp. 51–60.

————. "The Expelled." In *Stories and Texts for Nothing.* New York: Grove Press, 1967. Pp. 9–25.

————. *Film.* New York: Grove Press, 1969.

————. "First Love." In *First Love and Other Shorts.* New York: Grove Press, 1974. Pp. 9–36.

————. *Fizzles.* New York: Grove Press, 1976.

————. *Footfalls.* In *Ends and Odds.* New York: Grove Press, 1976. Pp. 39–49.

————. *From an Abandoned Work.* In *First Love and Other Shorts.* New York: Grove Press, 1974. Pp. 37–49.

————. *Ghost Trio.* In *Ends and Odds.* New York: Grove Press, 1976. Pp. 51–65.

————. *Happy Days.* New York: Grove Press, 1961.

————. *How It Is.* New York: Grove Press, 1964.

————. *Imagination Dead Imagine.* In *First Love and Other Shorts.* New York: Grove Press, 1974. Pp. 61–66.

————. *Krapp's Last Tape.* In *Krapp's Last Tape and Other Dramatic Pieces.* New York: Grove Press, 1960. Pp. 7–28.

————. *Lessness. New Statesman* 79 (1 May 1970): 635.

————. *The Lost Ones.* New York: Grove Press, 1972.

————. *Malone Dies.* In *Three Novels by Samuel Beckett.* New York: Grove Press, 1965. Pp. 177–288.

————. *Mercier and Camier.* New York: Grove Press, 1974.

————. *Molloy.* In *Three Novels by Samuel Beckett.* New York: Grove Press, 1965. Pp. 7–176.

————. *More Pricks Than Kicks.* New York: Grove Press, 1972.

————. *Murphy.* New York: Grove Press, 1957.

————. *Not I.* In *First Love and Other Shorts.* New York: Grove Press, 1974. Pp. 73–87.

————. *Ohio Impromptu.* In *Rockaby and Other Short Pieces.* New York: Grove Press, 1981. Pp. 25–35.

————. *A Piece of Monologue.* In *Rockaby and Other Short Pieces.* New York: Grove Press, 1981. Pp. 67–69.

————. *Ping*. In *First Love and Other Shorts*. New York: Grove Press, 1974. Pp. 67–72.

————. *Play*. In *Cascando and Other Short Dramatic Pieces*. New York: Grove Press, 1968. Pp. 43–63.

————. *Poems in English by Samuel Beckett*. New York: Grove Press, 1961.

————. *Proust*. New York: Grove Press, 1957.

————. *Rockaby*. In *Rockaby and Other Short Pieces*. New York: Grove Press, 1981. Pp. 7–23.

————. *Roughs for Theatre and Radio*. In *Ends and Odds*. New York: Grove Press, 1976. Pp. 69–128.

————. "Sedendo et Quiescendo." *Transition* 21 (March 1932): 13–20.

————. "Sounds," Appendix to John Pilling, "The Significance of Beckett's *Still*." *Essays in Criticism* 28, no. 2 (April 1978): 155–56.

————. "Still 3," Appendix to John Pilling, "The Significance of Beckett's *Still*." *Essays in Criticism* 28, no. 2 (April 1978): 156–57.

————. "Text." *New Review* (April 1932): 57.

————. *Texts for Nothing*. In *Stories and Texts for Nothing*. New York, Grove Press, 1965. Pp. 75–140.

————. *That Time*. In *Ends and Odds*. New York: Grove Press, 1976. Pp. 25–27,

————. "Three Dialogues." In *Samuel Beckett: A Collection of Critical Essays*, edited by Martin Esslin. Englewood Cliffs, N.J.: Prentice-Hall, 1965. Pp. 16–32.

————. *The Unnamable*. In *Three Novels by Samuel Beckett*. New York: Grove Press, 1965. Pp. 291–414.

————. *Waiting for Godot*. New York: Grove Press, 1954.

————. *Watt*. New York: Grove Press, 1959.

————. *Words and Music*. In *Cascando and Other Short Dramatic Pieces*. New York: Grove Press, 1968. Pp. 21–32.

Ben-Zvi, Linda. "Samuel Beckett, Fritz Mauthner, and the Limits of Language." *Publications of the Modern Language Association* 95, no. 2 (March 1980): 183–200.

Brater, Enoch. "Still/Beckett: The Essential and the Incidental." *Journal of Modern Literature* 6, no. 1 (Feb. 1977): 3–16.

Brienza, Susan, and Brater, Enoch. "Chance and Choice in Beckett's *Lessness*." *Journal of English Literary History* 43 (1976): 244–58.

Calder, John, ed. *Beckett at 60: A Festschrift*. London: Calder and Boyars, 1967.

Chambers, Ross. "Beckett's Brinkmanship." In *Samuel Beckett: A Collection of Critical Essays*, ed. Martin Esslin. Englewood Cliffs, N.J.: Prentice-Hall, 1965. Pp. 152–68.

Coe, Richard N. *Samuel Beckett*. New York: Grove Press, 1970.

Coetzee, J. M. "Samuel Beckett's *Lessness*: An Exercise in Decomposition." *Computers and the Humanities* 7, no. 4 (March 1973): 195–98.

Cohn, Ruby. *Back to Beckett*. Princeton, N.J.: Princeton University Press, 1973.

————. *Just Play: Beckett's Theatre*. Princeton, N.J.: Princeton University Press, 1980.

————. *Samuel Beckett: The Comic Gamut*. New Brunswick, N.J.: Rutgers University Press, 1962.

————, ed. *Casebook on "Waiting for Godot."* New York: Grove Press, 1967.

————. *Samuel Beckett: A Collection of Criticism Edited by Ruby Cohn*. New York: McGraw-Hill Book Company, 1975.

Croussy, Guy. *Beckett*. Paris: Librairie Hachette, 1971.

Driver, Tom F. "Beckett by the Madeleine." *Columbia University Forum* 4 (Summer 1961): 21–25.

Duckworth, Colin. *Angels of Darkness: Dramatic Effects in Samuel Beckett with Special Reference to Eugene Ionesco*. London: George Allen and Unwin, 1972.

————. "The Making of Godot." In *Casebook on "Waiting for Godot,"* ed. Ruby Cohn, New York: Grove Press, 1967. Pp. 89–100.

Esslin, Martin, ed. *Samuel Beckett: A Collection of Critical Essays*. Englewood Cliffs, N.J.: Prentice-Hall, 1965.

Federman, Raymond. *Journey to Chaos: Samuel Beckett's Early Fiction*. Berkeley: University of California Press, 1965.

————, and Fletcher, John. *Samuel Beckett: His Works and His Critics*. Berkeley: University of California Press, 1970.

Finney, Brian. *'Since how it is': A Study of Samuel Beckett's Later Fiction*. London: Covent Garden Press, 1972.

Fletcher, John. *The Novels of Samuel Beckett*. London: Chatto and Windus, 1964.

————. *Samuel Beckett's Art*. London: Chatto and Windus, 1967.

Friedman, Melvin J. *Samuel Beckett Now*. Chicago: The University of Chicago Press, 1970.

Graver, Lawrence, and Federman, Raymond, eds. *Samuel Beckett: The Critical Heritage*. London: Routledge and Kegan Paul, 1979.

Gruen, John. "Samuel Beckett Talks about Beckett." *Vogue* 154 (Dec. 1969): 210–11.

Harrison, Robert. *Samuel Beckett's Murphy: A Critical Excursion*. Athens: University of Georgia Press, 1968.

Harvey, Lawrence E. *Samuel Beckett: Poet and Critic*. Princeton, N.J.: Princeton University Press, 1970.

Helsa, David H. *The Shape of Chaos: An Interpretation of the Art of Samuel Beckett*. Minneapolis: The University of Minnesota Press, 1971.

Kennedy, Sighle. *Murphy's Bed*. Lewisburg: Bucknell University Press, 1971.

Kenner, Hugh. *Flaubert, Joyce and Beckett: The Stoic Comedians*. Boston: Beacon Press, 1962.

————. *A Reader's Guide to Samuel Beckett*. New York: Farrar, Straus and Giroux, 1973.

————. *Samuel Beckett: A Critical Study*. New ed. Berkeley: University of California Press, 1973.

Knowlson, James. *Light and Darkness in the Theatre of Samuel Beckett*. London: Turret Books, 1972.

————. *Samuel Beckett: An Exhibition*. London: Turret Books, 1971.

————, and Pilling, John. *Frescoes of the Skull: The Later Prose and Drama of Samuel Beckett*. New York: Grove Press, 1979.

Kolve, V. A. "Religious Language in *Waiting for Godot*." *The Centennial Review*, 11, no. 1 (Winter 1967): 102–27.

Mercier, Vivian. *Beckett/Beckett*. New York: Oxford University Press, 1977.

Morot-Sir, Edouard; Harper, Howard; and McMillan, Dougald, eds. *Samuel Beckett: The Art of Rhetoric*. Chapel Hill: North Carolina Studies in the Romance Languages and Literature, Symposium no. 5, 1976.

Nores, Dominique. *Les critiques de notre temps et Beckett*. Paris: Éditions Garnier Frères, 1971.

Pilling, John. *Samuel Beckett*. London: Routledge and Kegan Paul, 1976.

Rabinovitz, Rubin. "Time, Space, and Verisimilitude in Samuel Beckett's Fiction." *Journal of Beckett Studies*, no. 2 (1977): 40–46.

Robbe-Grillet, Alain. *For a New Novel: Essays on Fiction*. New York: Grove Press, 1965.

Rosen, Steven L. *Samuel Beckett and the Pessimistic Tradition*. New Brunswick, N.J.: Rutgers University Press, 1972.

Schneider, Alan. "Beckett's Letters on 'Endgame': Extracts from His Correspondence with Director Alan Schneider," *Village Voice* (19 March 1958): 8 and 15.

Shenker, Israel. "Moody Man of Letters: A Portrait of Samuel Beckett, Author of the Puzzling *Waiting for Godot*." *New York Times*, 6 May 1956, section 2.

Soloman, Philip H. *The Life After Birth: Imagery in Samuel Beckett's Trilogy*. Amherst, Mass.: Romance Monographs, University of Massachusetts, 1975.

Szanto, George H. *Narrative Consciousness*. Austin: University of Texas Press, 1972.

Tanner, James T. F., and Vann, J. Don. *Samuel Beckett: A Checklist of Criticism*. Kent, Ohio: The Kent State University Press, 1969.

Webb, Eugene. *Samuel Beckett: A Study of His Novels*. Seattle and London: University of Washington Press.

Worth, Katharine, ed. *Beckett the Shape Changer*. London: Routledge and Kegan Paul, 1975.

Index